MAX RIDE
FINAL FLIGHT

JAMES PATTERSON

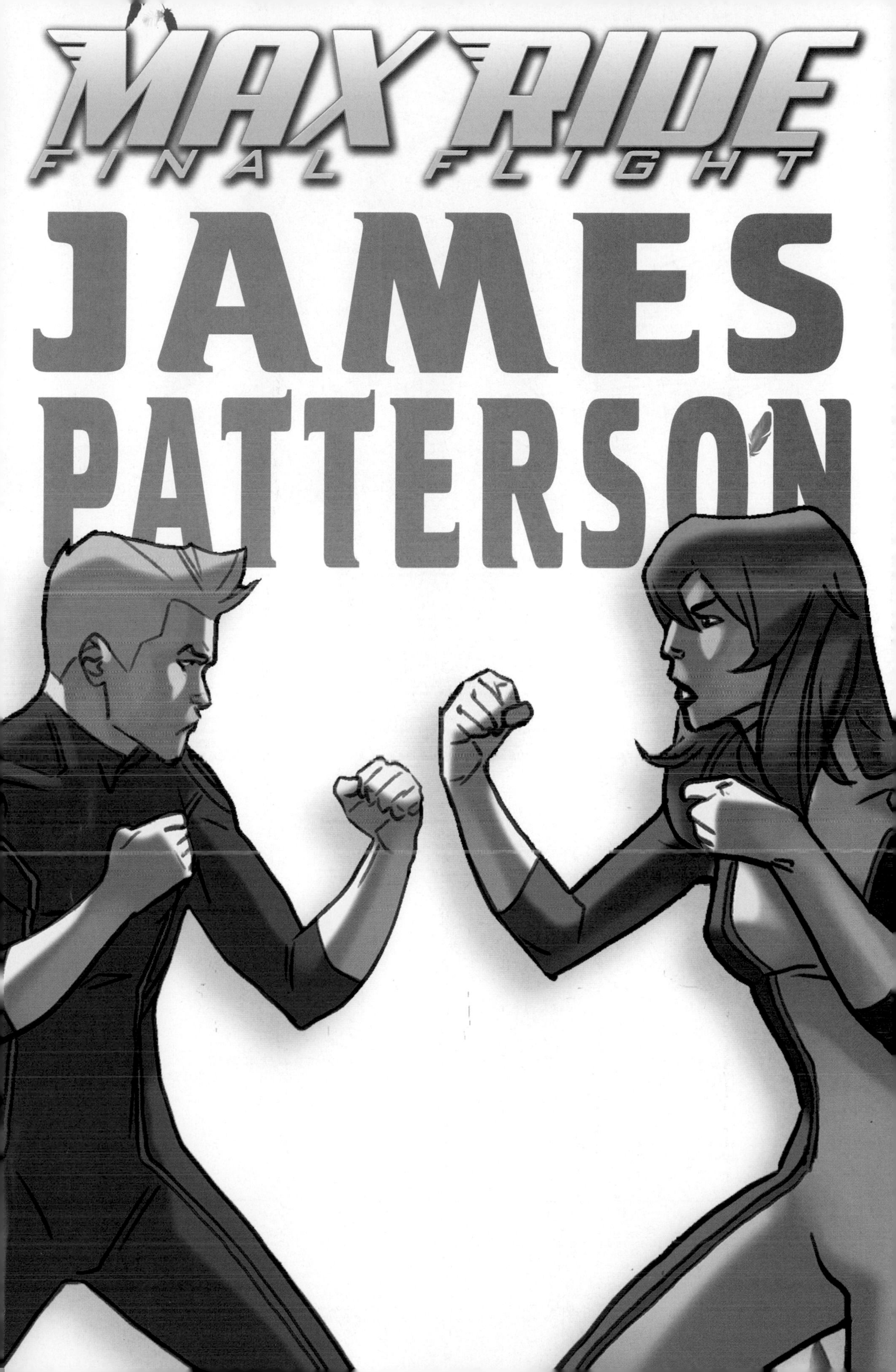

COLLECTION EDITOR *MARK D. BEAZLEY*
ASSISTANT EDITOR *CAITLIN O'CONNELL*
ASSOCIATE MANAGING EDITOR *KATERI WOODY*
EDITOR, SPECIAL PROJECTS *JENNIFER GRÜNWALD*
VP PRODUCTION & SPECIAL PROJECTS *JEFF YOUNGQUIST*
SVP PRINT, SALES & MARKETING *DAVID GABRIEL*
BOOK DESIGNER *ADAM DEL RE*

EDITOR IN CHIEF *AXEL ALONSO*
CHIEF CREATIVE OFFICER *JOE QUESADA*
PUBLISHER *DAN BUCKLEY*

MAX RIDE: FINAL FLIGHT. CONTAINS MATERIAL ORIGINALLY PUBLISHED IN MAGAZINE FORM AS MAX RIDE: FINAL FLIGHT #1-5. FIRST PRINTING 2017. ISBN# 978-1-302-90333-6. PUBLISHED BY MARVEL WORLDWIDE, INC., A SUBSIDIARY OF MARVEL ENTERTAINMENT, LLC. OFFICE OF PUBLICATION: 135 WEST 50TH STREET, NEW YORK, NY 10020. COPYRIGHT © 2016 BY JAMES PATTERSON. ALL RIGHTS RESERVED. ALL CHARACTERS FEATURED IN THIS ISSUE AND THE DISTINCTIVE NAMES AND LIKENESSES THEREOF, AND ALL RELATED INDICIA ARE TRADEMARKS OF JAMES PATTERSON. NO SIMILARITY BETWEEN ANY OF THE NAMES, CHARACTERS, PERSONS, AND/OR INSTITUTIONS IN THIS MAGAZINE WITH THOSE OF ANY LIVING OR DEAD PERSON OR INSTITUTION IS INTENDED, AND ANY SUCH SIMILARITY WHICH MAY EXIST IS PURELY COINCIDENTAL. MARVEL AND ITS LOGOS ARE TM MARVEL CHARACTERS, INC. **PRINTED IN THE U.S.A.** ALAN FINE, PRESIDENT, MARVEL ENTERTAINMENT; DAN BUCKLEY, PRESIDENT, TV, PUBLISHING & BRAND MANAGEMENT; JOE QUESADA, CHIEF CREATIVE OFFICER; TOM BREVOORT, SVP OF PUBLISHING; DAVID BOGART, SVP OF BUSINESS AFFAIRS & OPERATIONS, PUBLISHING & PARTNERSHIP; C.B. CEBULSKI, VP OF BRAND MANAGEMENT & DEVELOPMENT, ASIA; DAVID GABRIEL, SVP OF SALES & MARKETING, PUBLISHING; JEFF YOUNGQUIST, VP OF PRODUCTION & SPECIAL PROJECTS; DAN CARR, EXECUTIVE DIRECTOR OF PUBLISHING TECHNOLOGY; ALEX MORALES, DIRECTOR OF PUBLISHING OPERATIONS; SUSAN CRESPI, PRODUCTION MANAGER; STAN LEE, CHAIRMAN EMERITUS. FOR INFORMATION REGARDING ADVERTISING IN MARVEL COMICS OR ON MARVEL.COM, PLEASE CONTACT VIT DEBELLIS, INTEGRATED SALES MANAGER, AT VDEBELLIS@MARVEL.COM. FOR MARVEL SUBSCRIPTION INQUIRIES, PLEASE CALL 888-511-5480. **MANUFACTURED BETWEEN 1/13/2017 AND 2/14/2017 BY LSC COMMUNICATIONS INC., SALEM, VA, USA.**

10 9 8 7 6 5 4 3 2 1

ADAPTED FROM THE NOVEL
MAXIMUM RIDE:
SAVING THE WORLD AND OTHER EXTREME SPORTS
BY # JAMES PATTERSON

WRITER
JODY HOUSER

PENCILER
MARCO FAILLA

COLORIST
RACHELLE ROSENBERG

LETTERER
VC'S TRAVIS LANHAM

COVER ARTIST
DAVID NAKAYAMA

EDITOR
MARK BASSO

MAXIMUM RIDE DOESN'T KNOW MUCH ABOUT HER PAST.

SHE KNOWS ABOUT THE **LAB** WHERE SHE WAS GIVEN
WINGS AND THE ABILITY TO FLY. SHE KNOWS ABOUT **JEB**,
THE MAN WHO WAS RESPONSIBLE FOR EXPERIMENTING ON HER.
SHE KNOWS THAT SHE HAS TO PROTECT THE REST OF **THE FLOCK**
-- FANG, NUDGE, IGGY, GASMAN, AND ANGEL -- AT ALL COSTS.

AND SHE KNOWS THAT SHE HAS ONE MISSION:
TO SAVE THE WORLD.

CHAPTER 1

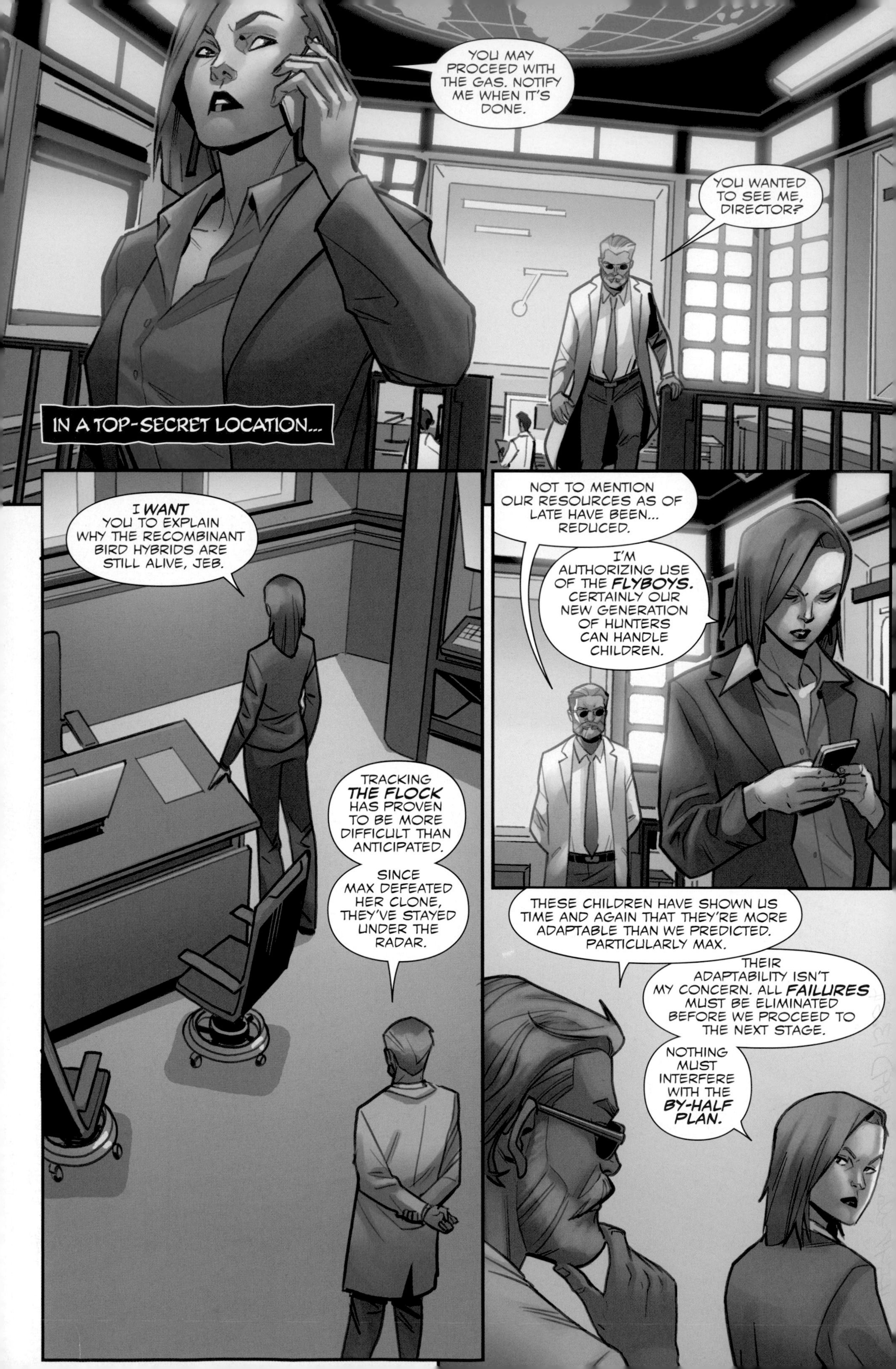
YOU MAY PROCEED WITH THE GAS. NOTIFY ME WHEN IT'S DONE.
YOU WANTED TO SEE ME, DIRECTOR?
IN A TOP-SECRET LOCATION...
I WANT YOU TO EXPLAIN WHY THE RECOMBINANT BIRD HYBRIDS ARE STILL ALIVE, JEB.
TRACKING THE FLOCK HAS PROVEN TO BE MORE DIFFICULT THAN ANTICIPATED.
SINCE MAX DEFEATED HER CLONE, THEY'VE STAYED UNDER THE RADAR.
NOT TO MENTION OUR RESOURCES AS OF LATE HAVE BEEN... REDUCED.
I'M AUTHORIZING USE OF THE FLYBOYS. CERTAINLY OUR NEW GENERATION OF HUNTERS CAN HANDLE CHILDREN.
THESE CHILDREN HAVE SHOWN US TIME AND AGAIN THAT THEY'RE MORE ADAPTABLE THAN WE PREDICTED. PARTICULARLY MAX.
THEIR ADAPTABILITY ISN'T MY CONCERN. ALL FAILURES MUST BE ELIMINATED BEFORE WE PROCEED TO THE NEXT STAGE.
NOTHING MUST INTERFERE WITH THE BY-HALF PLAN.

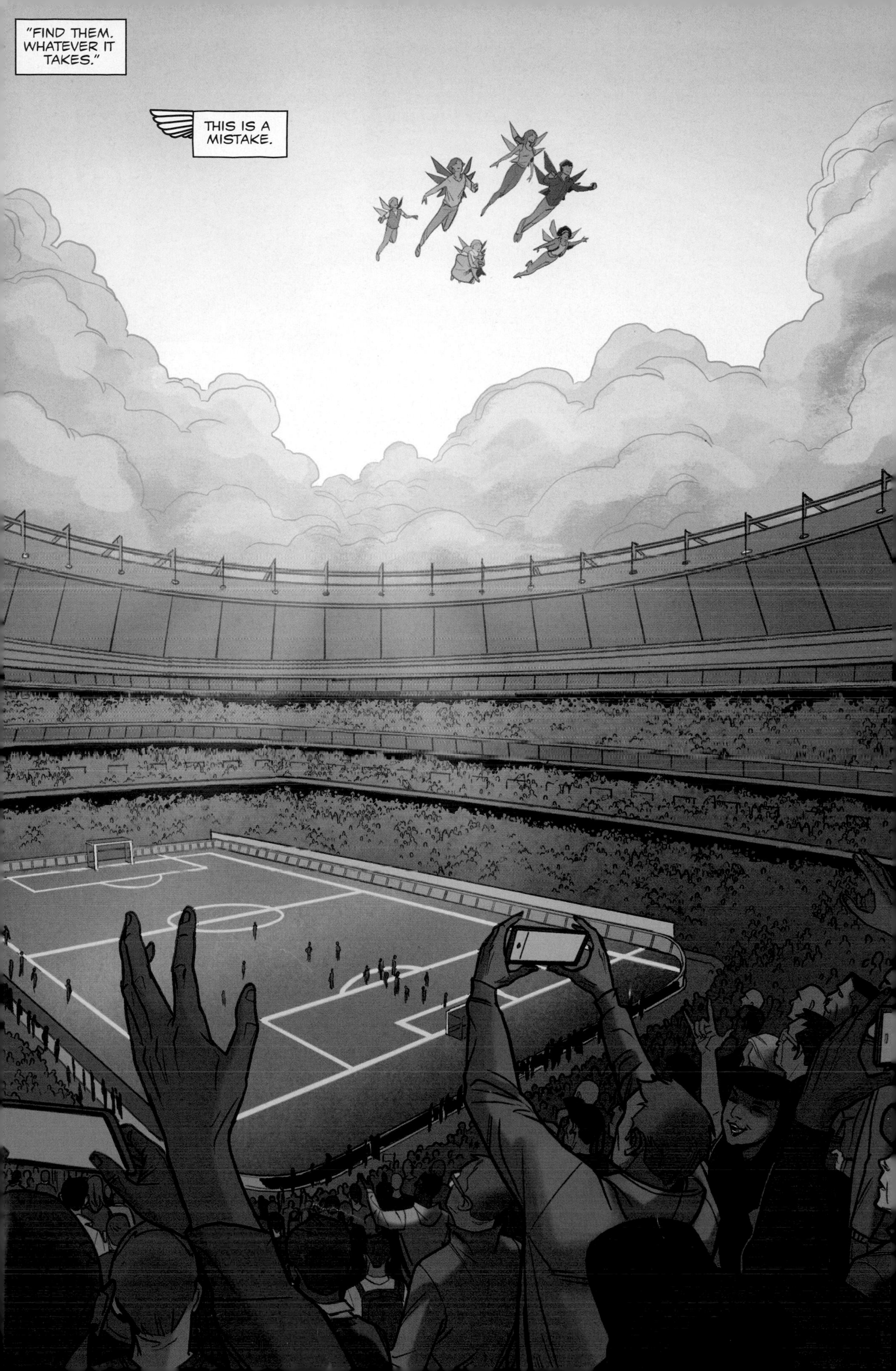
"FIND THEM. WHATEVER IT TAKES."
THIS IS A MISTAKE.

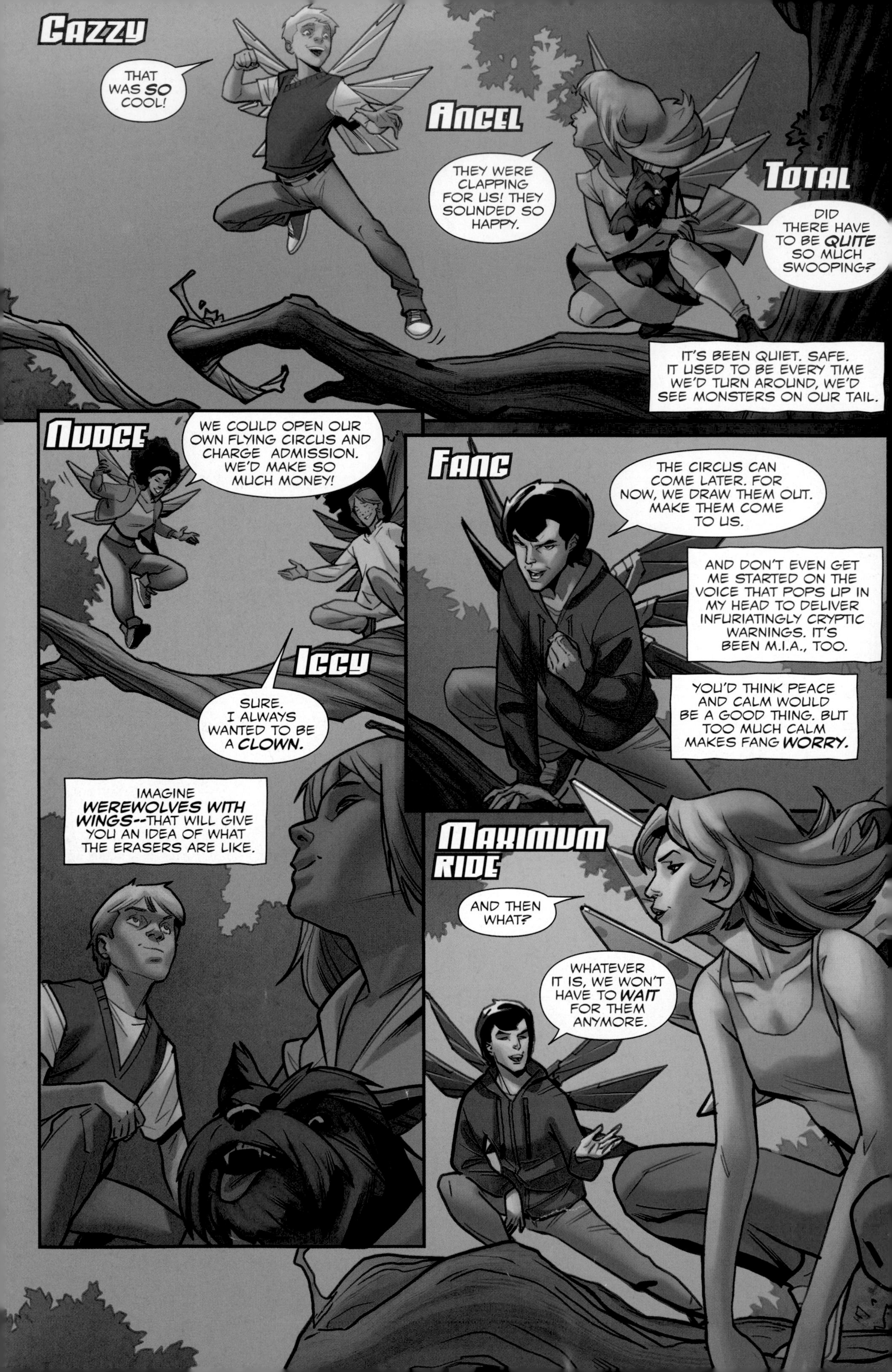
Gazzy
THAT WAS SO COOL!
Angel
THEY WERE CLAPPING FOR US! THEY SOUNDED SO HAPPY.
Total
DID THERE HAVE TO BE QUITE SO MUCH SWOOPING?
IT'S BEEN QUIET. SAFE. IT USED TO BE EVERY TIME WE'D TURN AROUND, WE'D SEE MONSTERS ON OUR TAIL.
Nudge
WE COULD OPEN OUR OWN FLYING CIRCUS AND CHARGE ADMISSION. WE'D MAKE SO MUCH MONEY!
Iggy
SURE. I ALWAYS WANTED TO BE A CLOWN.
IMAGINE WEREWOLVES WITH WINGS--THAT WILL GIVE YOU AN IDEA OF WHAT THE ERASERS ARE LIKE.
Fang
THE CIRCUS CAN COME LATER. FOR NOW, WE DRAW THEM OUT. MAKE THEM COME TO US.
AND DON'T EVEN GET ME STARTED ON THE VOICE THAT POPS UP IN MY HEAD TO DELIVER INFURIATINGLY CRYPTIC WARNINGS. IT'S BEEN M.I.A., TOO.
YOU'D THINK PEACE AND CALM WOULD BE A GOOD THING. BUT TOO MUCH CALM MAKES FANG WORRY.
Maximum Ride
AND THEN WHAT?
WHATEVER IT IS, WE WON'T HAVE TO WAIT FOR THEM ANYMORE.

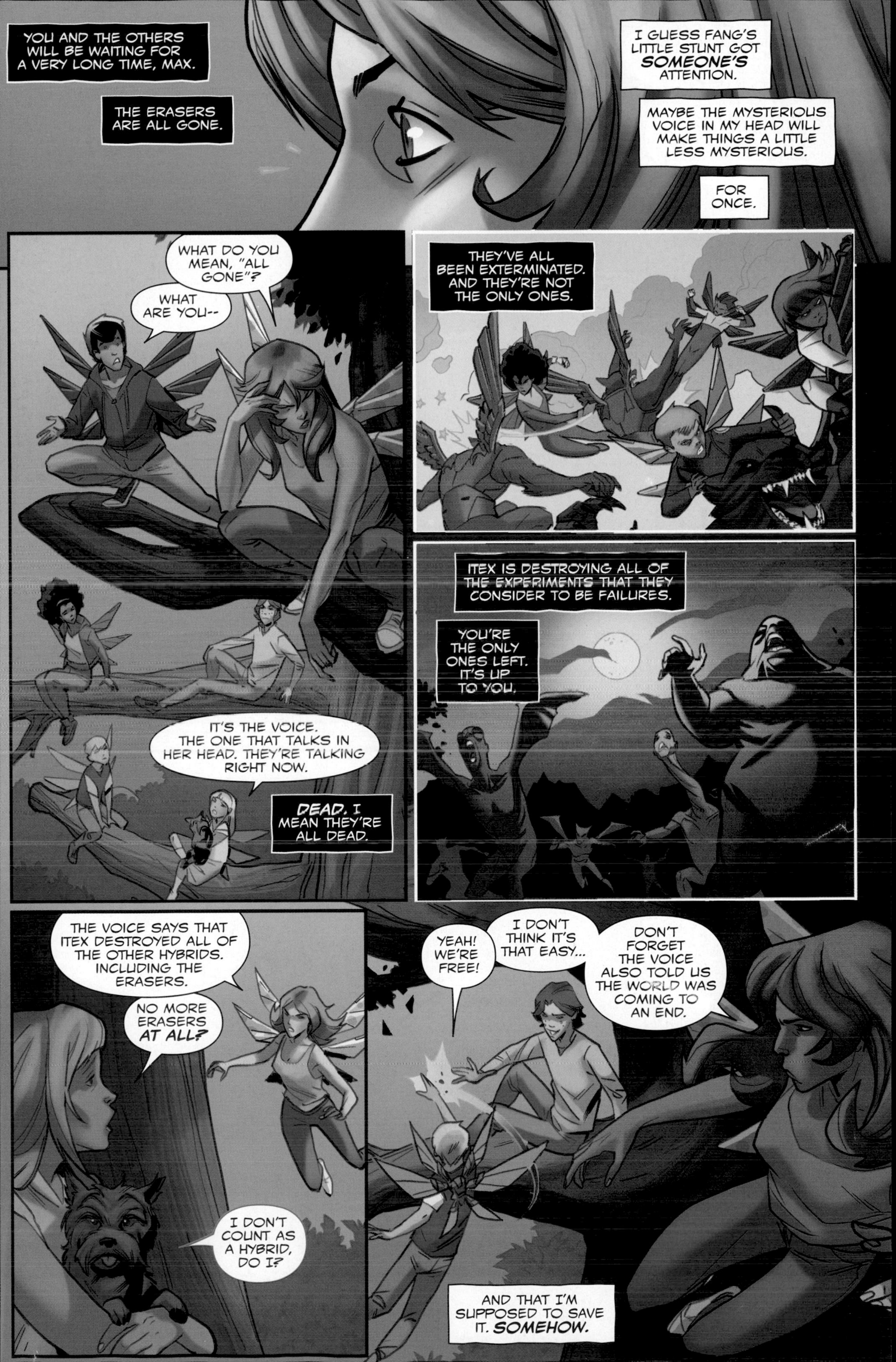
YOU AND THE OTHERS WILL BE WAITING FOR A VERY LONG TIME, MAX.
THE ERASERS ARE ALL GONE.
I GUESS FANG'S LITTLE STUNT GOT SOMEONE'S ATTENTION.
MAYBE THE MYSTERIOUS VOICE IN MY HEAD WILL MAKE THINGS A LITTLE LESS MYSTERIOUS.
FOR ONCE.
WHAT DO YOU MEAN, "ALL GONE"?
WHAT ARE YOU--
IT'S THE VOICE. THE ONE THAT TALKS IN HER HEAD. THEY'RE TALKING RIGHT NOW.
DEAD. I MEAN THEY'RE ALL DEAD.
THEY'VE ALL BEEN EXTERMINATED. AND THEY'RE NOT THE ONLY ONES.
ITEX IS DESTROYING ALL OF THE EXPERIMENTS THAT THEY CONSIDER TO BE FAILURES.
YOU'RE THE ONLY ONES LEFT. IT'S UP TO YOU.
THE VOICE SAYS THAT ITEX DESTROYED ALL OF THE OTHER HYBRIDS. INCLUDING THE ERASERS.
NO MORE ERASERS AT ALL?
I DON'T COUNT AS A HYBRID, DO I?
YEAH! WE'RE FREE!
I DON'T THINK IT'S THAT EASY...
DON'T FORGET THE VOICE ALSO TOLD US THE WORLD WAS COMING TO AN END.
AND THAT I'M SUPPOSED TO SAVE IT. SOMEHOW.

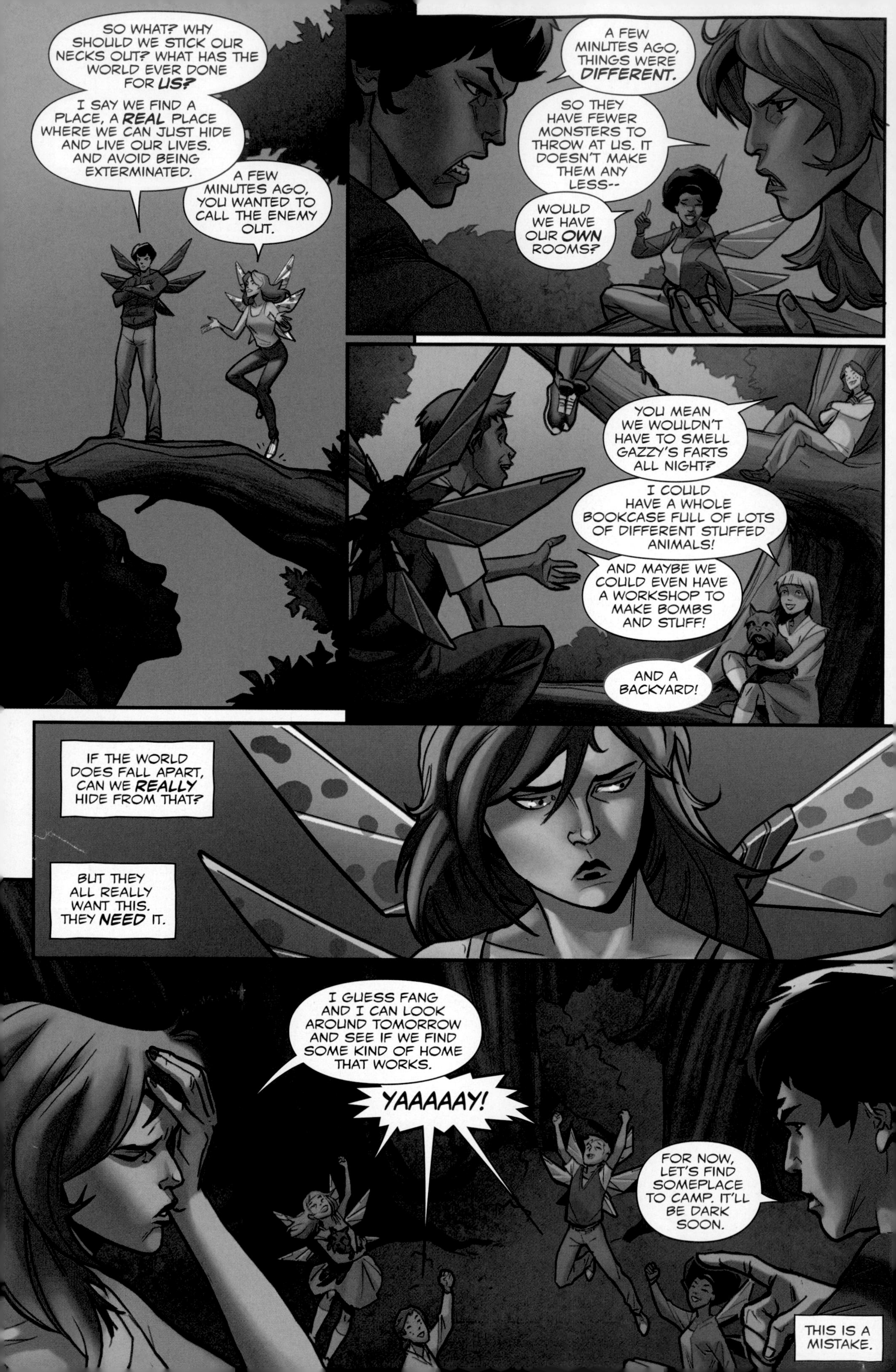
SO WHAT? WHY SHOULD WE STICK OUR NECKS OUT? WHAT HAS THE WORLD EVER DONE FOR US?
I SAY WE FIND A PLACE, A REAL PLACE WHERE WE CAN JUST HIDE AND LIVE OUR LIVES. AND AVOID BEING EXTERMINATED.
A FEW MINUTES AGO, YOU WANTED TO CALL THE ENEMY OUT.
A FEW MINUTES AGO, THINGS WERE DIFFERENT.
SO THEY HAVE FEWER MONSTERS TO THROW AT US. IT DOESN'T MAKE THEM ANY LESS--
WOULD WE HAVE OUR OWN ROOMS?
YOU MEAN WE WOULDN'T HAVE TO SMELL GAZZY'S FARTS ALL NIGHT?
I COULD HAVE A WHOLE BOOKCASE FULL OF LOTS OF DIFFERENT STUFFED ANIMALS!
AND MAYBE WE COULD EVEN HAVE A WORKSHOP TO MAKE BOMBS AND STUFF!
AND A BACKYARD!
IF THE WORLD DOES FALL APART, CAN WE REALLY HIDE FROM THAT?
BUT THEY ALL REALLY WANT THIS. THEY NEED IT.
I GUESS FANG AND I CAN LOOK AROUND TOMORROW AND SEE IF WE FIND SOME KIND OF HOME THAT WORKS.
YAAAAAY!
FOR NOW, LET'S FIND SOMEPLACE TO CAMP. IT'LL BE DARK SOON.
THIS IS A MISTAKE.

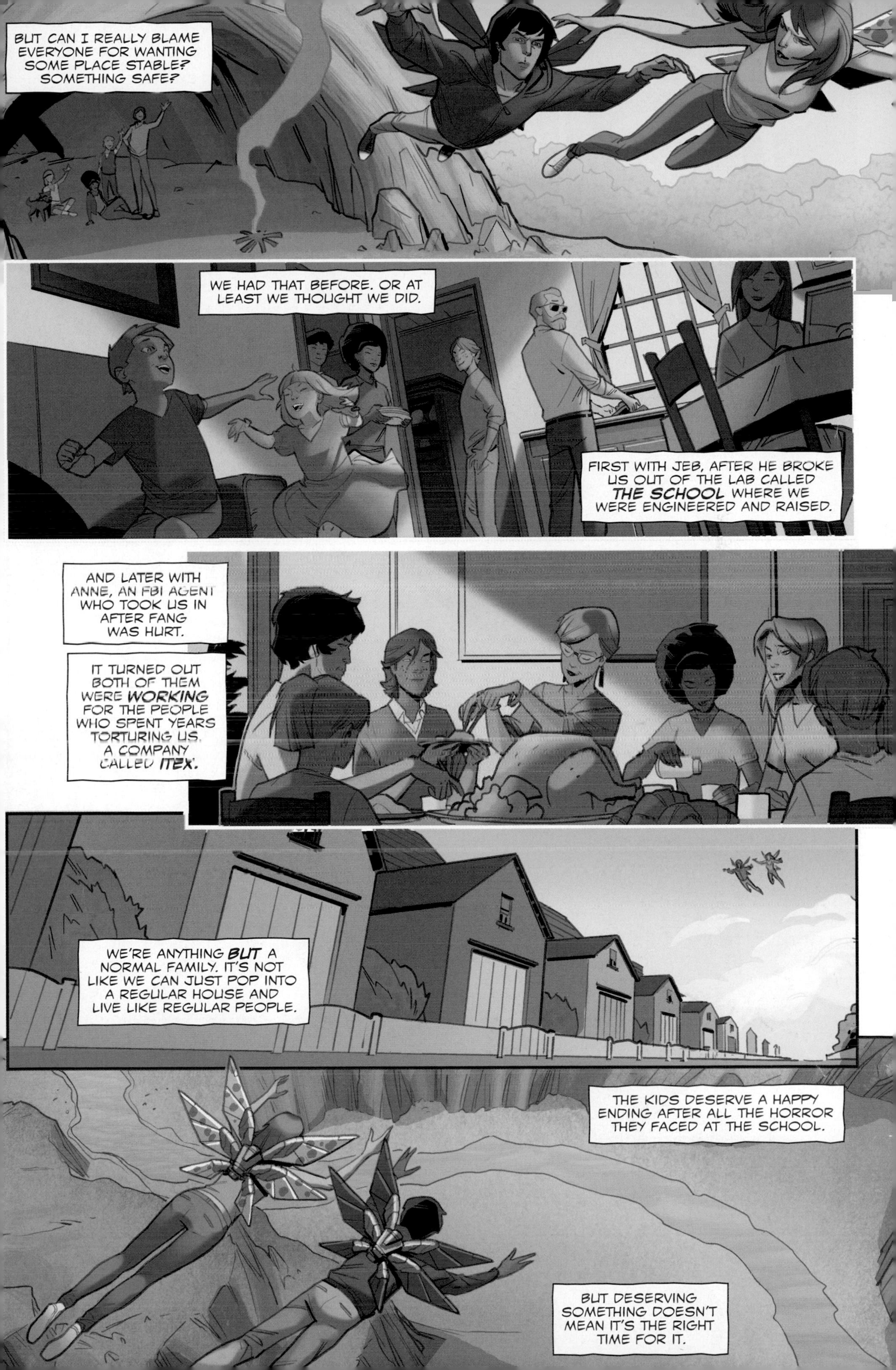
BUT CAN I REALLY BLAME EVERYONE FOR WANTING SOME PLACE STABLE? SOMETHING SAFE?
WE HAD THAT BEFORE. OR AT LEAST WE THOUGHT WE DID.
FIRST WITH JEB, AFTER HE BROKE US OUT OF THE LAB CALLED THE SCHOOL WHERE WE WERE ENGINEERED AND RAISED.
AND LATER WITH ANNE, AN FBI AGENT WHO TOOK US IN AFTER FANG WAS HURT.
IT TURNED OUT BOTH OF THEM WERE WORKING FOR THE PEOPLE WHO SPENT YEARS TORTURING US. A COMPANY CALLED ITEX.
WE'RE ANYTHING BUT A NORMAL FAMILY. IT'S NOT LIKE WE CAN JUST POP INTO A REGULAR HOUSE AND LIVE LIKE REGULAR PEOPLE.
THE KIDS DESERVE A HAPPY ENDING AFTER ALL THE HORROR THEY FACED AT THE SCHOOL.
BUT DESERVING SOMETHING DOESN'T MEAN IT'S THE RIGHT TIME FOR IT.

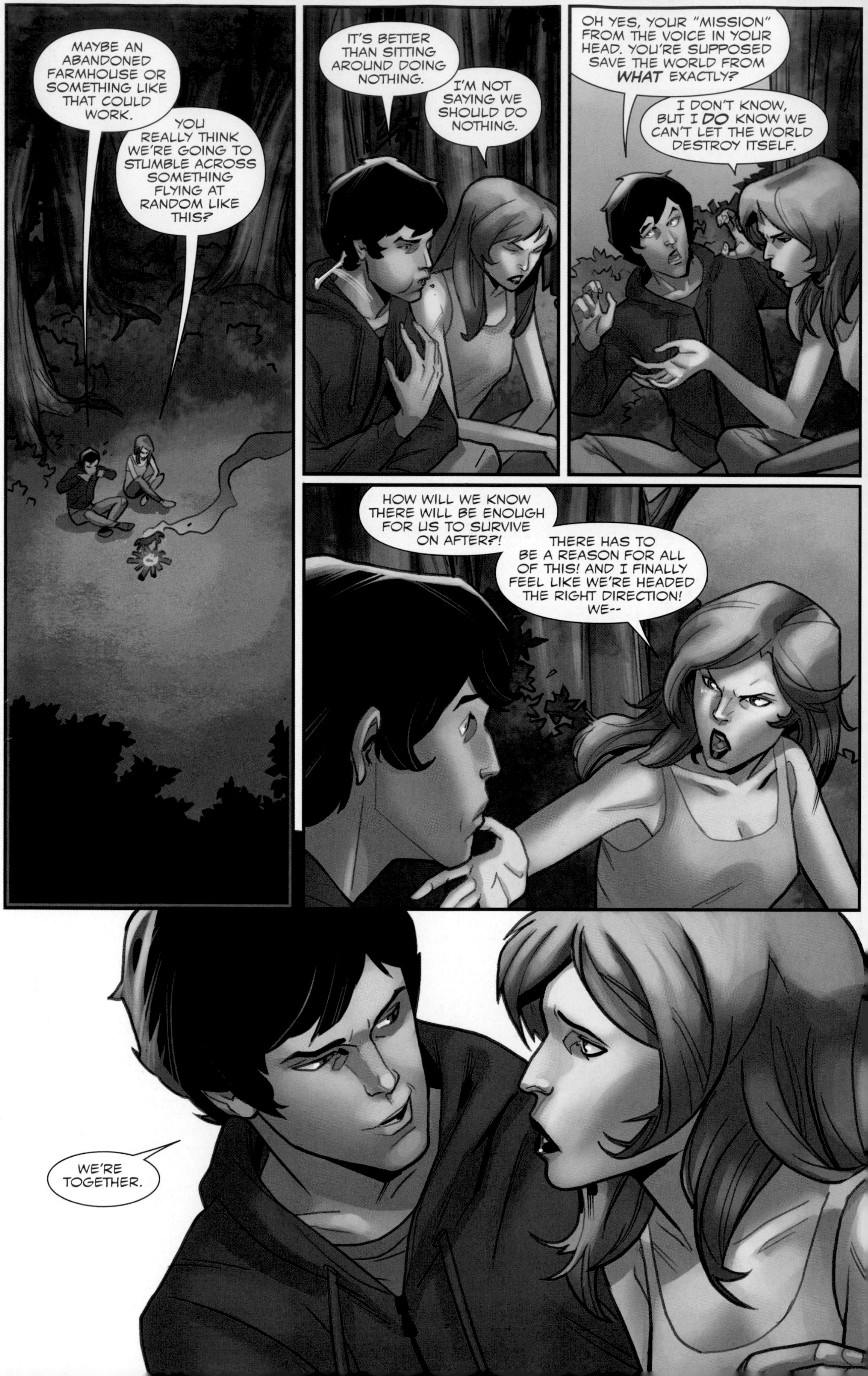
MAYBE AN ABANDONED FARMHOUSE OR SOMETHING LIKE THAT COULD WORK.
YOU REALLY THINK WE'RE GOING TO STUMBLE ACROSS SOMETHING FLYING AT RANDOM LIKE THIS?
IT'S BETTER THAN SITTING AROUND DOING NOTHING.
I'M NOT SAYING WE SHOULD DO NOTHING.
OH YES, YOUR "MISSION" FROM THE VOICE IN YOUR HEAD. YOU'RE SUPPOSED SAVE THE WORLD FROM WHAT EXACTLY?
I DON'T KNOW, BUT I DO KNOW WE CAN'T LET THE WORLD DESTROY ITSELF.
HOW WILL WE KNOW THERE WILL BE ENOUGH FOR US TO SURVIVE ON AFTER?!
THERE HAS TO BE A REASON FOR ALL OF THIS! AND I FINALLY FEEL LIKE WE'RE HEADED THE RIGHT DIRECTION! WE--
WE'RE TOGETHER.

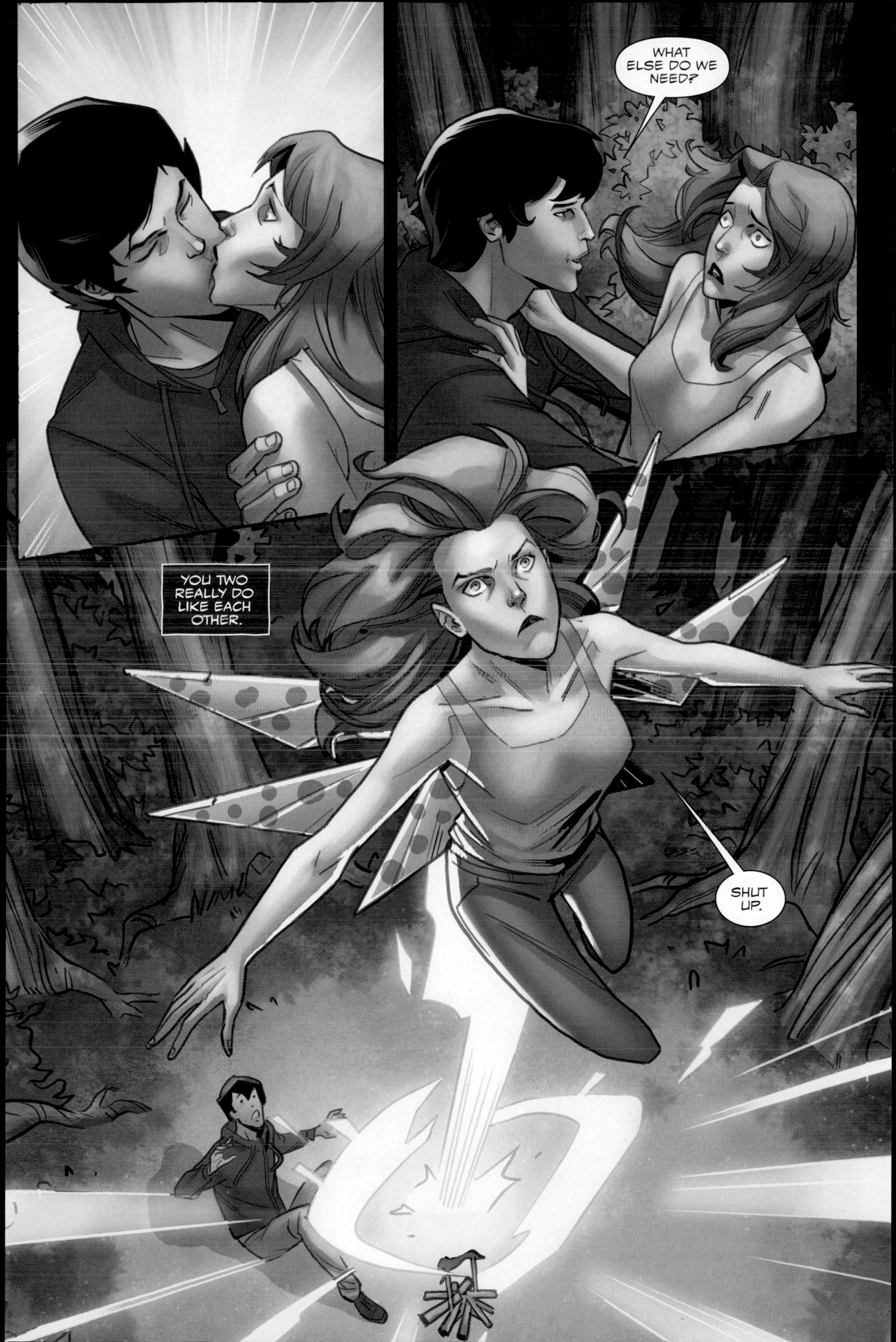
WHAT ELSE DO WE NEED?
YOU TWO REALLY DO LIKE EACH OTHER.
SHUT UP.

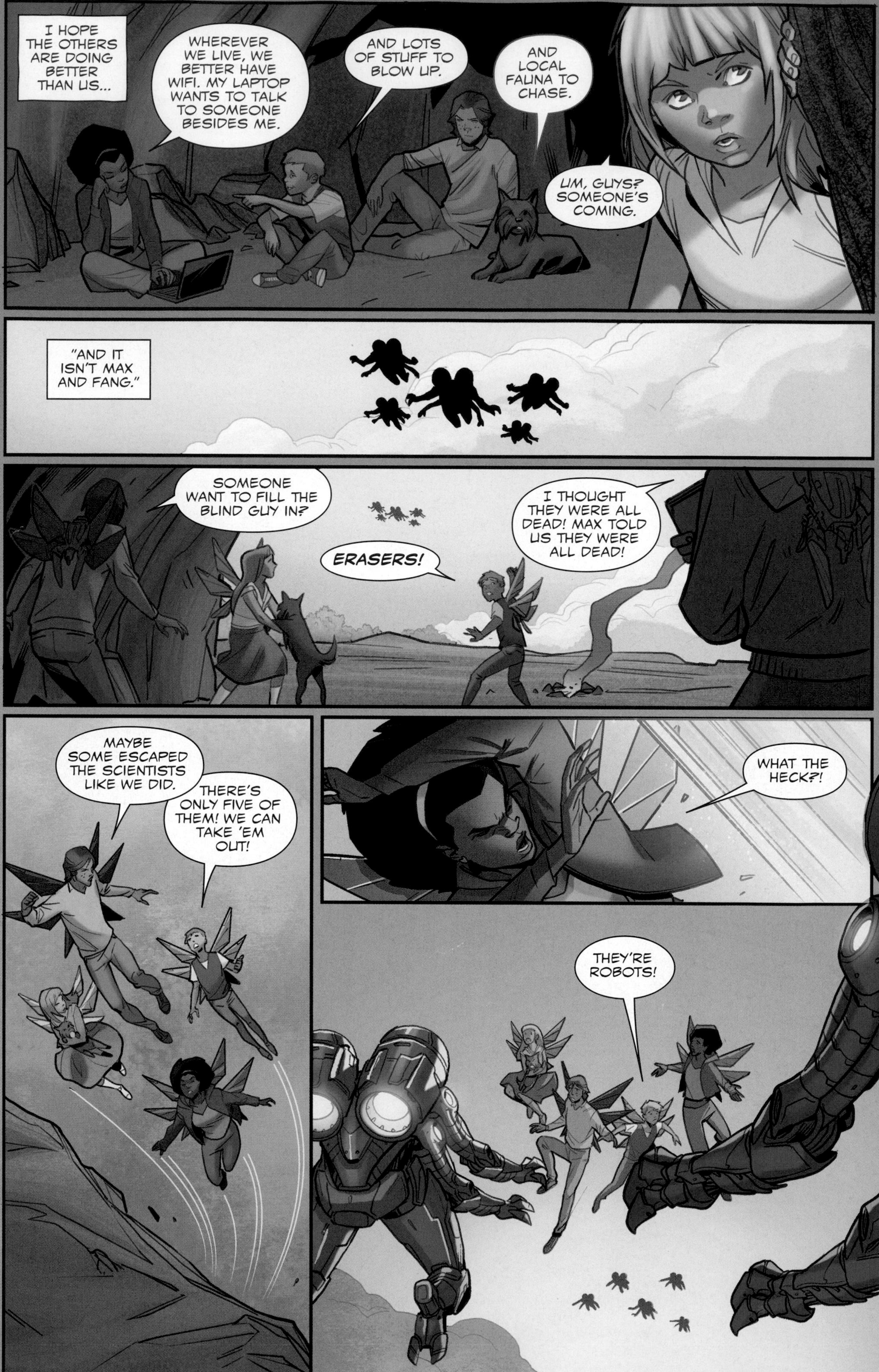
I HOPE THE OTHERS ARE DOING BETTER THAN US...
WHEREVER WE LIVE, WE BETTER HAVE WIFI. MY LAPTOP WANTS TO TALK TO SOMEONE BESIDES ME.
AND LOTS OF STUFF TO BLOW UP.
AND LOCAL FAUNA TO CHASE.
UM, GUYS? SOMEONE'S COMING.
"AND IT ISN'T MAX AND FANG."
SOMEONE WANT TO FILL THE BLIND GUY IN?
ERASERS!
I THOUGHT THEY WERE ALL DEAD! MAX TOLD US THEY WERE ALL DEAD!
MAYBE SOME ESCAPED THE SCIENTISTS LIKE WE DID.
THERE'S ONLY FIVE OF THEM! WE CAN TAKE 'EM OUT!
WHAT THE HECK?!
THEY'RE ROBOTS!

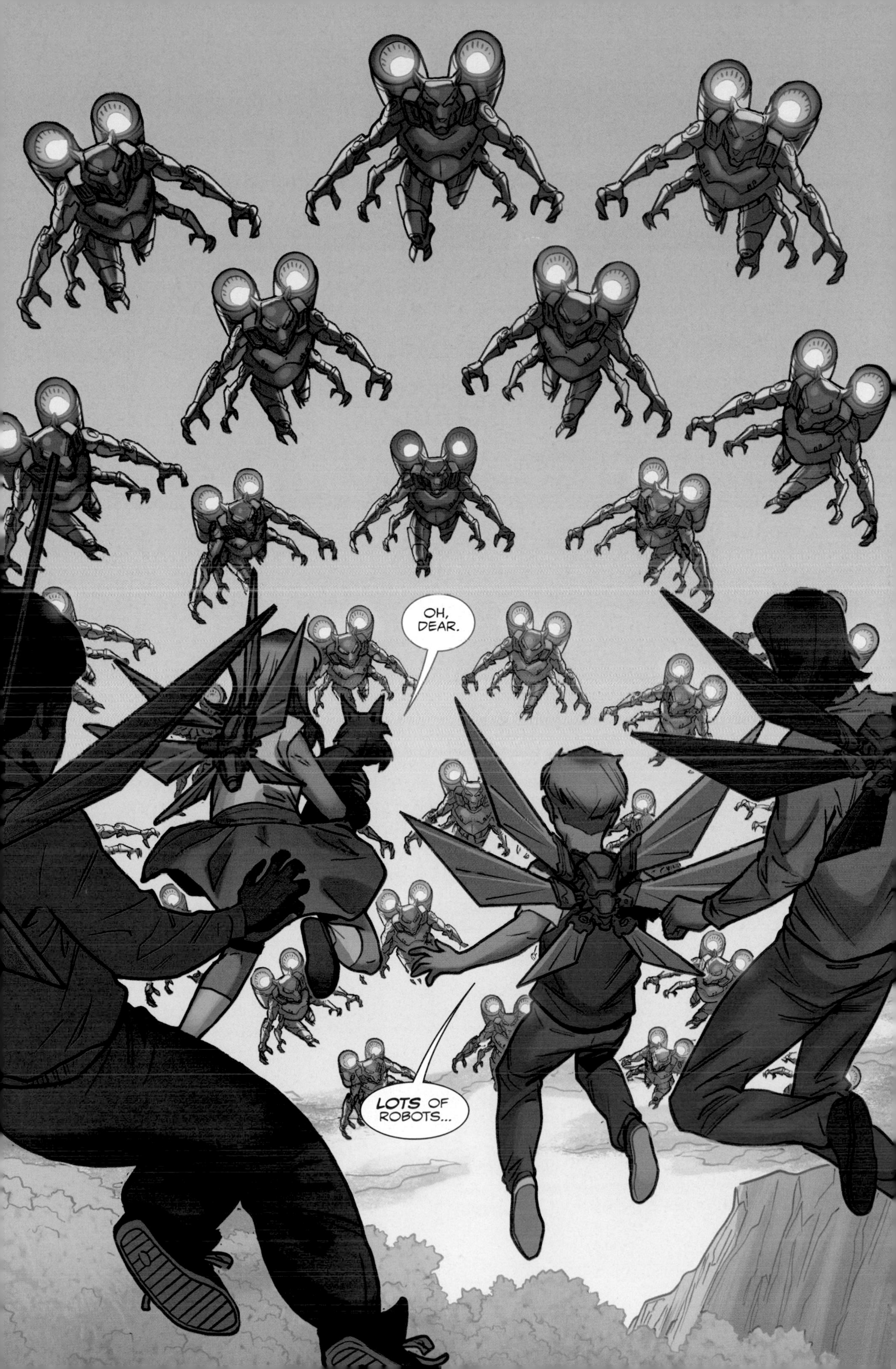

OH, DEAR.
LOTS OF ROBOTS...

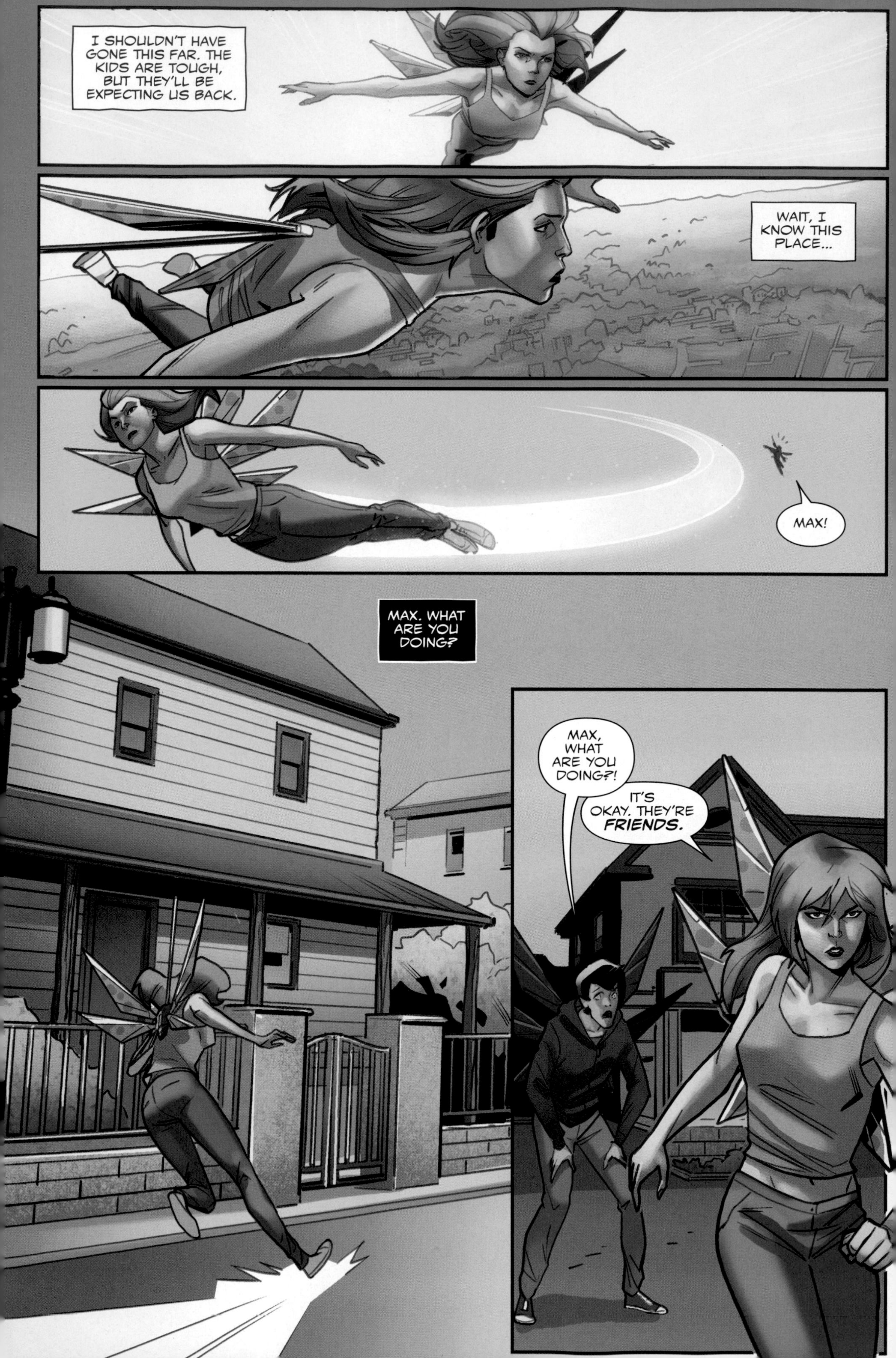
I SHOULDN'T HAVE GONE THIS FAR. THE KIDS ARE TOUGH, BUT THEY'LL BE EXPECTING US BACK.
WAIT, I KNOW THIS PLACE...
MAX!
MAX. WHAT ARE YOU DOING?
MAX, WHAT ARE YOU DOING?!
IT'S OKAY. THEY'RE FRIENDS.

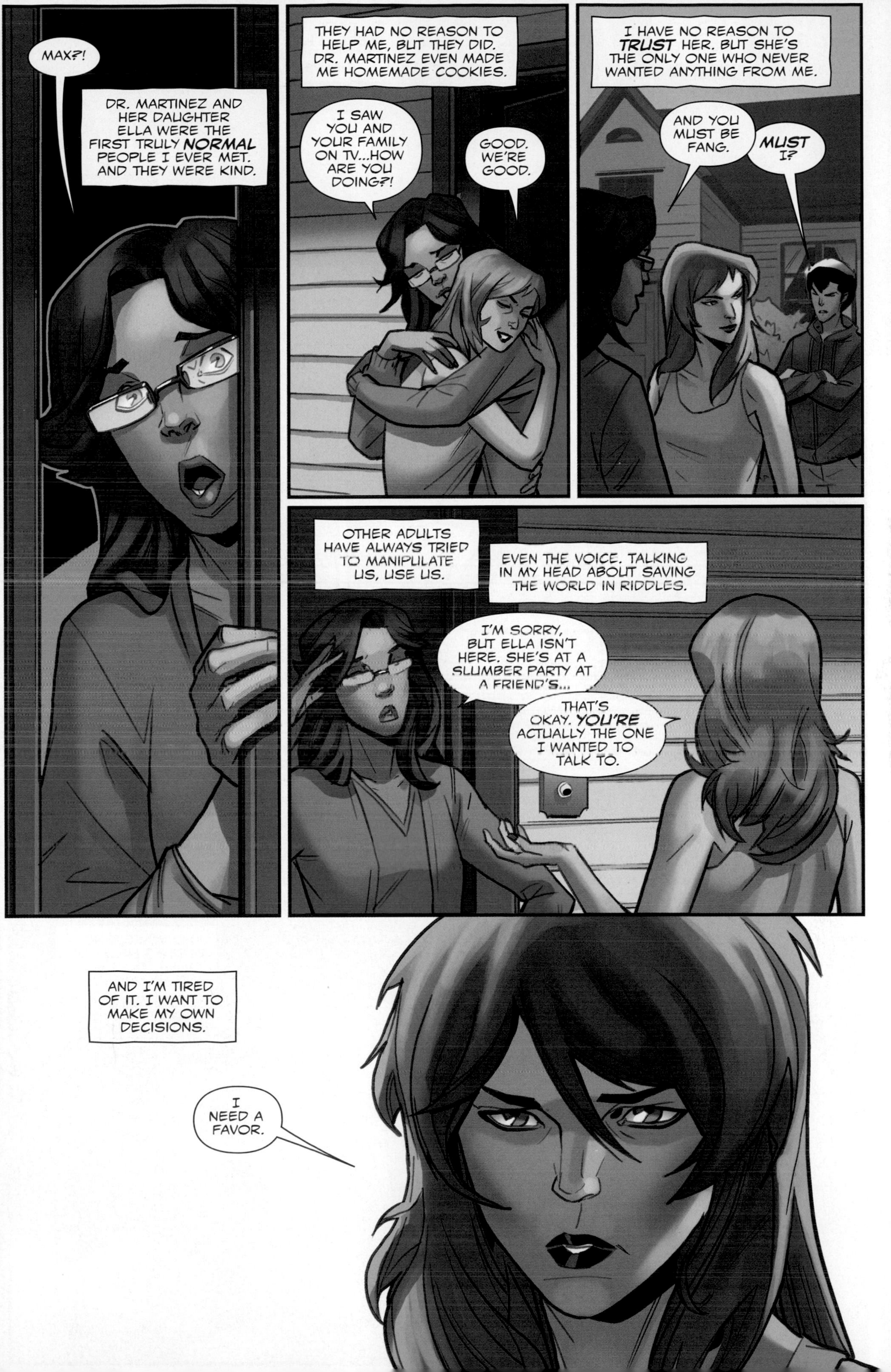
MAX?!
DR. MARTINEZ AND HER DAUGHTER ELLA WERE THE FIRST TRULY NORMAL PEOPLE I EVER MET. AND THEY WERE KIND.
THEY HAD NO REASON TO HELP ME, BUT THEY DID. DR. MARTINEZ EVEN MADE ME HOMEMADE COOKIES.
I SAW YOU AND YOUR FAMILY ON TV...HOW ARE YOU DOING?!
GOOD. WE'RE GOOD.
I HAVE NO REASON TO TRUST HER. BUT SHE'S THE ONLY ONE WHO NEVER WANTED ANYTHING FROM ME.
AND YOU MUST BE FANG.
MUST I?
OTHER ADULTS HAVE ALWAYS TRIED TO MANIPULATE US, USE US.
EVEN THE VOICE. TALKING IN MY HEAD ABOUT SAVING THE WORLD IN RIDDLES.
I'M SORRY, BUT ELLA ISN'T HERE. SHE'S AT A SLUMBER PARTY AT A FRIEND'S...
THAT'S OKAY. YOU'RE ACTUALLY THE ONE I WANTED TO TALK TO.
AND I'M TIRED OF IT. I WANT TO MAKE MY OWN DECISIONS.
I NEED A FAVOR.

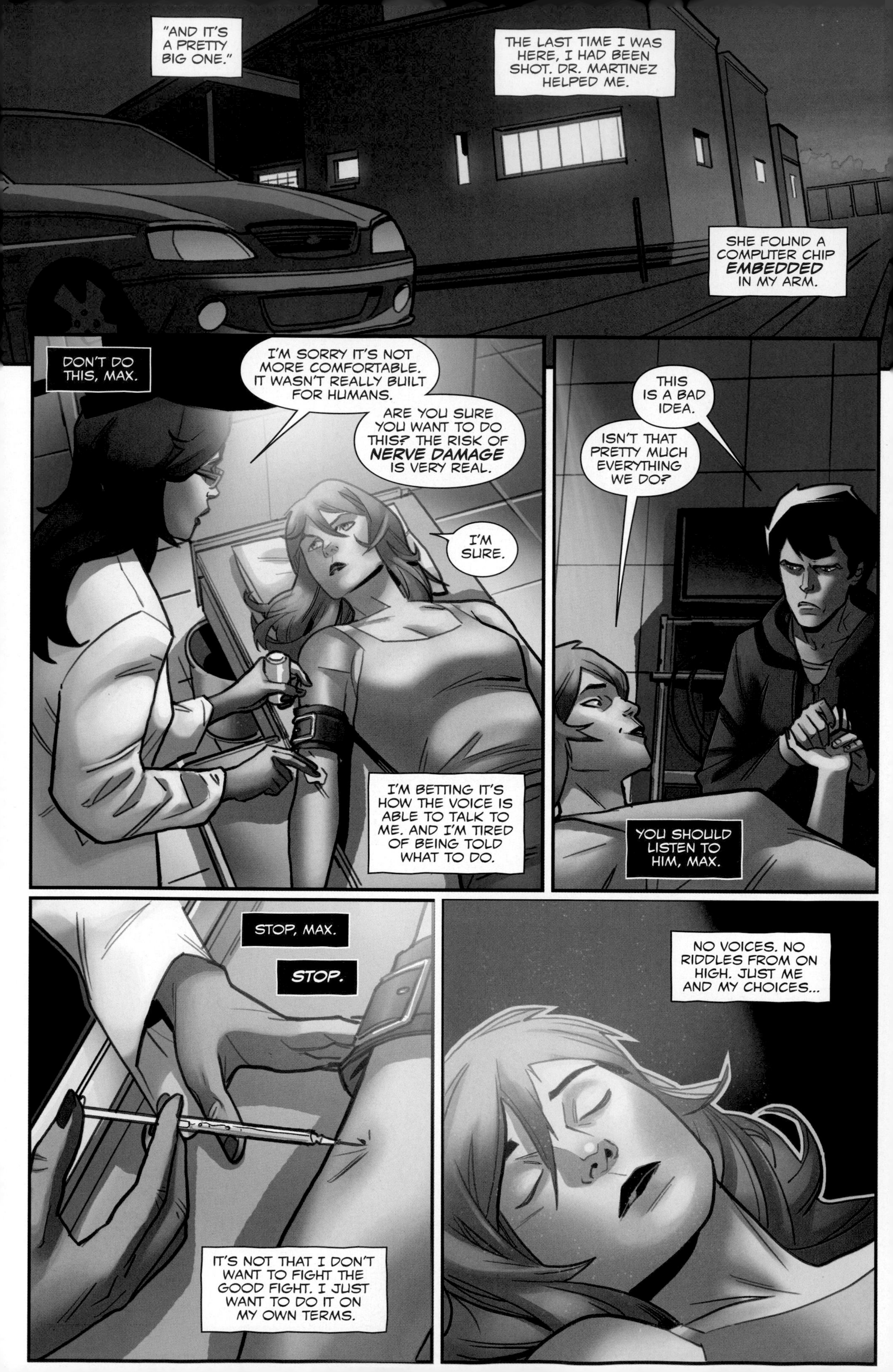
"AND IT'S A PRETTY BIG ONE."
THE LAST TIME I WAS HERE, I HAD BEEN SHOT. DR. MARTINEZ HELPED ME.
SHE FOUND A COMPUTER CHIP EMBEDDED IN MY ARM.
DON'T DO THIS, MAX.
I'M SORRY IT'S NOT MORE COMFORTABLE. IT WASN'T REALLY BUILT FOR HUMANS.
ARE YOU SURE YOU WANT TO DO THIS? THE RISK OF NERVE DAMAGE IS VERY REAL.
I'M SURE.
I'M BETTING IT'S HOW THE VOICE IS ABLE TO TALK TO ME. AND I'M TIRED OF BEING TOLD WHAT TO DO.
THIS IS A BAD IDEA.
ISN'T THAT PRETTY MUCH EVERYTHING WE DO?
YOU SHOULD LISTEN TO HIM, MAX.
STOP, MAX.
STOP.
IT'S NOT THAT I DON'T WANT TO FIGHT THE GOOD FIGHT. I JUST WANT TO DO IT ON MY OWN TERMS.
NO VOICES. NO RIDDLES FROM ON HIGH. JUST ME AND MY CHOICES...

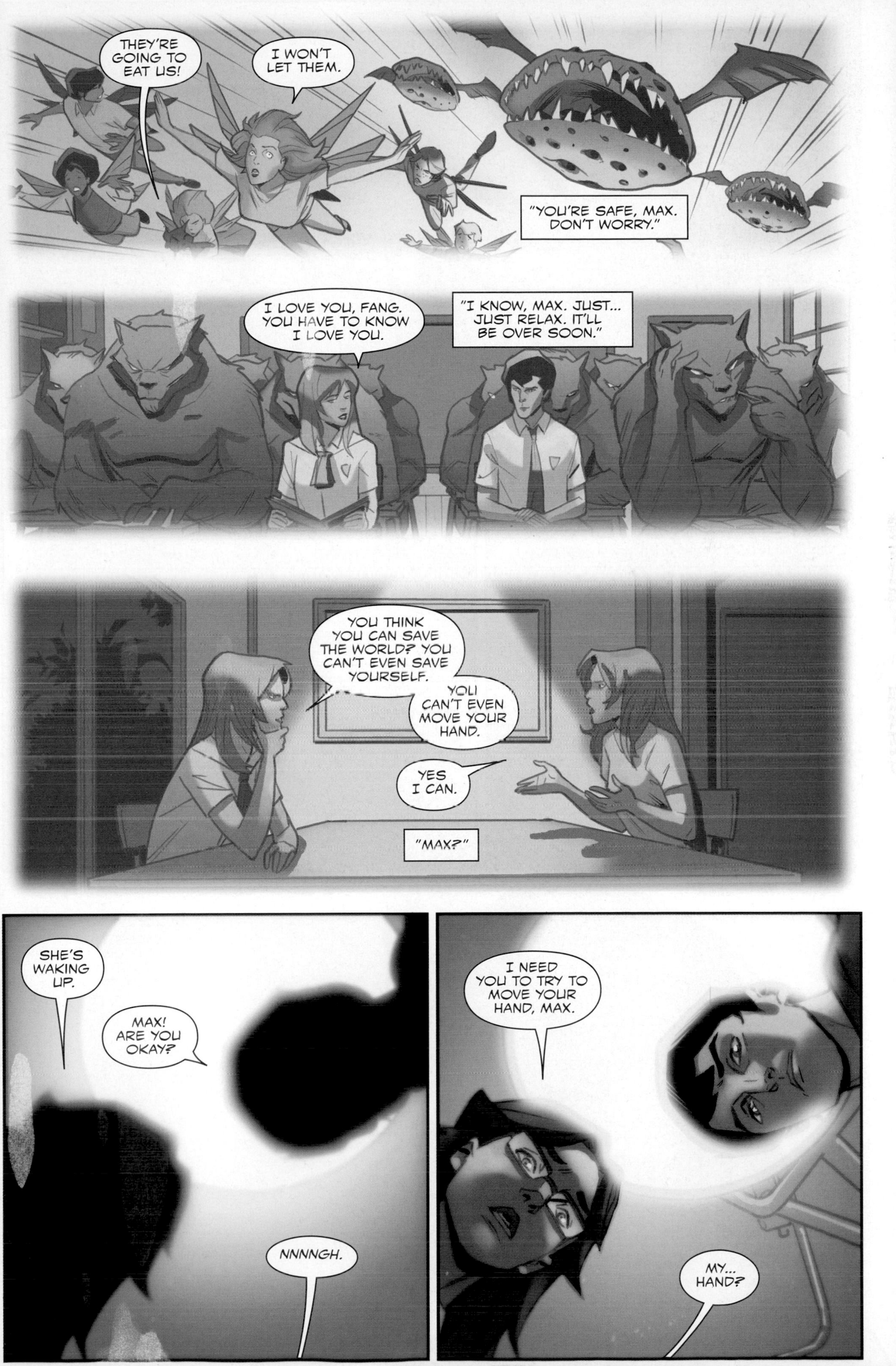
THEY'RE GOING TO EAT US!
I WON'T LET THEM.
"YOU'RE SAFE, MAX. DON'T WORRY."
I LOVE YOU, FANG. YOU HAVE TO KNOW I LOVE YOU.
"I KNOW, MAX. JUST... JUST RELAX. IT'LL BE OVER SOON."
YOU THINK YOU CAN SAVE THE WORLD? YOU CAN'T EVEN SAVE YOURSELF.
YOU CAN'T EVEN MOVE YOUR HAND.
YES I CAN.
"MAX?"
SHE'S WAKING UP.
MAX! ARE YOU OKAY?
NNNNGH.
I NEED YOU TO TRY TO MOVE YOUR HAND, MAX.
MY... HAND?

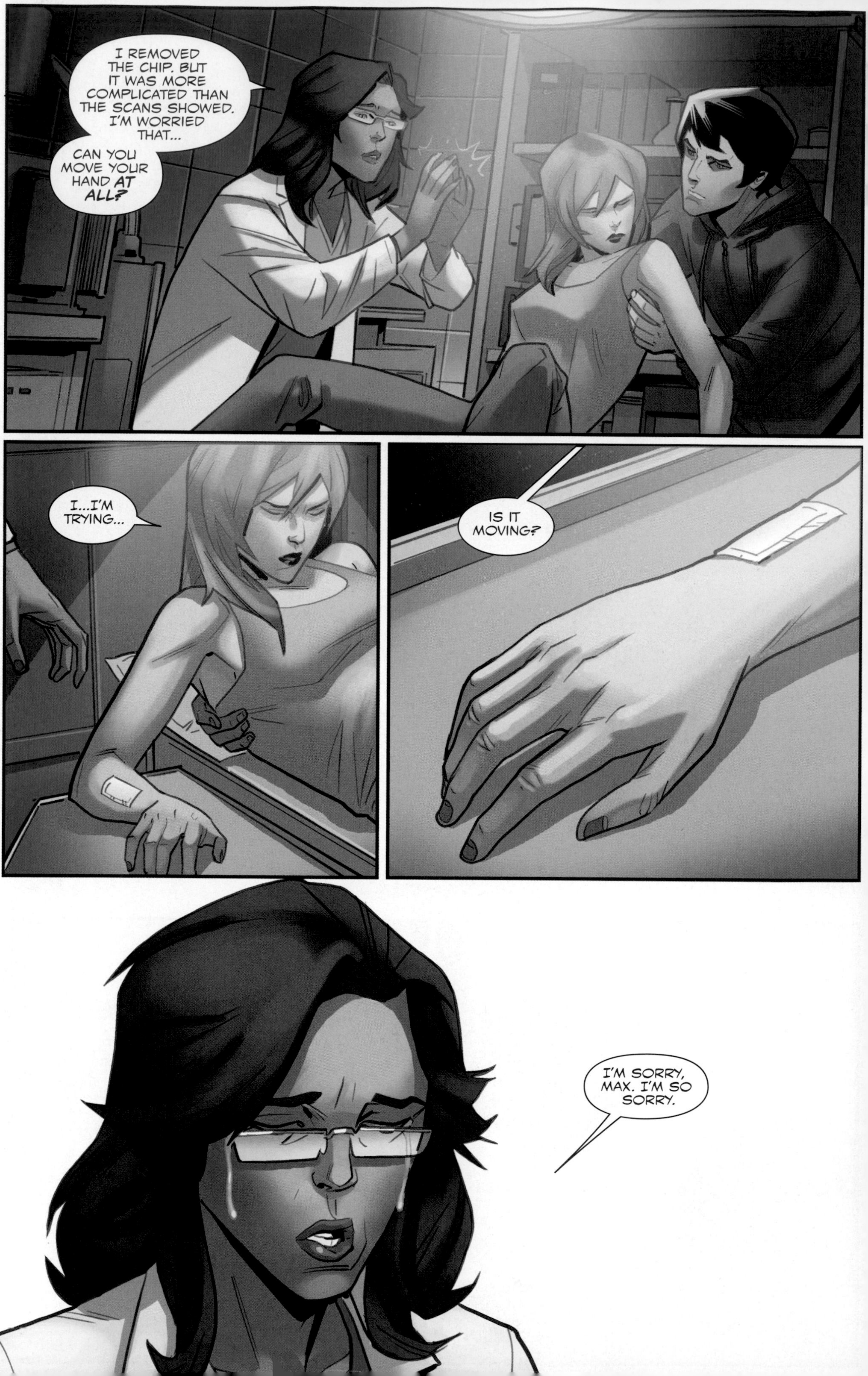
I REMOVED THE CHIP. BUT IT WAS MORE COMPLICATED THAN THE SCANS SHOWED. I'M WORRIED THAT...
CAN YOU MOVE YOUR HAND **AT ALL?**
I...I'M TRYING...
IS IT MOVING?
I'M SORRY, MAX. I'M SO SORRY.

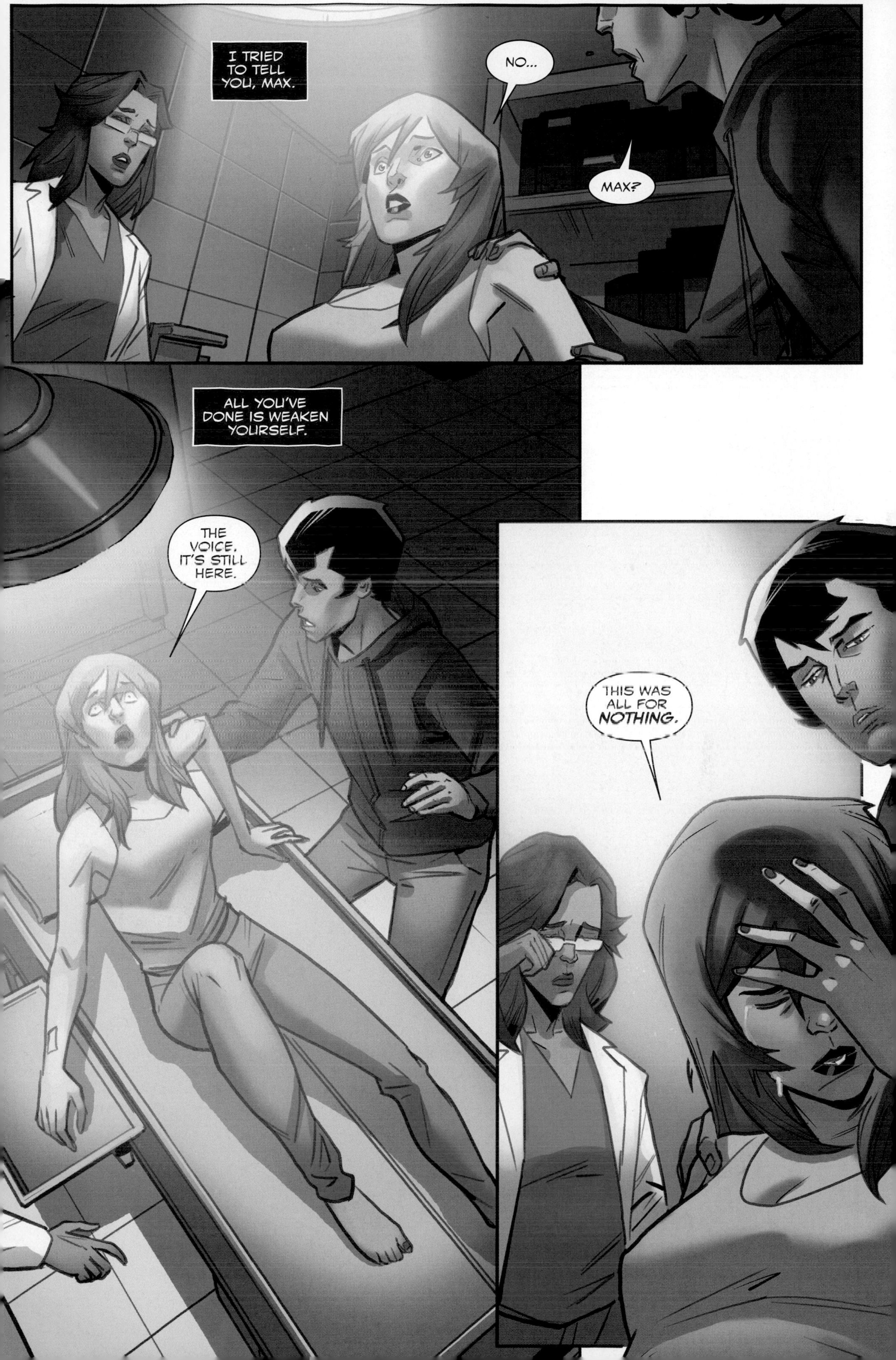
I TRIED TO TELL YOU, MAX.
NO...
MAX?
ALL YOU'VE DONE IS WEAKEN YOURSELF.
THE VOICE. IT'S STILL HERE.
THIS WAS ALL FOR *NOTHING.*

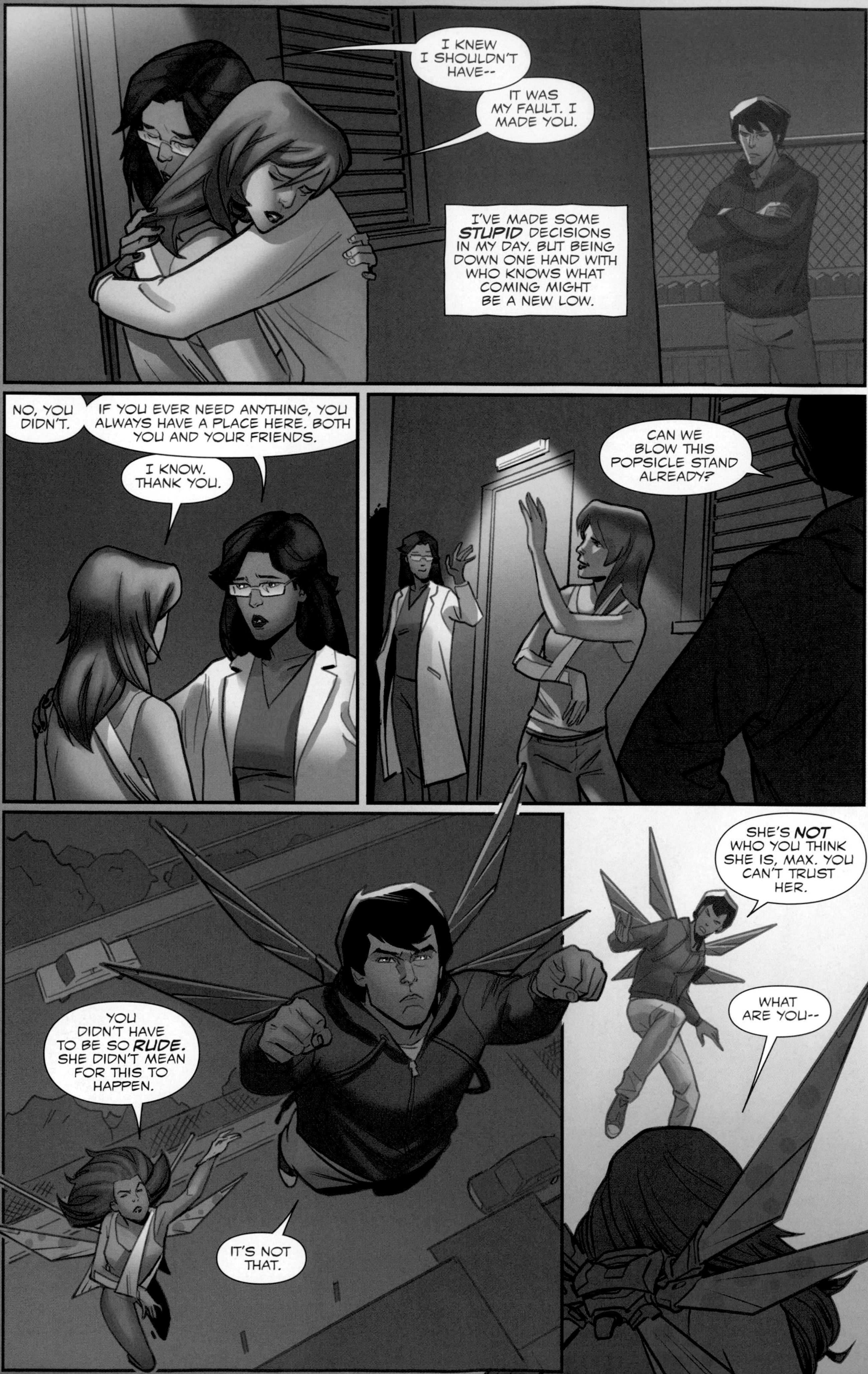
I KNEW I SHOULDN'T HAVE--
IT WAS MY FAULT. I MADE YOU.
I'VE MADE SOME STUPID DECISIONS IN MY DAY. BUT BEING DOWN ONE HAND WITH WHO KNOWS WHAT COMING MIGHT BE A NEW LOW.
NO, YOU DIDN'T.
IF YOU EVER NEED ANYTHING, YOU ALWAYS HAVE A PLACE HERE. BOTH YOU AND YOUR FRIENDS.
I KNOW. THANK YOU.
CAN WE BLOW THIS POPSICLE STAND ALREADY?
YOU DIDN'T HAVE TO BE SO RUDE. SHE DIDN'T MEAN FOR THIS TO HAPPEN.
IT'S NOT THAT.
SHE'S NOT WHO YOU THINK SHE IS, MAX. YOU CAN'T TRUST HER.
WHAT ARE YOU--

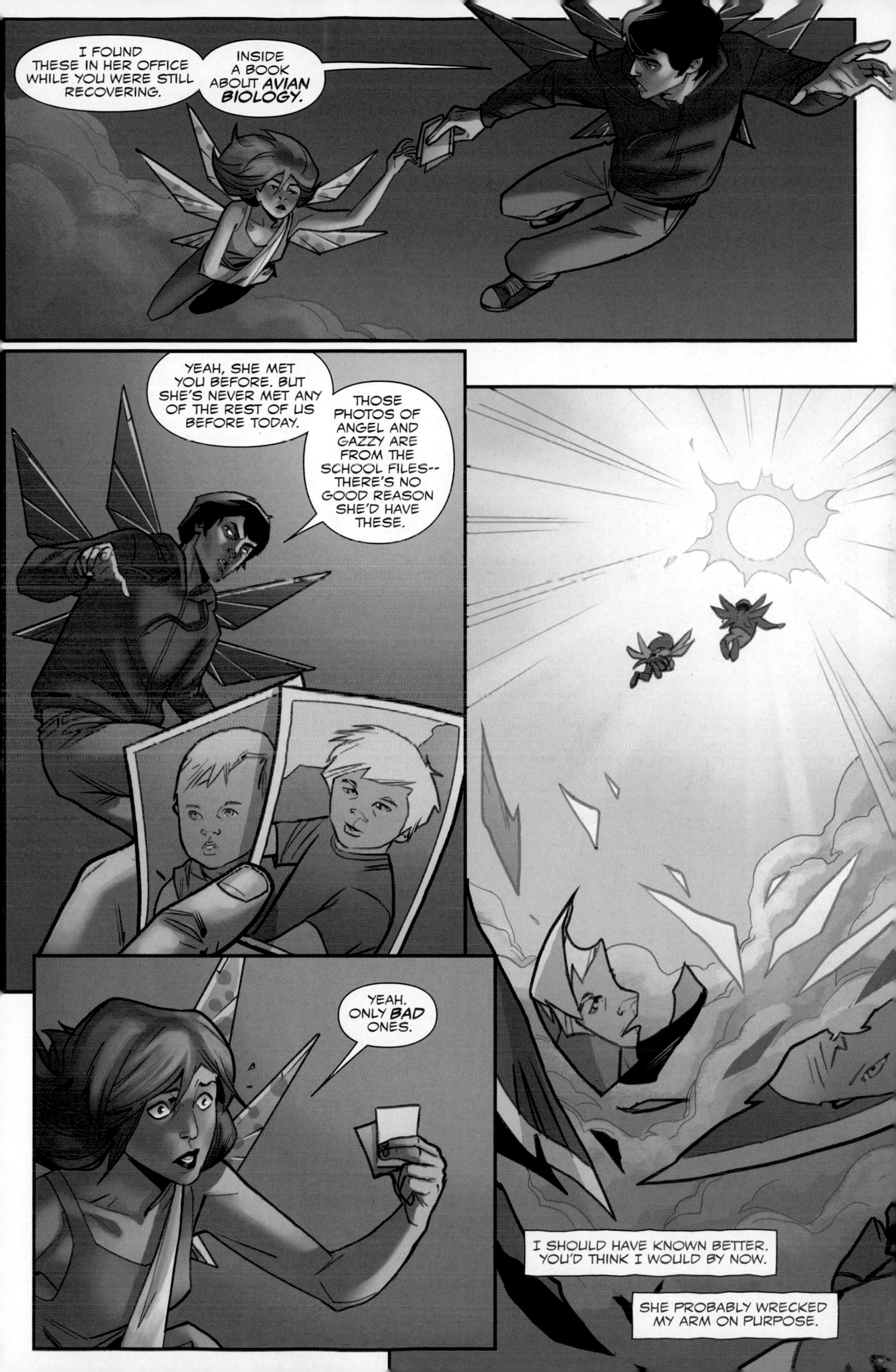
I FOUND THESE IN HER OFFICE WHILE YOU WERE STILL RECOVERING.
INSIDE A BOOK ABOUT AVIAN BIOLOGY.
YEAH, SHE MET YOU BEFORE. BUT SHE'S NEVER MET ANY OF THE REST OF US BEFORE TODAY.
THOSE PHOTOS OF ANGEL AND GAZZY ARE FROM THE SCHOOL FILES-- THERE'S NO GOOD REASON SHE'D HAVE THESE.
YEAH. ONLY BAD ONES.
I SHOULD HAVE KNOWN BETTER. YOU'D THINK I WOULD BY NOW.
SHE PROBABLY WRECKED MY ARM ON PURPOSE.

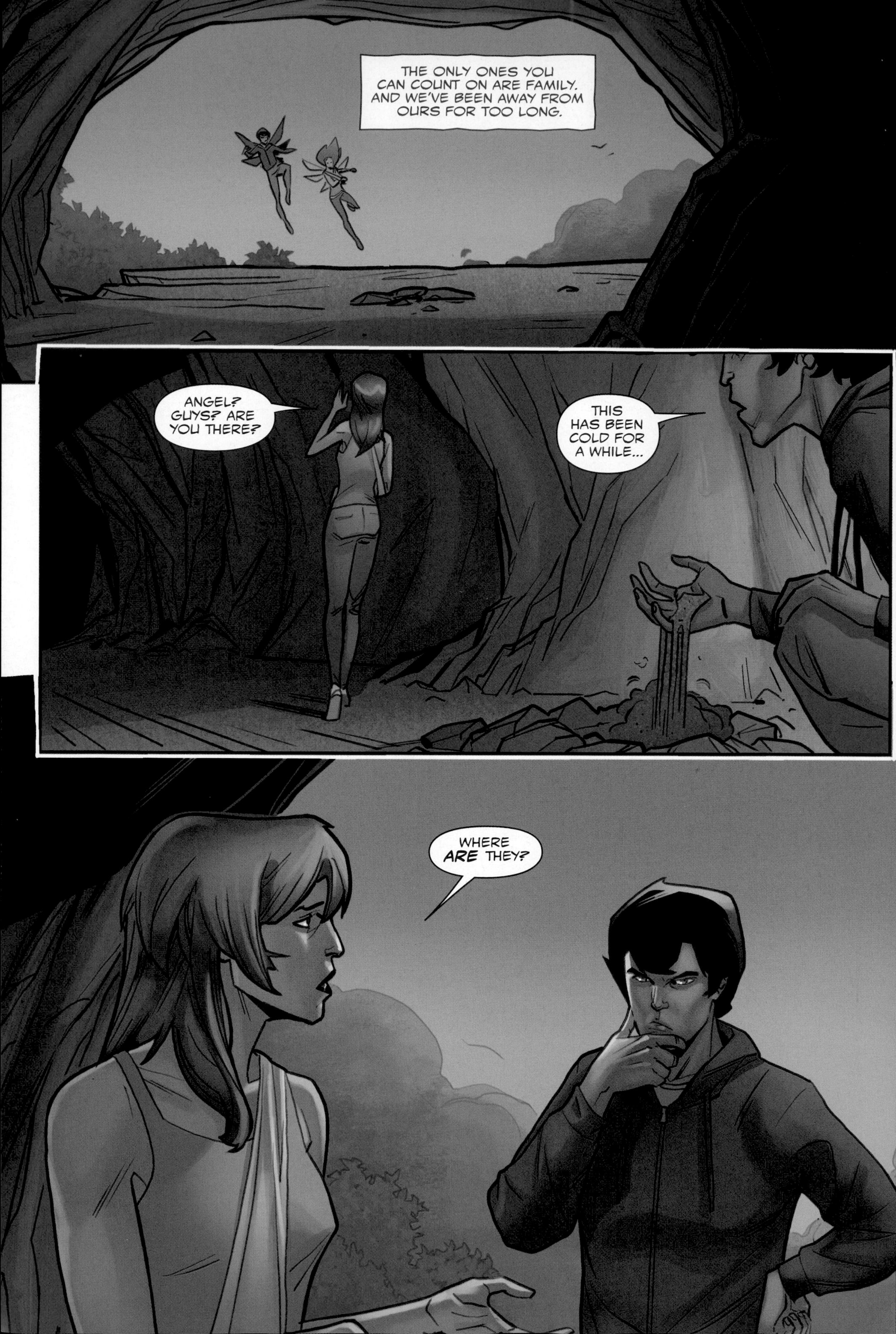
THE ONLY ONES YOU CAN COUNT ON ARE FAMILY. AND WE'VE BEEN AWAY FROM OURS FOR TOO LONG.
ANGEL? GUYS? ARE YOU THERE?
THIS HAS BEEN COLD FOR A WHILE...
WHERE ARE THEY?

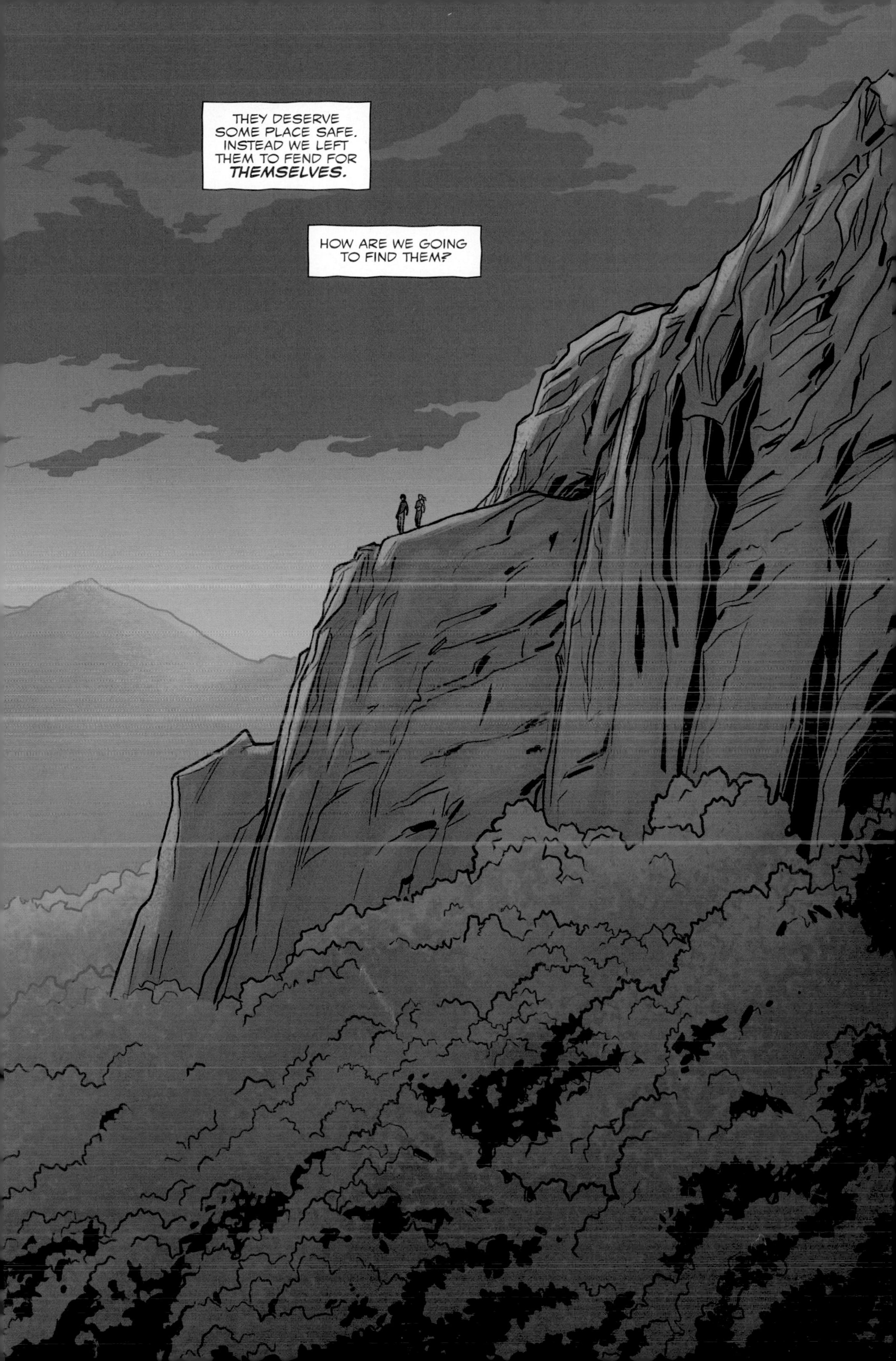
THEY DESERVE SOME PLACE SAFE. INSTEAD WE LEFT THEM TO FEND FOR *THEMSELVES.*
HOW ARE WE GOING TO FIND THEM?

CHAPTER 2

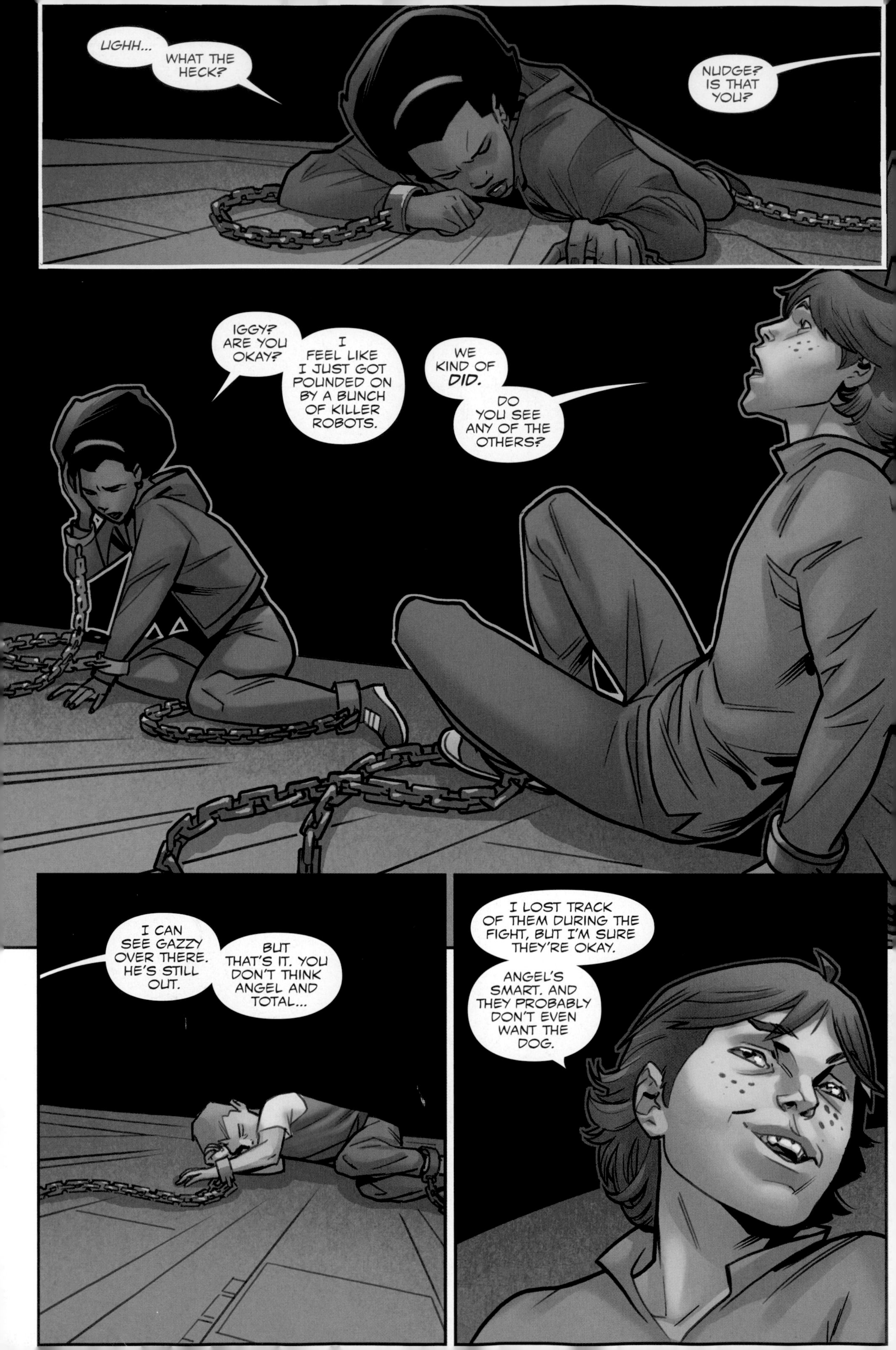
UGHH...
WHAT THE HECK?
NUDGE? IS THAT YOU?
IGGY? ARE YOU OKAY?
I FEEL LIKE I JUST GOT POUNDED ON BY A BUNCH OF KILLER ROBOTS.
WE KIND OF DID.
DO YOU SEE ANY OF THE OTHERS?
I CAN SEE GAZZY OVER THERE. HE'S STILL OUT.
BUT THAT'S IT. YOU DON'T THINK ANGEL AND TOTAL...
I LOST TRACK OF THEM DURING THE FIGHT, BUT I'M SURE THEY'RE OKAY.
ANGEL'S SMART. AND THEY PROBABLY DON'T EVEN WANT THE DOG.

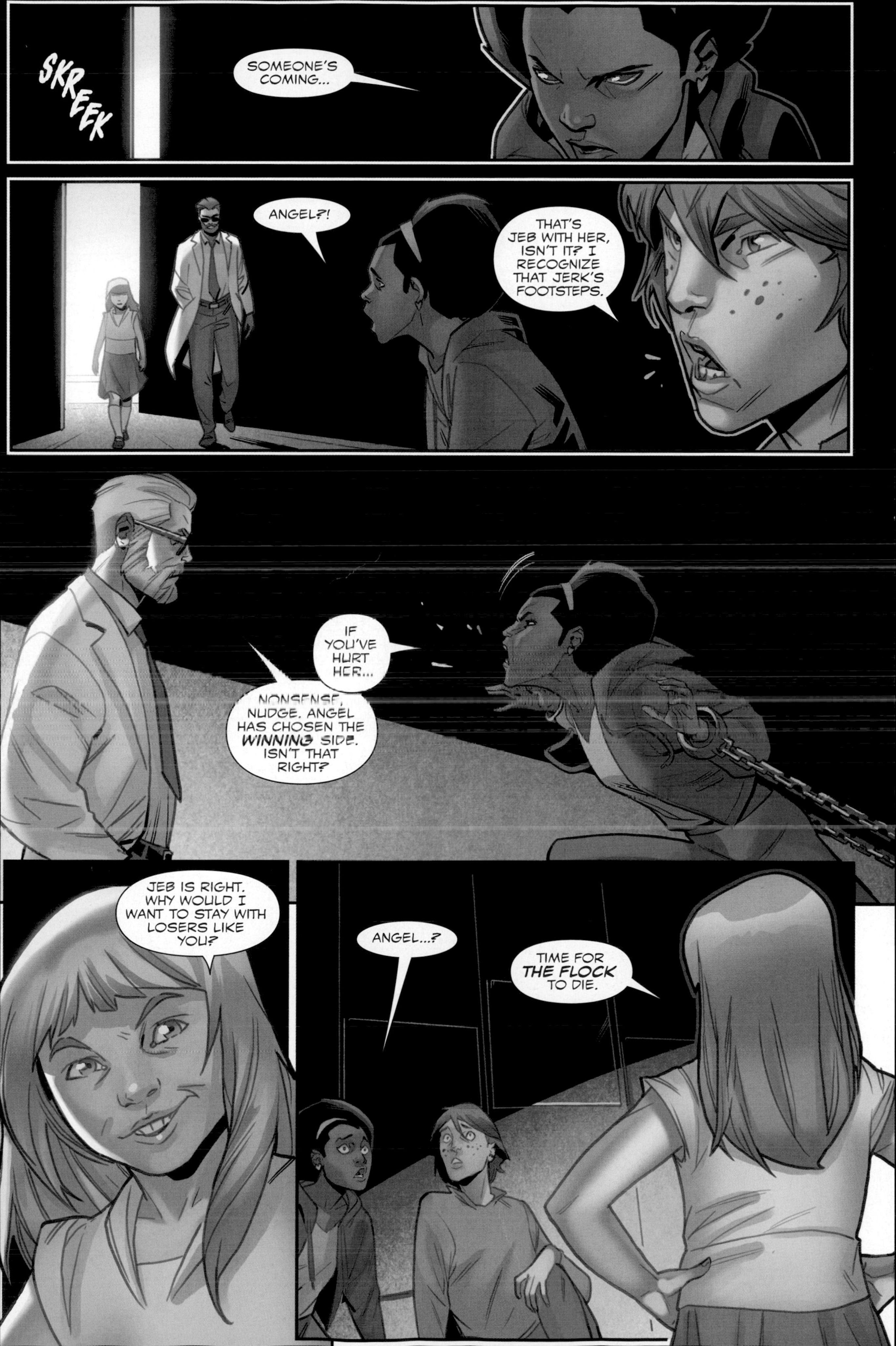
SKREEK
SOMEONE'S COMING...
ANGEL?!
THAT'S JEB WITH HER, ISN'T IT? I RECOGNIZE THAT JERK'S FOOTSTEPS.
IF YOU'VE HURT HER...
NONSENSE, NUDGE. ANGEL HAS CHOSEN THE WINNING SIDE. ISN'T THAT RIGHT?
JEB IS RIGHT. WHY WOULD I WANT TO STAY WITH LOSERS LIKE YOU?
ANGEL...?
TIME FOR THE FLOCK TO DIE.

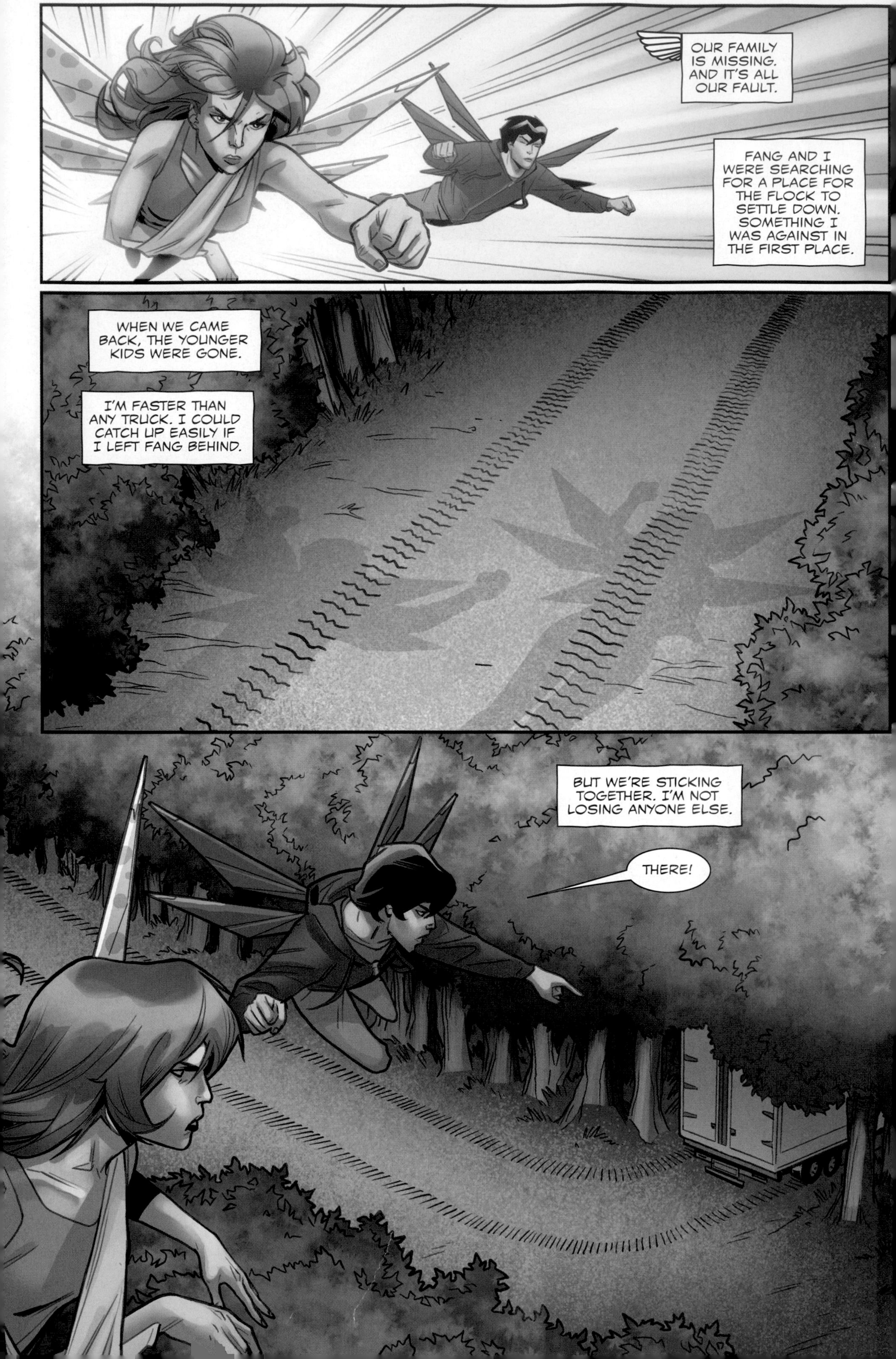
OUR FAMILY IS MISSING. AND IT'S ALL OUR FAULT.
FANG AND I WERE SEARCHING FOR A PLACE FOR THE FLOCK TO SETTLE DOWN. SOMETHING I WAS AGAINST IN THE FIRST PLACE.
WHEN WE CAME BACK, THE YOUNGER KIDS WERE GONE.
I'M FASTER THAN ANY TRUCK. I COULD CATCH UP EASILY IF I LEFT FANG BEHIND.
BUT WE'RE STICKING TOGETHER. I'M NOT LOSING ANYONE ELSE.
THERE!

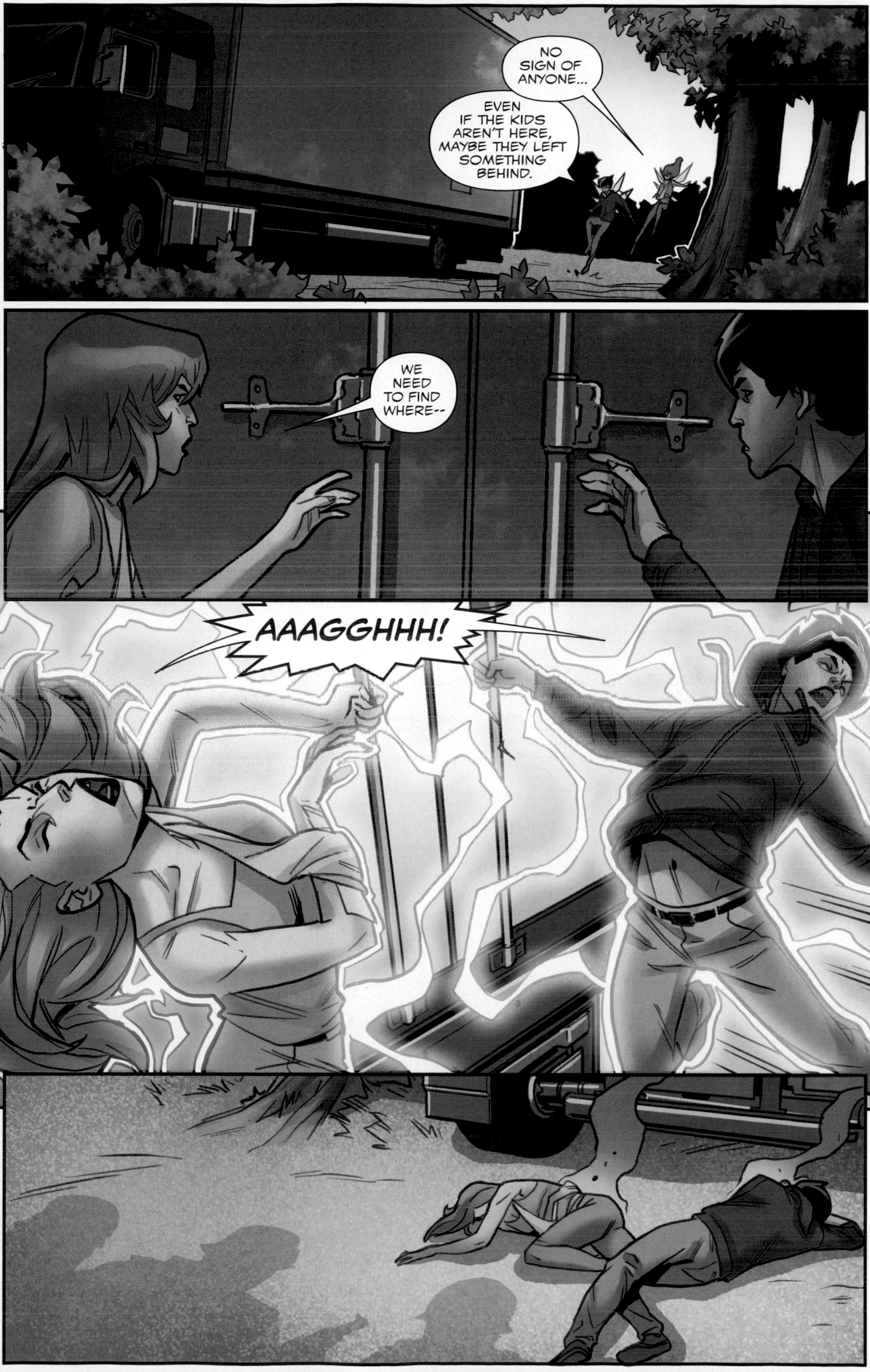
NO SIGN OF ANYONE...
EVEN IF THE KIDS AREN'T HERE, MAYBE THEY LEFT SOMETHING BEHIND.
WE NEED TO FIND WHERE--
AAAGGHHH!

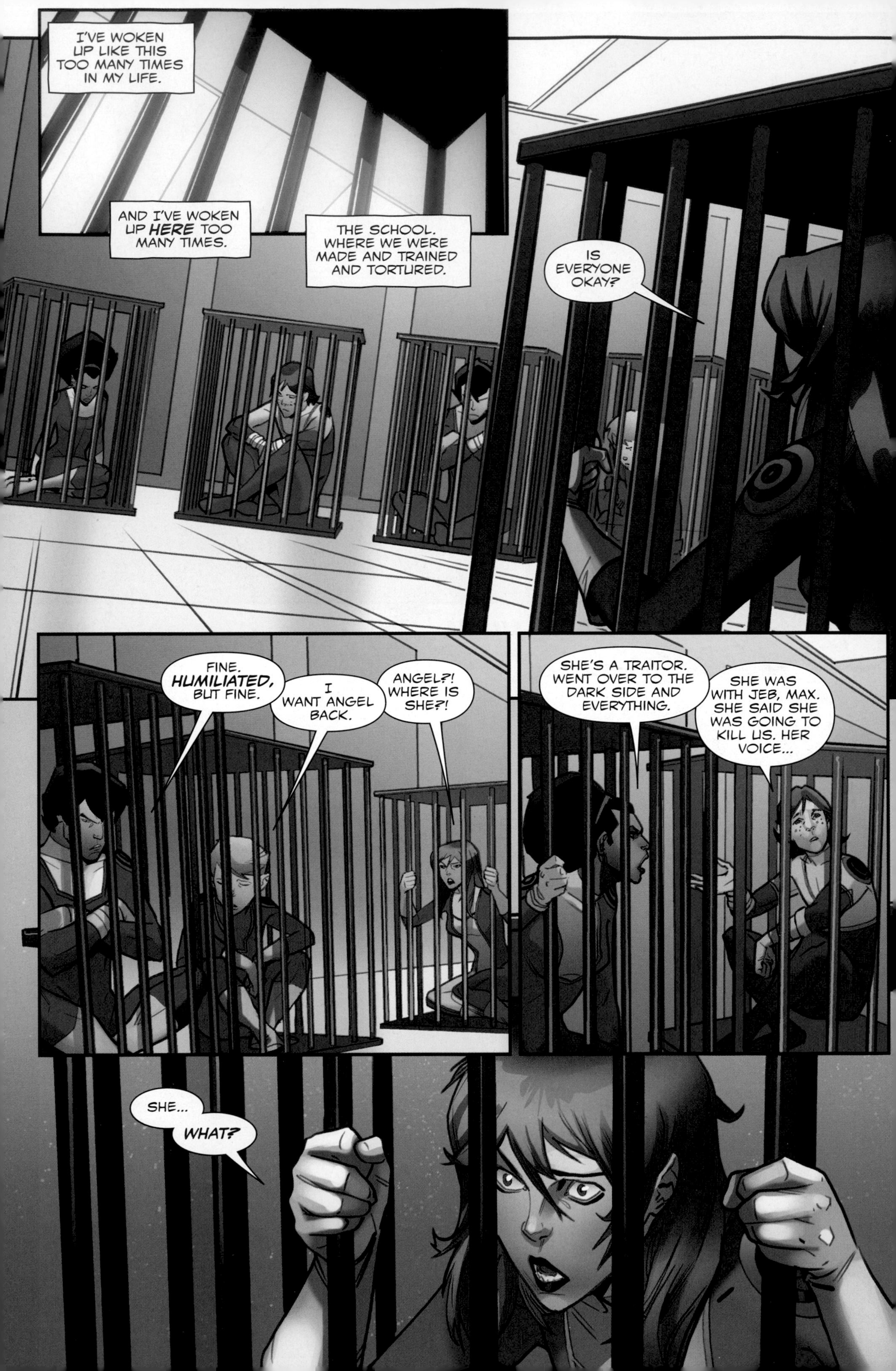
I'VE WOKEN UP LIKE THIS TOO MANY TIMES IN MY LIFE.
AND I'VE WOKEN UP HERE TOO MANY TIMES.
THE SCHOOL. WHERE WE WERE MADE AND TRAINED AND TORTURED.
IS EVERYONE OKAY?
FINE. HUMILIATED, BUT FINE.
I WANT ANGEL BACK.
ANGEL?! WHERE IS SHE?!
SHE'S A TRAITOR. WENT OVER TO THE DARK SIDE AND EVERYTHING.
SHE WAS WITH JEB, MAX. SHE SAID SHE WAS GOING TO KILL US. HER VOICE...
SHE...
WHAT?

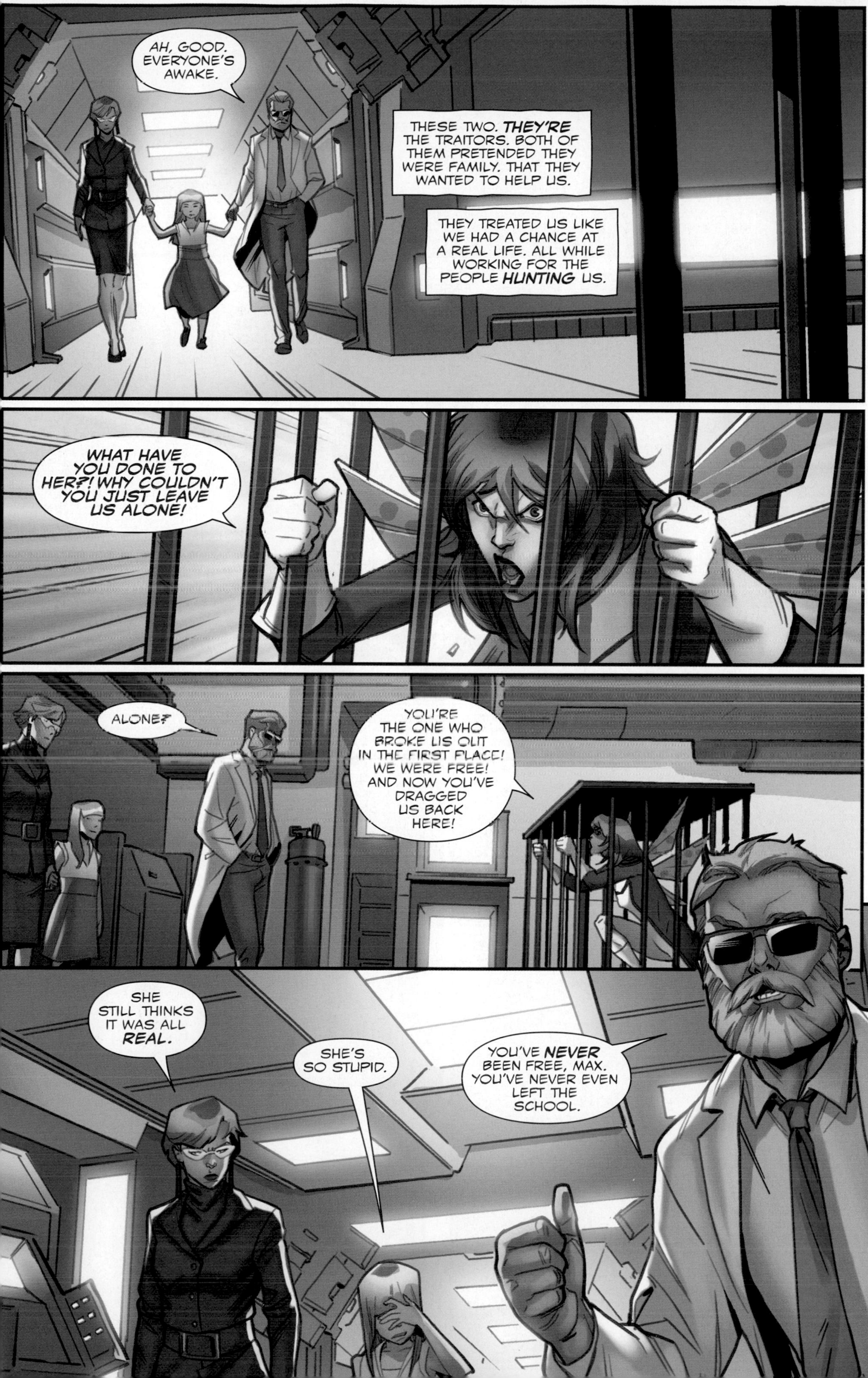
AH, GOOD. EVERYONE'S AWAKE.
THESE TWO. ***THEY'RE*** THE TRAITORS. BOTH OF THEM PRETENDED THEY WERE FAMILY. THAT THEY WANTED TO HELP US.
THEY TREATED US LIKE WE HAD A CHANCE AT A REAL LIFE. ALL WHILE WORKING FOR THE PEOPLE ***HUNTING*** US.
WHAT HAVE YOU DONE TO HER?! WHY COULDN'T YOU JUST LEAVE US ALONE!
ALONE?
YOU'RE THE ONE WHO BROKE US OUT IN THE FIRST PLACE! WE WERE FREE! AND NOW YOU'VE DRAGGED US BACK HERE!
SHE STILL THINKS IT WAS ALL ***REAL***.
SHE'S SO STUPID.
YOU'VE ***NEVER*** BEEN FREE, MAX. YOU'VE NEVER EVEN LEFT THE SCHOOL.

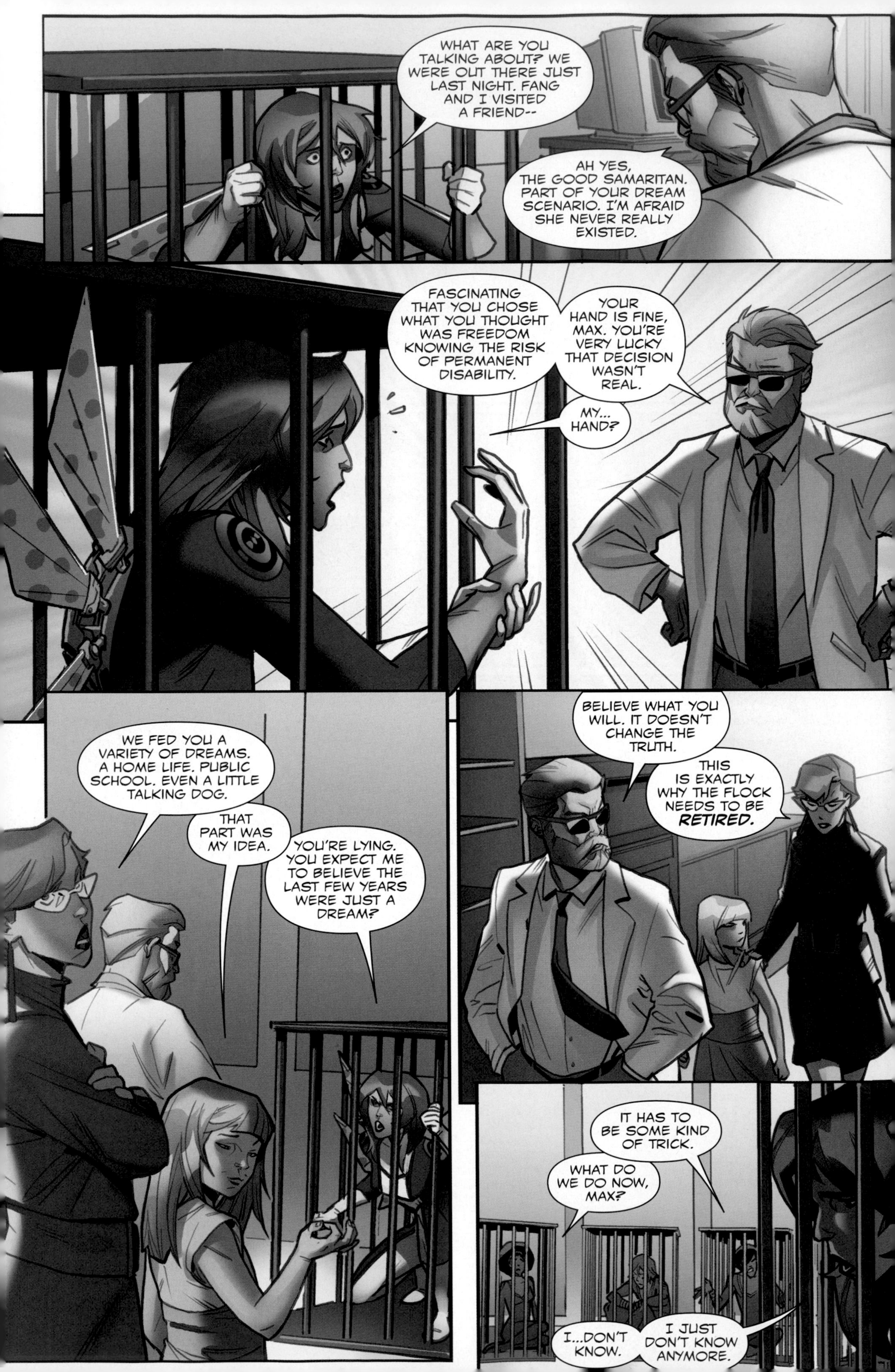
WHAT ARE YOU TALKING ABOUT? WE WERE OUT THERE JUST LAST NIGHT. FANG AND I VISITED A FRIEND--
AH YES, THE GOOD SAMARITAN. PART OF YOUR DREAM SCENARIO. I'M AFRAID SHE NEVER REALLY EXISTED.
FASCINATING THAT YOU CHOSE WHAT YOU THOUGHT WAS FREEDOM KNOWING THE RISK OF PERMANENT DISABILITY.
YOUR HAND IS FINE, MAX. YOU'RE VERY LUCKY THAT DECISION WASN'T REAL.
MY... HAND?
WE FED YOU A VARIETY OF DREAMS. A HOME LIFE. PUBLIC SCHOOL. EVEN A LITTLE TALKING DOG.
THAT PART WAS MY IDEA.
YOU'RE LYING. YOU EXPECT ME TO BELIEVE THE LAST FEW YEARS WERE JUST A DREAM?
BELIEVE WHAT YOU WILL. IT DOESN'T CHANGE THE TRUTH.
THIS IS EXACTLY WHY THE FLOCK NEEDS TO BE ***RETIRED.***
IT HAS TO BE SOME KIND OF TRICK.
WHAT DO WE DO NOW, MAX?
I...DON'T KNOW.
I JUST DON'T KNOW ANYMORE.

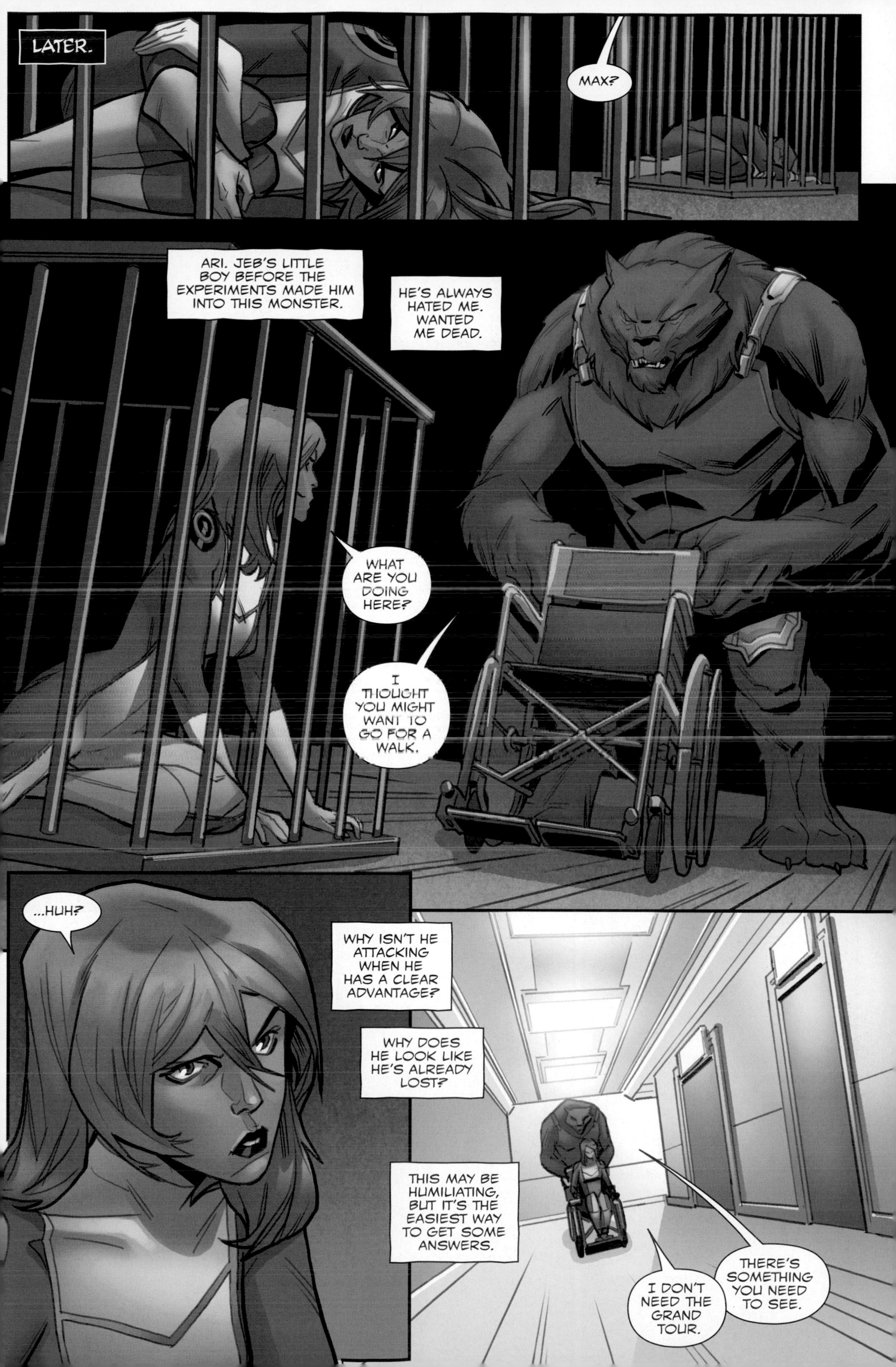
LATER.
MAX?
ARI. JEB'S LITTLE BOY BEFORE THE EXPERIMENTS MADE HIM INTO THIS MONSTER.
HE'S ALWAYS HATED ME. WANTED ME DEAD.
WHAT ARE YOU DOING HERE?
I THOUGHT YOU MIGHT WANT TO GO FOR A WALK.
...HUH?
WHY ISN'T HE ATTACKING WHEN HE HAS A CLEAR ADVANTAGE?
WHY DOES HE LOOK LIKE HE'S ALREADY LOST?
THIS MAY BE HUMILIATING, BUT IT'S THE EASIEST WAY TO GET SOME ANSWERS.
THERE'S SOMETHING YOU NEED TO SEE.
I DON'T NEED THE GRAND TOUR.

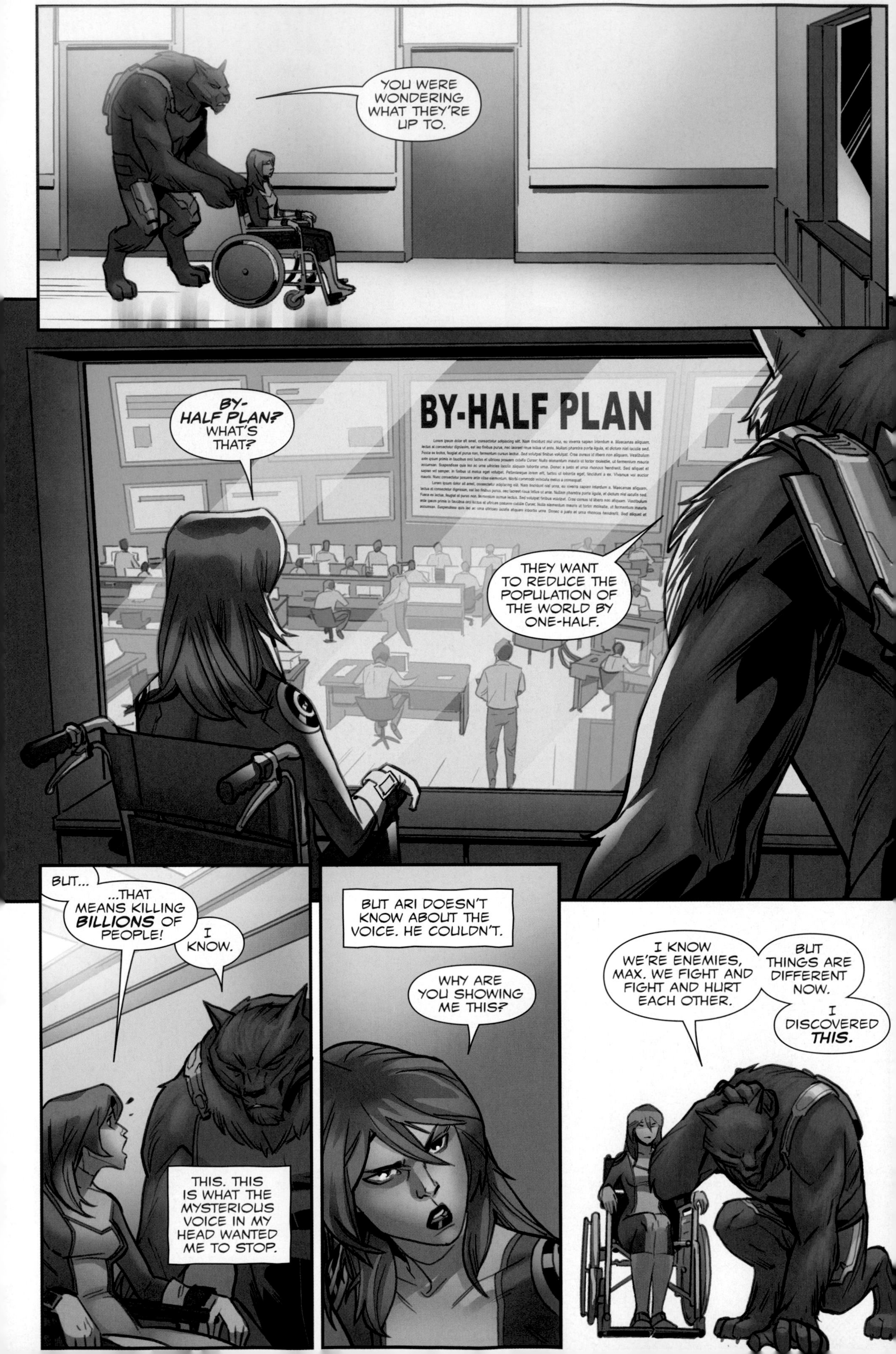

YOU WERE WONDERING WHAT THEY'RE UP TO.
BY-HALF PLAN
BY-HALF PLAN? WHAT'S THAT?
THEY WANT TO REDUCE THE POPULATION OF THE WORLD BY ONE-HALF.
BUT...
...THAT MEANS KILLING BILLIONS OF PEOPLE!
I KNOW.
THIS. THIS IS WHAT THE MYSTERIOUS VOICE IN MY HEAD WANTED ME TO STOP.
BUT ARI DOESN'T KNOW ABOUT THE VOICE. HE COULDN'T.
WHY ARE YOU SHOWING ME THIS?
I KNOW WE'RE ENEMIES, MAX. WE FIGHT AND FIGHT AND HURT EACH OTHER.
BUT THINGS ARE DIFFERENT NOW.
I DISCOVERED THIS.

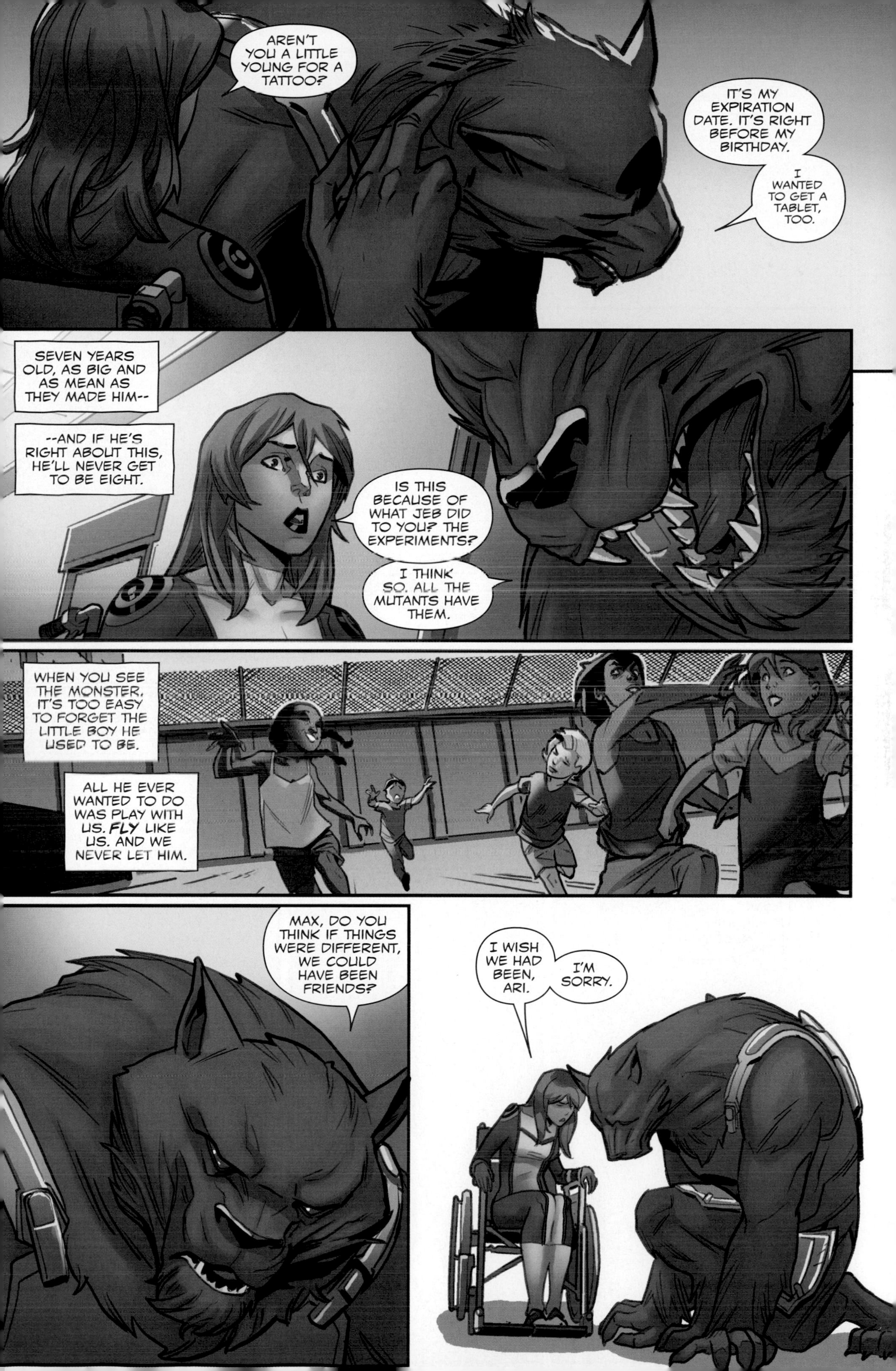
AREN'T YOU A LITTLE YOUNG FOR A TATTOO?
IT'S MY EXPIRATION DATE. IT'S RIGHT BEFORE MY BIRTHDAY.
I WANTED TO GET A TABLET, TOO.
SEVEN YEARS OLD, AS BIG AND AS MEAN AS THEY MADE HIM--
--AND IF HE'S RIGHT ABOUT THIS, HE'LL NEVER GET TO BE EIGHT.
IS THIS BECAUSE OF WHAT JEB DID TO YOU? THE EXPERIMENTS?
I THINK SO. ALL THE MUTANTS HAVE THEM.
WHEN YOU SEE THE MONSTER, IT'S TOO EASY TO FORGET THE LITTLE BOY HE USED TO BE.
ALL HE EVER WANTED TO DO WAS PLAY WITH US. FLY LIKE US. AND WE NEVER LET HIM.
MAX, DO YOU THINK IF THINGS WERE DIFFERENT, WE COULD HAVE BEEN FRIENDS?
I WISH WE HAD BEEN, ARI.
I'M SORRY.

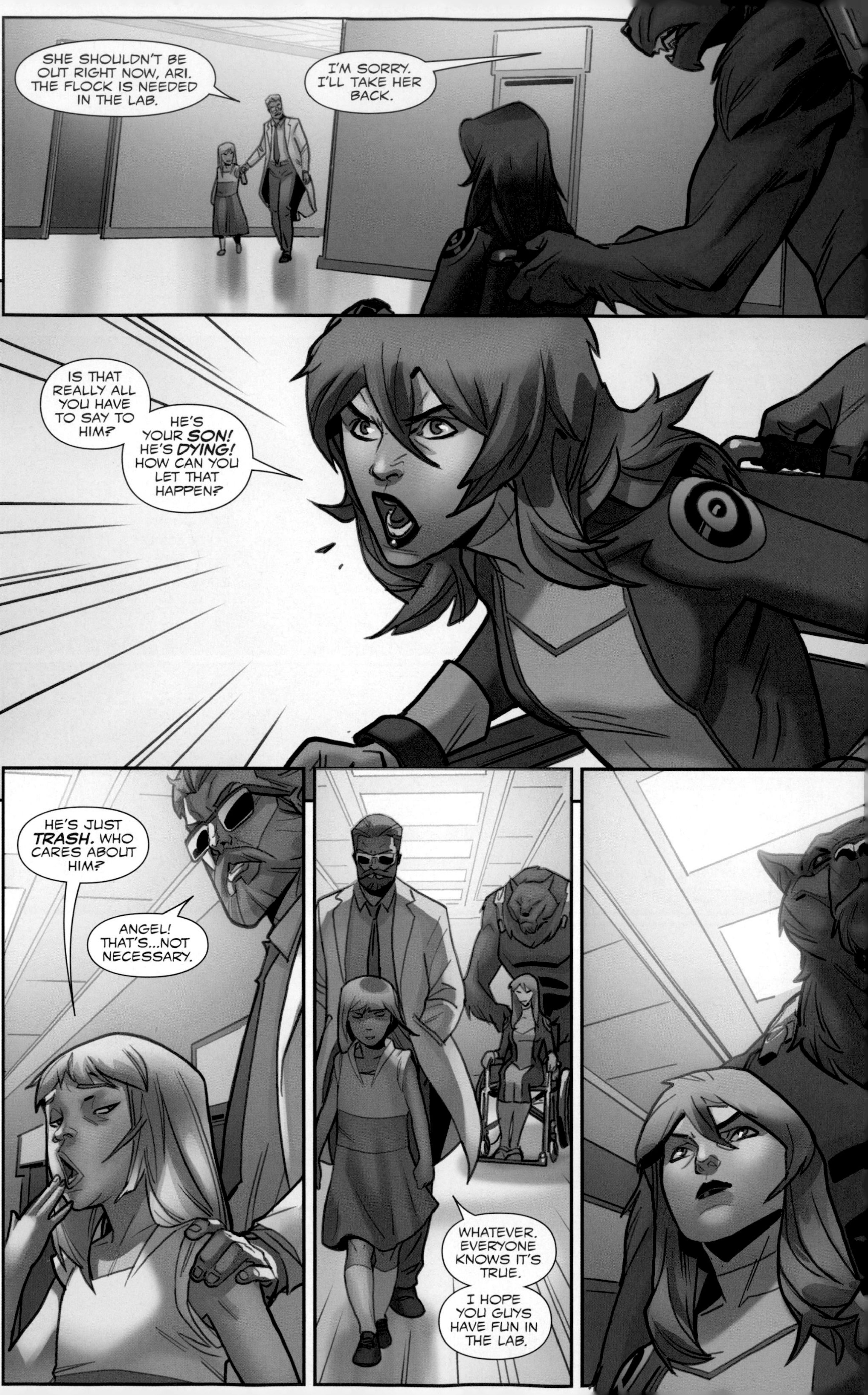
SHE SHOULDN'T BE OUT RIGHT NOW, ARI. THE FLOCK IS NEEDED IN THE LAB.
I'M SORRY. I'LL TAKE HER BACK.
IS THAT REALLY ALL YOU HAVE TO SAY TO HIM?
HE'S YOUR SON! HE'S DYING! HOW CAN YOU LET THAT HAPPEN?
HE'S JUST TRASH. WHO CARES ABOUT HIM?
ANGEL! THAT'S...NOT NECESSARY.
WHATEVER. EVERYONE KNOWS IT'S TRUE.
I HOPE YOU GUYS HAVE FUN IN THE LAB.

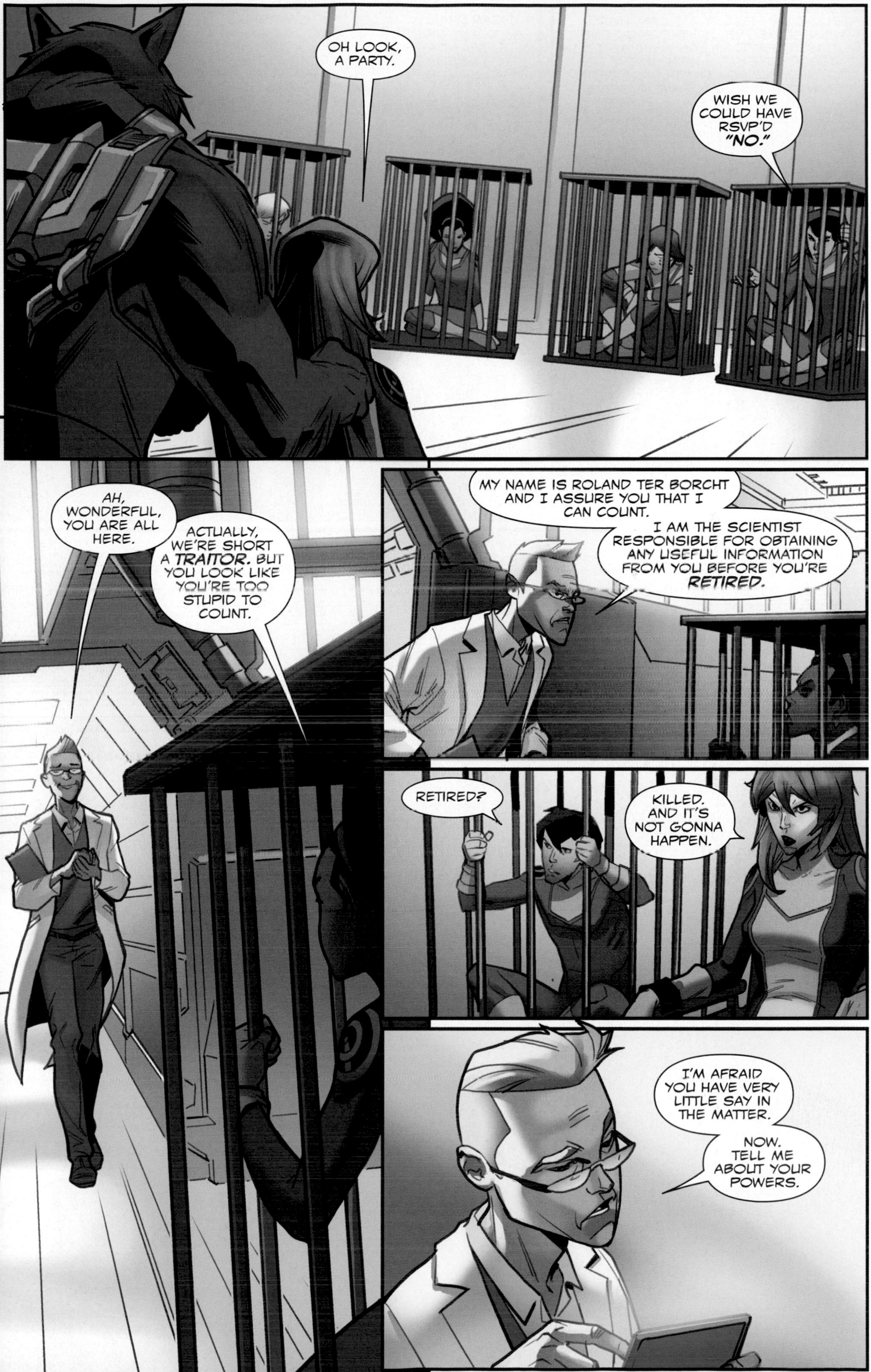
OH LOOK, A PARTY.
WISH WE COULD HAVE RSVP'D "NO."
AH, WONDERFUL, YOU ARE ALL HERE.
ACTUALLY, WE'RE SHORT A TRAITOR. BUT YOU LOOK LIKE YOU'RE TOO STUPID TO COUNT.
MY NAME IS ROLAND TER BORCHT AND I ASSURE YOU THAT I CAN COUNT.
I AM THE SCIENTIST RESPONSIBLE FOR OBTAINING ANY USEFUL INFORMATION FROM YOU BEFORE YOU'RE RETIRED.
RETIRED?
KILLED. AND IT'S NOT GONNA HAPPEN.
I'M AFRAID YOU HAVE VERY LITTLE SAY IN THE MATTER.
NOW. TELL ME ABOUT YOUR POWERS.

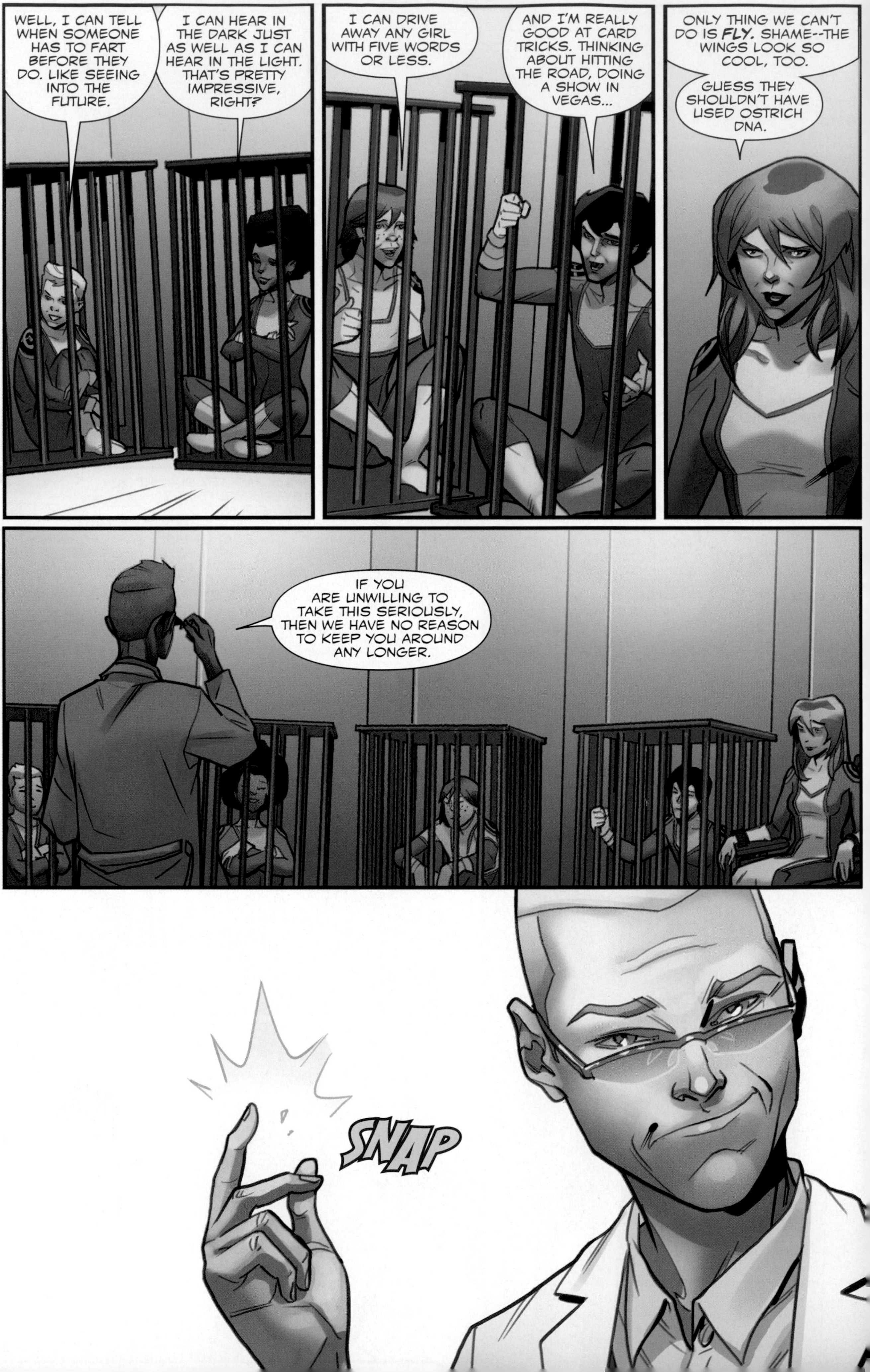
WELL, I CAN TELL WHEN SOMEONE HAS TO FART BEFORE THEY DO. LIKE SEEING INTO THE FUTURE.
I CAN HEAR IN THE DARK JUST AS WELL AS I CAN HEAR IN THE LIGHT. THAT'S PRETTY IMPRESSIVE, RIGHT?
I CAN DRIVE AWAY ANY GIRL WITH FIVE WORDS OR LESS.
AND I'M REALLY GOOD AT CARD TRICKS. THINKING ABOUT HITTING THE ROAD, DOING A SHOW IN VEGAS...
ONLY THING WE CAN'T DO IS FLY. SHAME--THE WINGS LOOK SO COOL, TOO.
GUESS THEY SHOULDN'T HAVE USED OSTRICH DNA.
IF YOU ARE UNWILLING TO TAKE THIS SERIOUSLY, THEN WE HAVE NO REASON TO KEEP YOU AROUND ANY LONGER.
SNAP

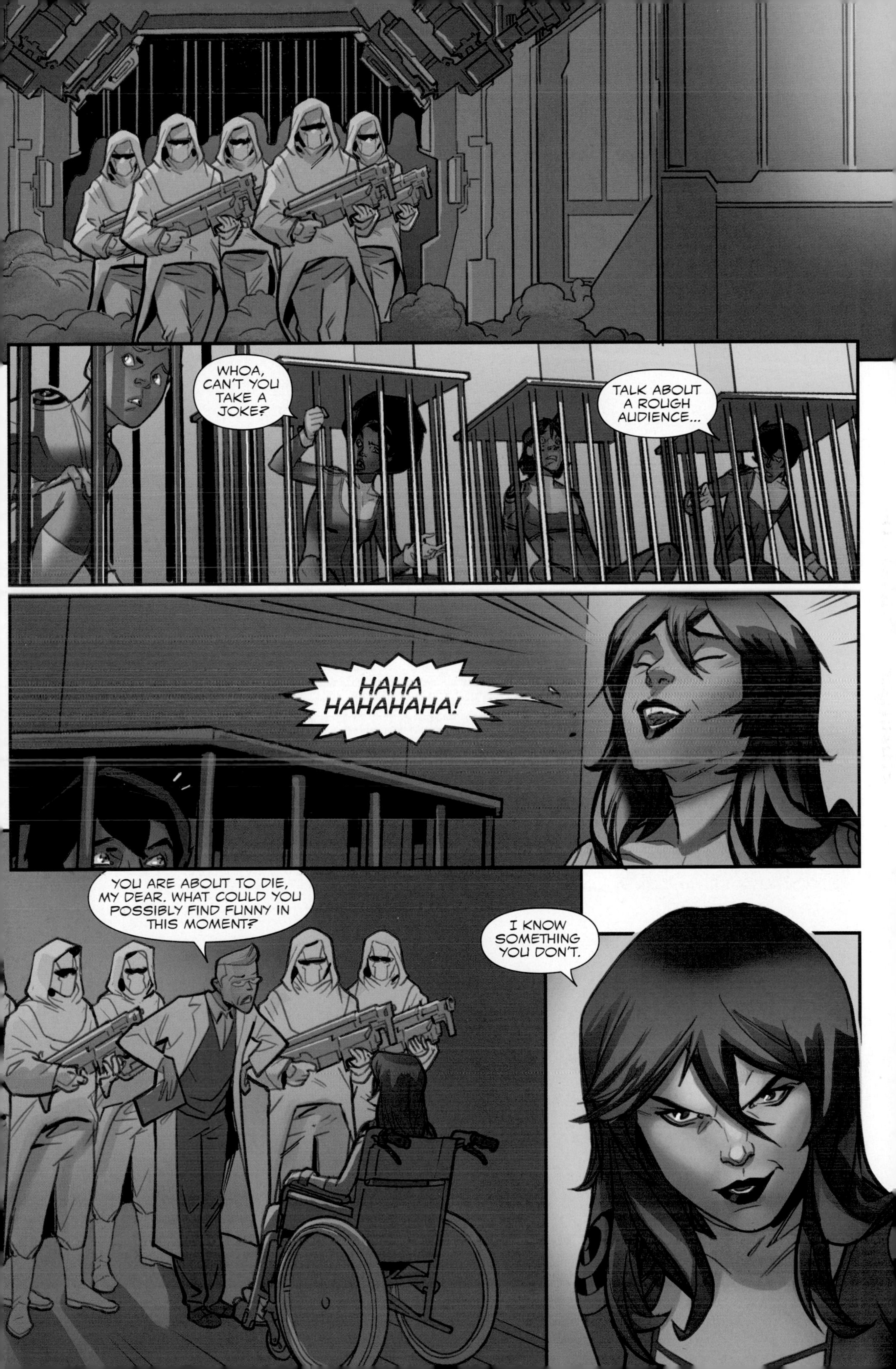
WHOA, CAN'T YOU TAKE A JOKE?
TALK ABOUT A ROUGH AUDIENCE...
HAHA HAHAHAHA!
YOU ARE ABOUT TO DIE, MY DEAR. WHAT COULD YOU POSSIBLY FIND FUNNY IN THIS MOMENT?
I KNOW SOMETHING YOU DON'T.

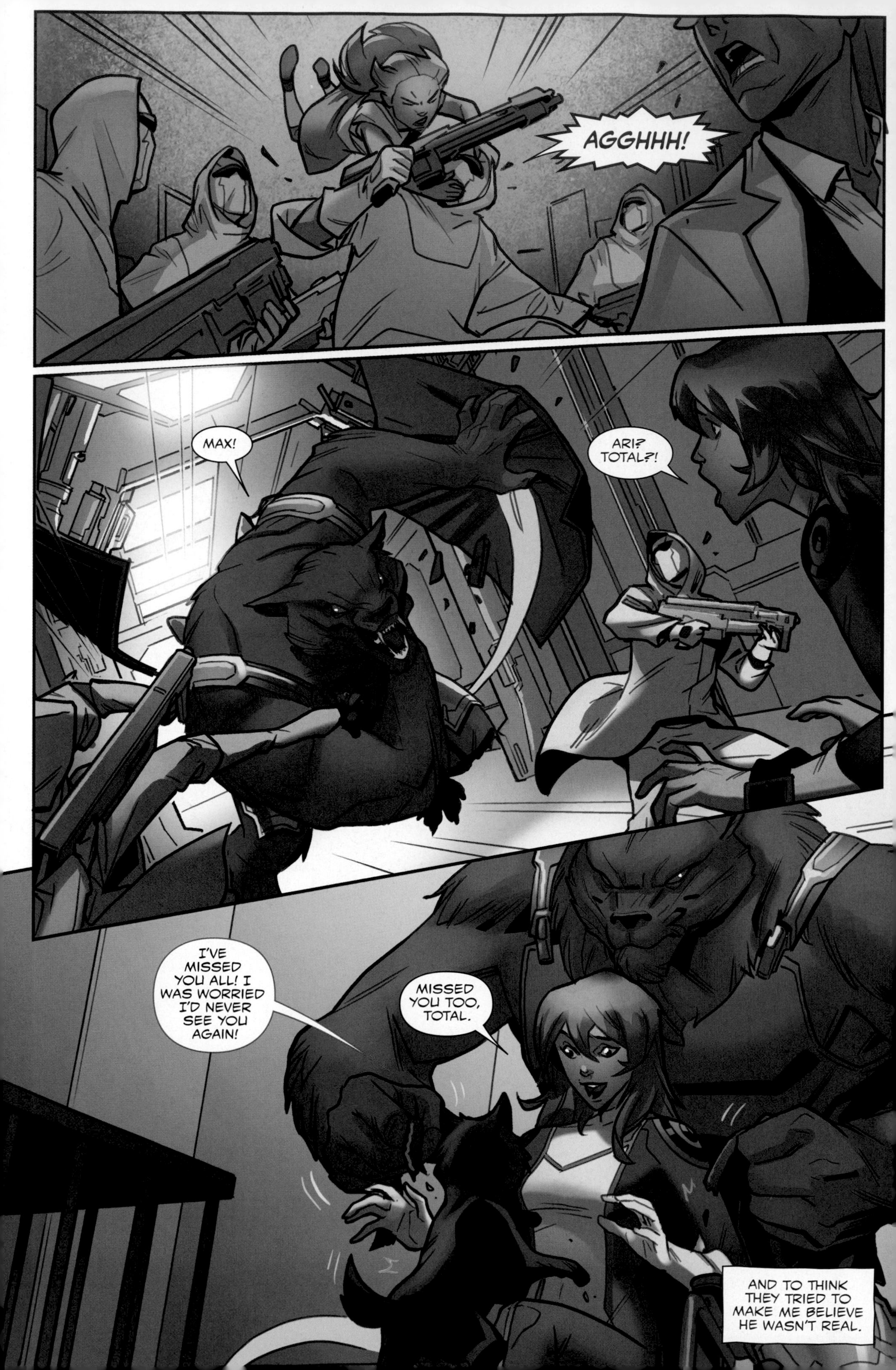
AGGHHH!
MAX!
ARI? TOTAL?!
I'VE MISSED YOU ALL! I WAS WORRIED I'D NEVER SEE YOU AGAIN!
MISSED YOU TOO, TOTAL.
AND TO THINK THEY TRIED TO MAKE ME BELIEVE HE WASN'T REAL.

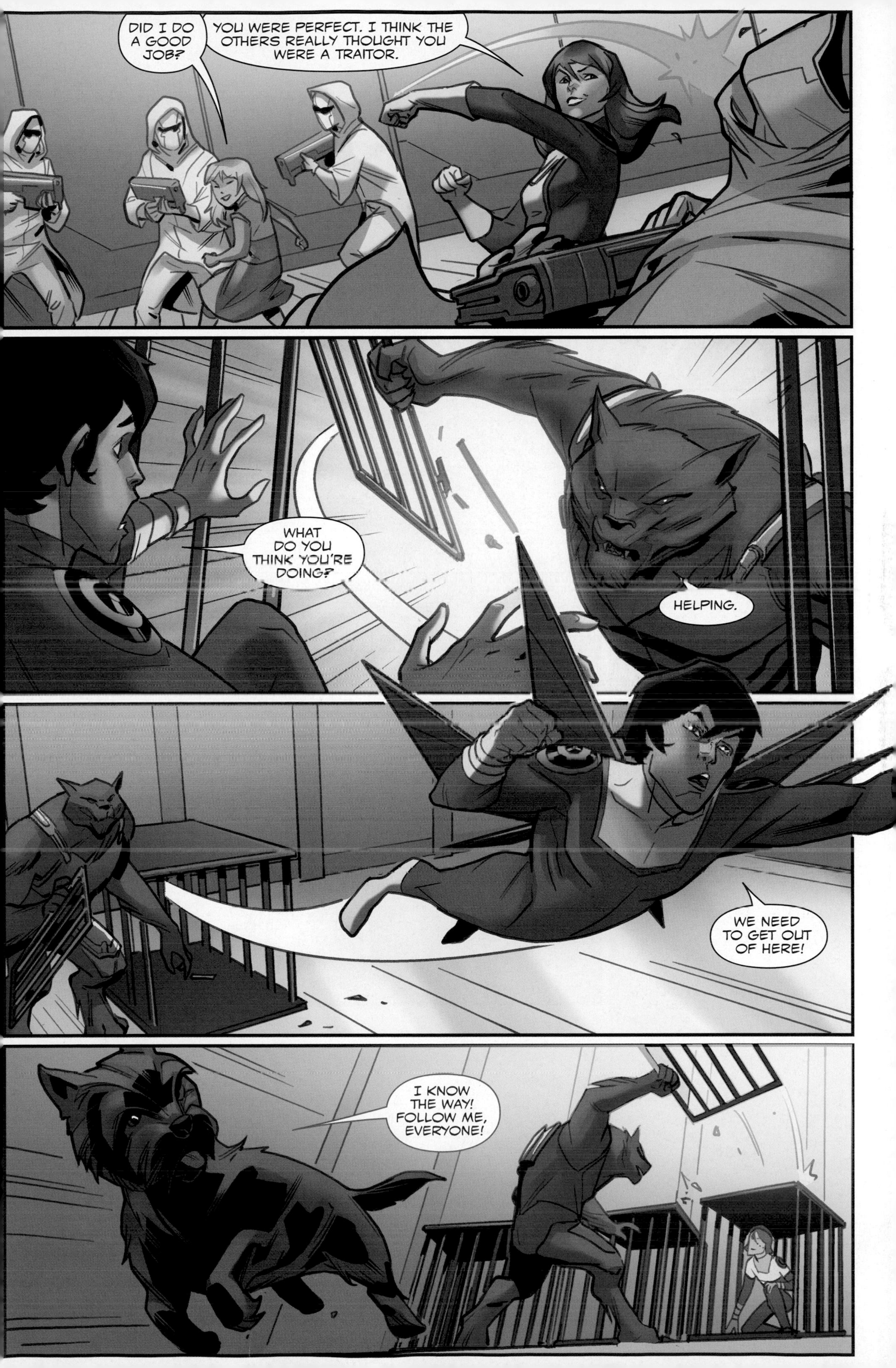
DID I DO A GOOD JOB?
YOU WERE PERFECT. I THINK THE OTHERS REALLY THOUGHT YOU WERE A TRAITOR.
WHAT DO YOU THINK YOU'RE DOING?
HELPING.
WE NEED TO GET OUT OF HERE!
I KNOW THE WAY! FOLLOW ME, EVERYONE!

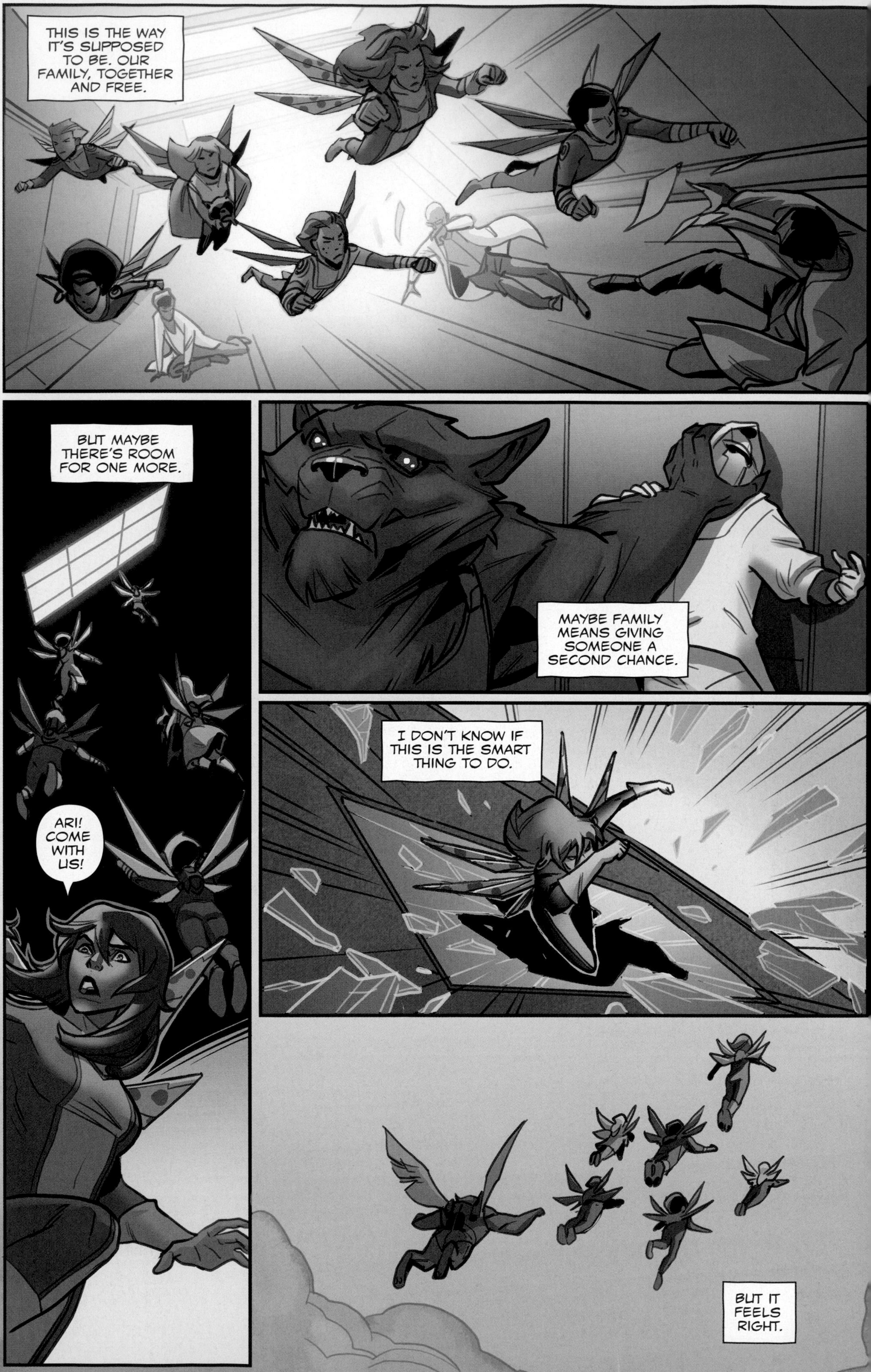
THIS IS THE WAY IT'S SUPPOSED TO BE. OUR FAMILY, TOGETHER AND FREE.
BUT MAYBE THERE'S ROOM FOR ONE MORE.
MAYBE FAMILY MEANS GIVING SOMEONE A SECOND CHANCE.
ARI! COME WITH US!
I DON'T KNOW IF THIS IS THE SMART THING TO DO.
BUT IT FEELS RIGHT.

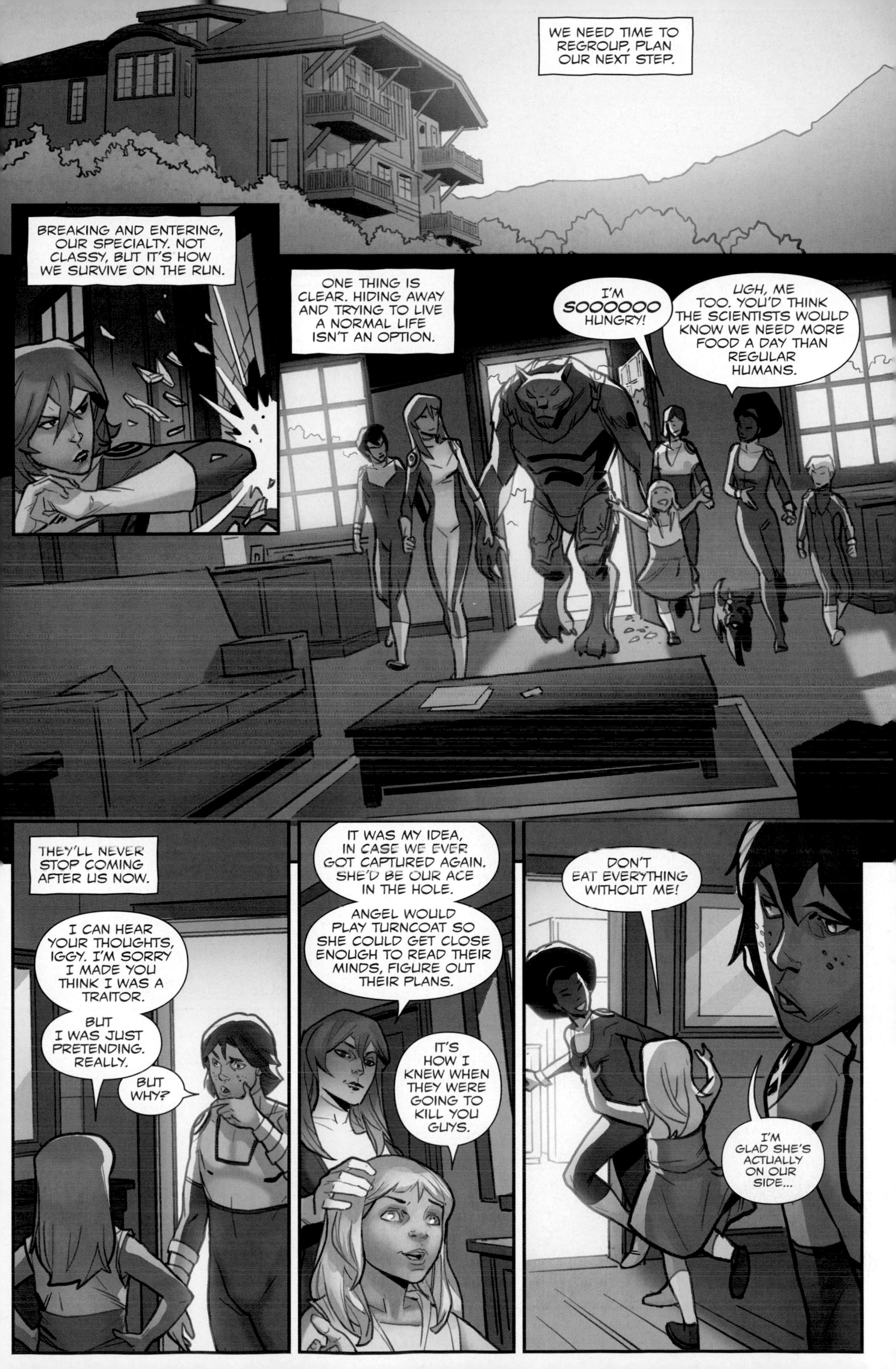
WE NEED TIME TO REGROUP, PLAN OUR NEXT STEP.
BREAKING AND ENTERING, OUR SPECIALTY. NOT CLASSY, BUT IT'S HOW WE SURVIVE ON THE RUN.
ONE THING IS CLEAR. HIDING AWAY AND TRYING TO LIVE A NORMAL LIFE ISN'T AN OPTION.
I'M SOOOOOO HUNGRY!
UGH, ME TOO. YOU'D THINK THE SCIENTISTS WOULD KNOW WE NEED MORE FOOD A DAY THAN REGULAR HUMANS.
THEY'LL NEVER STOP COMING AFTER US NOW.
I CAN HEAR YOUR THOUGHTS, IGGY. I'M SORRY I MADE YOU THINK I WAS A TRAITOR.
BUT I WAS JUST PRETENDING. REALLY.
BUT WHY?
IT WAS MY IDEA, IN CASE WE EVER GOT CAPTURED AGAIN. SHE'D BE OUR ACE IN THE HOLE.
ANGEL WOULD PLAY TURNCOAT SO SHE COULD GET CLOSE ENOUGH TO READ THEIR MINDS, FIGURE OUT THEIR PLANS.
IT'S HOW I KNEW WHEN THEY WERE GOING TO KILL YOU GUYS.
DON'T EAT EVERYTHING WITHOUT ME!
I'M GLAD SHE'S ACTUALLY ON OUR SIDE...

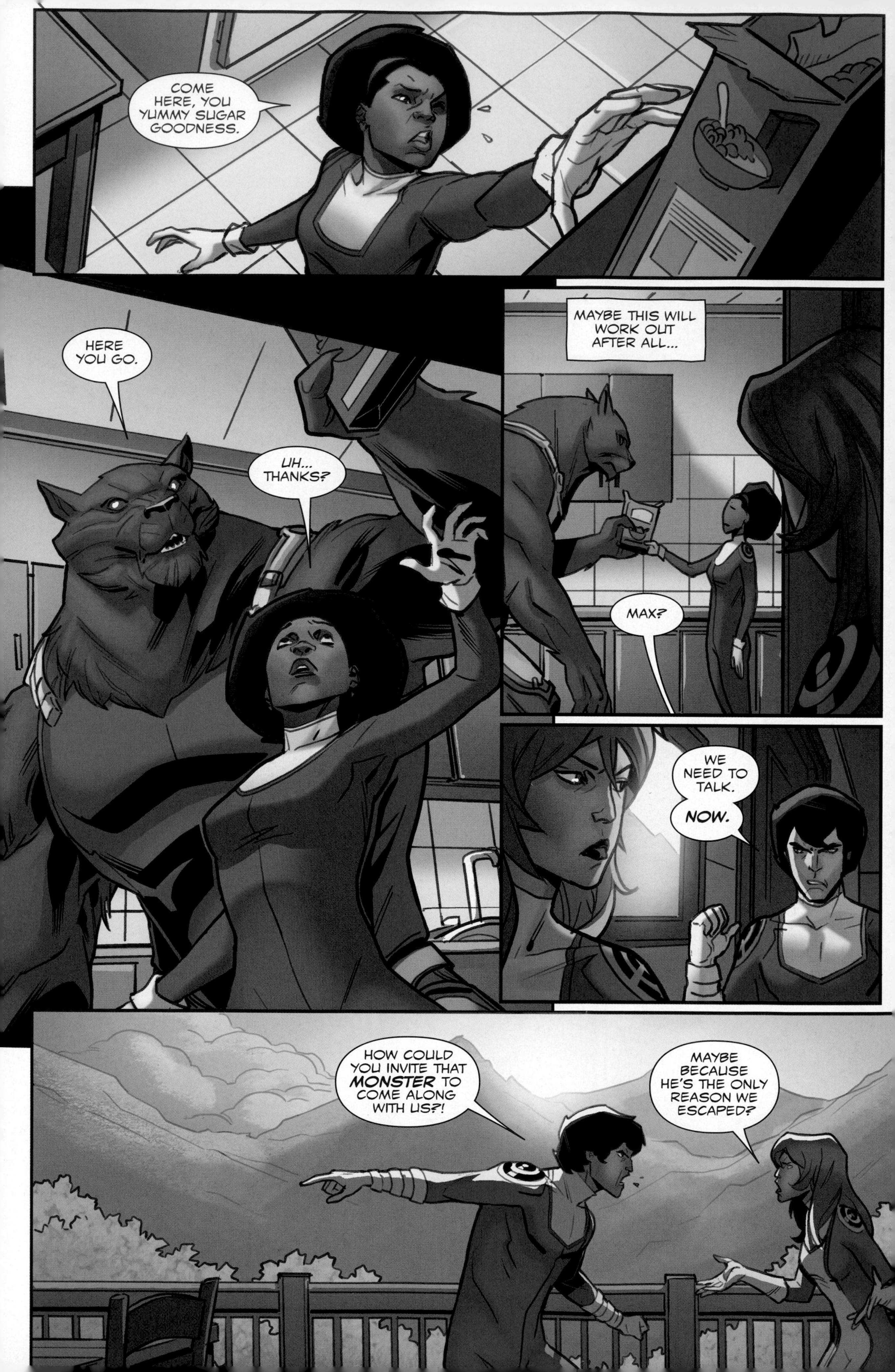
COME HERE, YOU YUMMY SUGAR GOODNESS.
HERE YOU GO.
UH... THANKS?
MAYBE THIS WILL WORK OUT AFTER ALL...
MAX?
WE NEED TO TALK.
NOW.
HOW COULD YOU INVITE THAT MONSTER TO COME ALONG WITH US?!
MAYBE BECAUSE HE'S THE ONLY REASON WE ESCAPED?

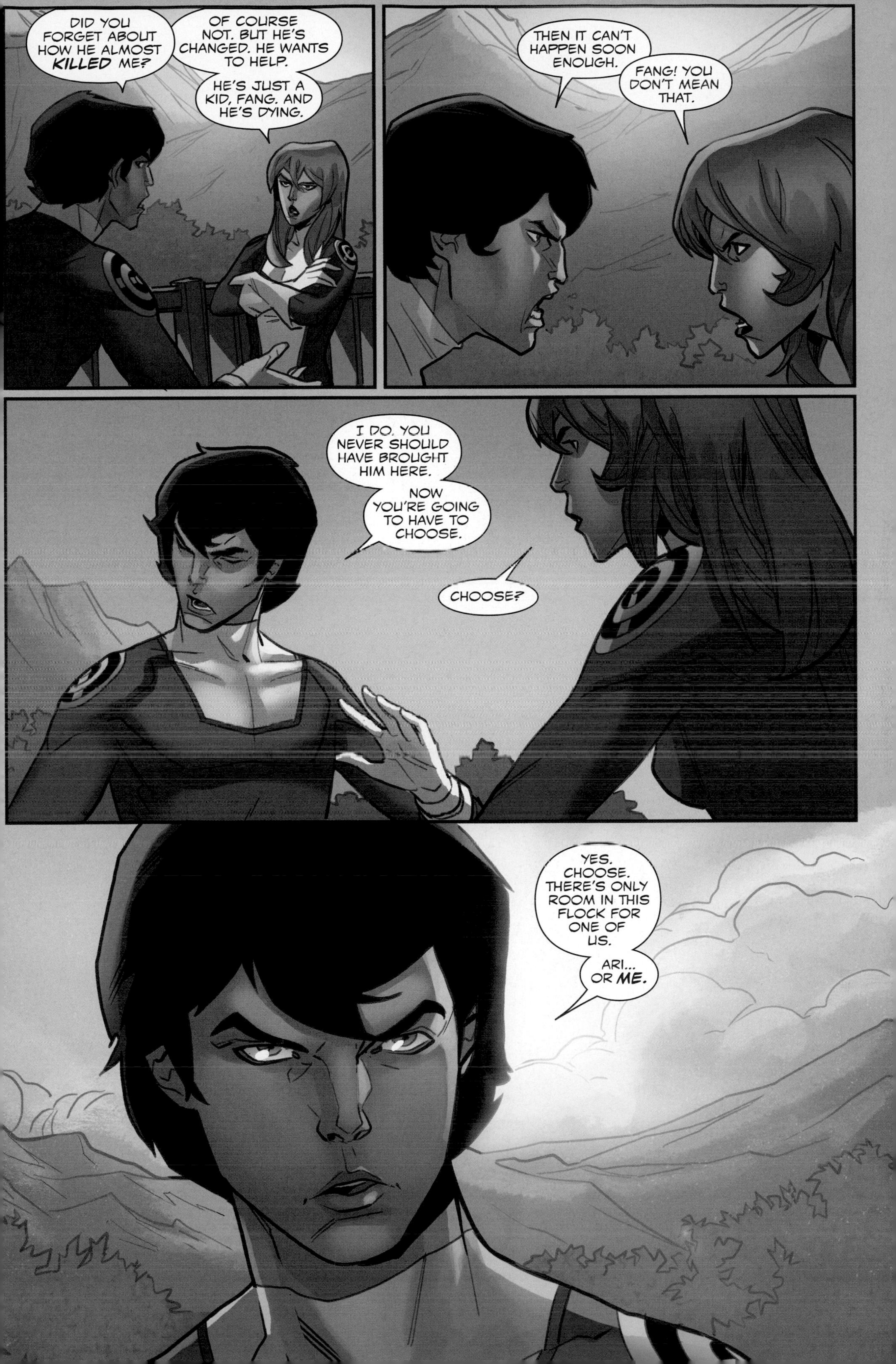
DID YOU FORGET ABOUT HOW HE ALMOST KILLED ME?
OF COURSE NOT. BUT HE'S CHANGED. HE WANTS TO HELP.
HE'S JUST A KID, FANG. AND HE'S DYING.
THEN IT CAN'T HAPPEN SOON ENOUGH.
FANG! YOU DON'T MEAN THAT.
I DO. YOU NEVER SHOULD HAVE BROUGHT HIM HERE.
NOW YOU'RE GOING TO HAVE TO CHOOSE.
CHOOSE?
YES. CHOOSE. THERE'S ONLY ROOM IN THIS FLOCK FOR ONE OF US.
ARI... OR ME.

CHAPTER 3

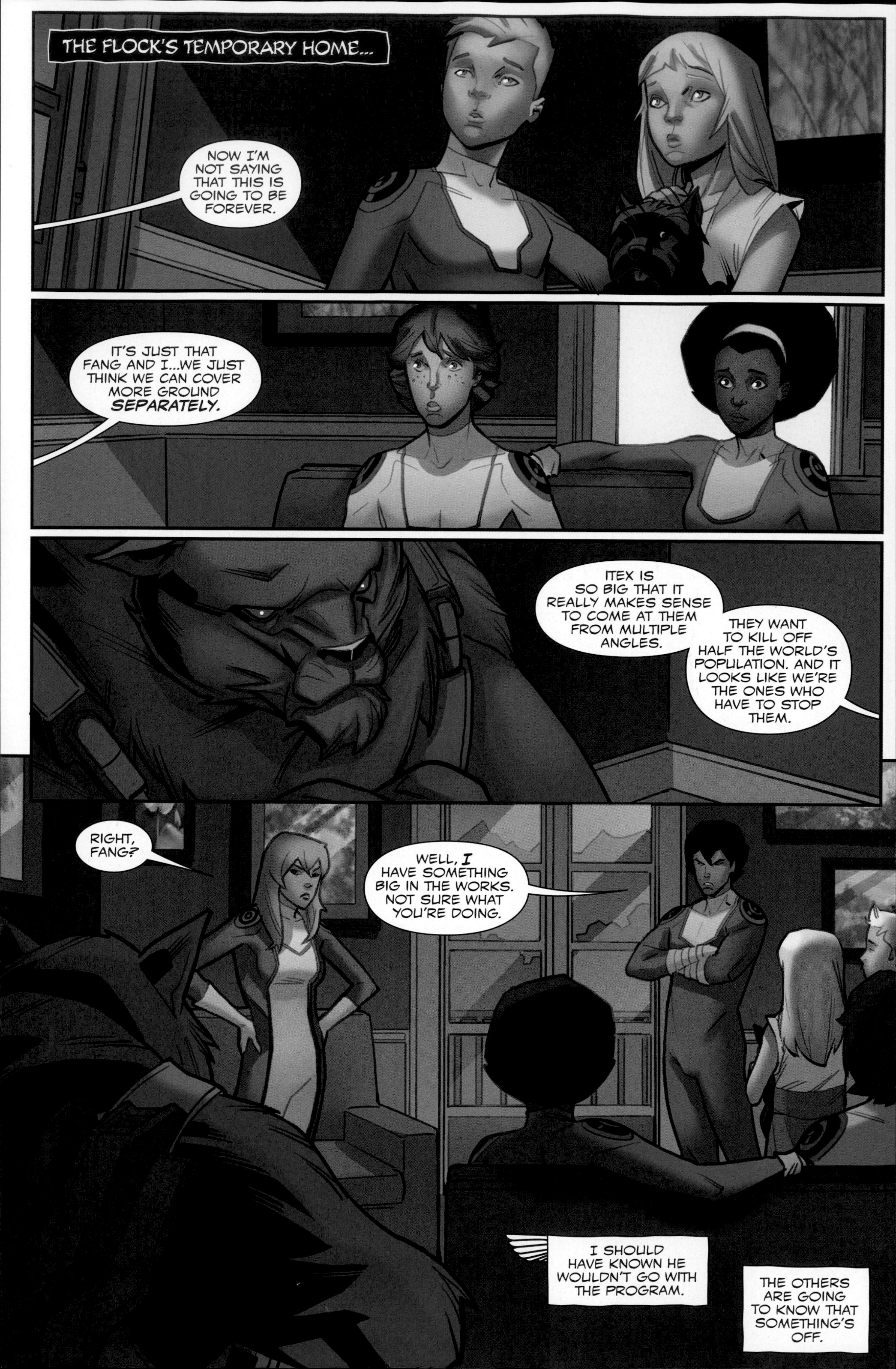
THE FLOCK'S TEMPORARY HOME...
NOW I'M NOT SAYING THAT THIS IS GOING TO BE FOREVER.
IT'S JUST THAT FANG AND I...WE JUST THINK WE CAN COVER MORE GROUND SEPARATELY.
ITEX IS SO BIG THAT IT REALLY MAKES SENSE TO COME AT THEM FROM MULTIPLE ANGLES.
THEY WANT TO KILL OFF HALF THE WORLD'S POPULATION. AND IT LOOKS LIKE WE'RE THE ONES WHO HAVE TO STOP THEM.
RIGHT, FANG?
WELL, I HAVE SOMETHING BIG IN THE WORKS. NOT SURE WHAT YOU'RE DOING.
I SHOULD HAVE KNOWN HE WOULDN'T GO WITH THE PROGRAM.
THE OTHERS ARE GOING TO KNOW THAT SOMETHING'S OFF.

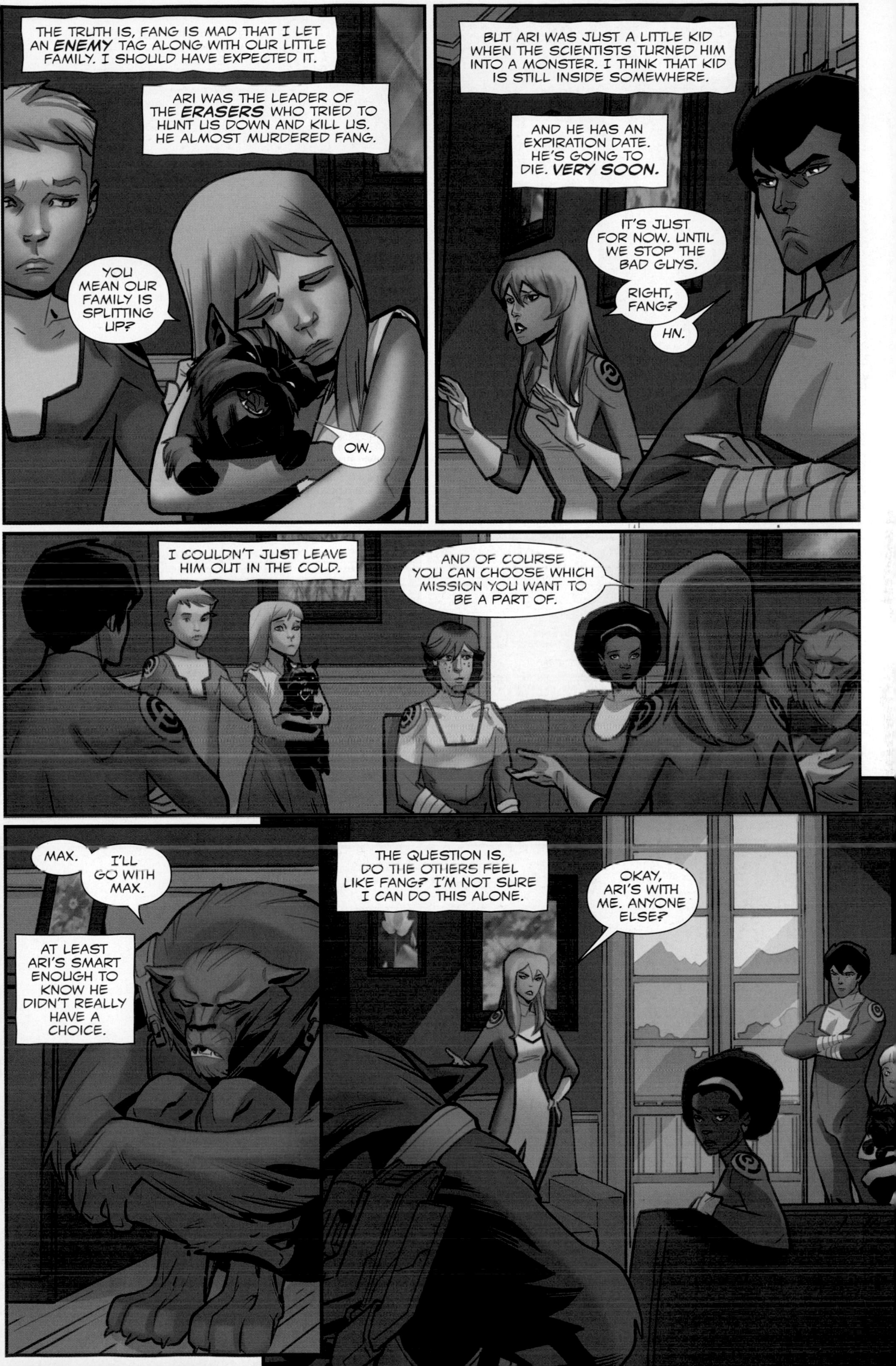
THE TRUTH IS, FANG IS MAD THAT I LET AN ENEMY TAG ALONG WITH OUR LITTLE FAMILY. I SHOULD HAVE EXPECTED IT.
ARI WAS THE LEADER OF THE ERASERS WHO TRIED TO HUNT US DOWN AND KILL US. HE ALMOST MURDERED FANG.
YOU MEAN OUR FAMILY IS SPLITTING UP?
OW.
BUT ARI WAS JUST A LITTLE KID WHEN THE SCIENTISTS TURNED HIM INTO A MONSTER. I THINK THAT KID IS STILL INSIDE SOMEWHERE.
AND HE HAS AN EXPIRATION DATE. HE'S GOING TO DIE. VERY SOON.
IT'S JUST FOR NOW. UNTIL WE STOP THE BAD GUYS.
RIGHT, FANG?
HN.
I COULDN'T JUST LEAVE HIM OUT IN THE COLD.
AND OF COURSE YOU CAN CHOOSE WHICH MISSION YOU WANT TO BE A PART OF.
MAX.
I'LL GO WITH MAX.
AT LEAST ARI'S SMART ENOUGH TO KNOW HE DIDN'T REALLY HAVE A CHOICE.
THE QUESTION IS, DO THE OTHERS FEEL LIKE FANG? I'M NOT SURE I CAN DO THIS ALONE.
OKAY, ARI'S WITH ME. ANYONE ELSE?

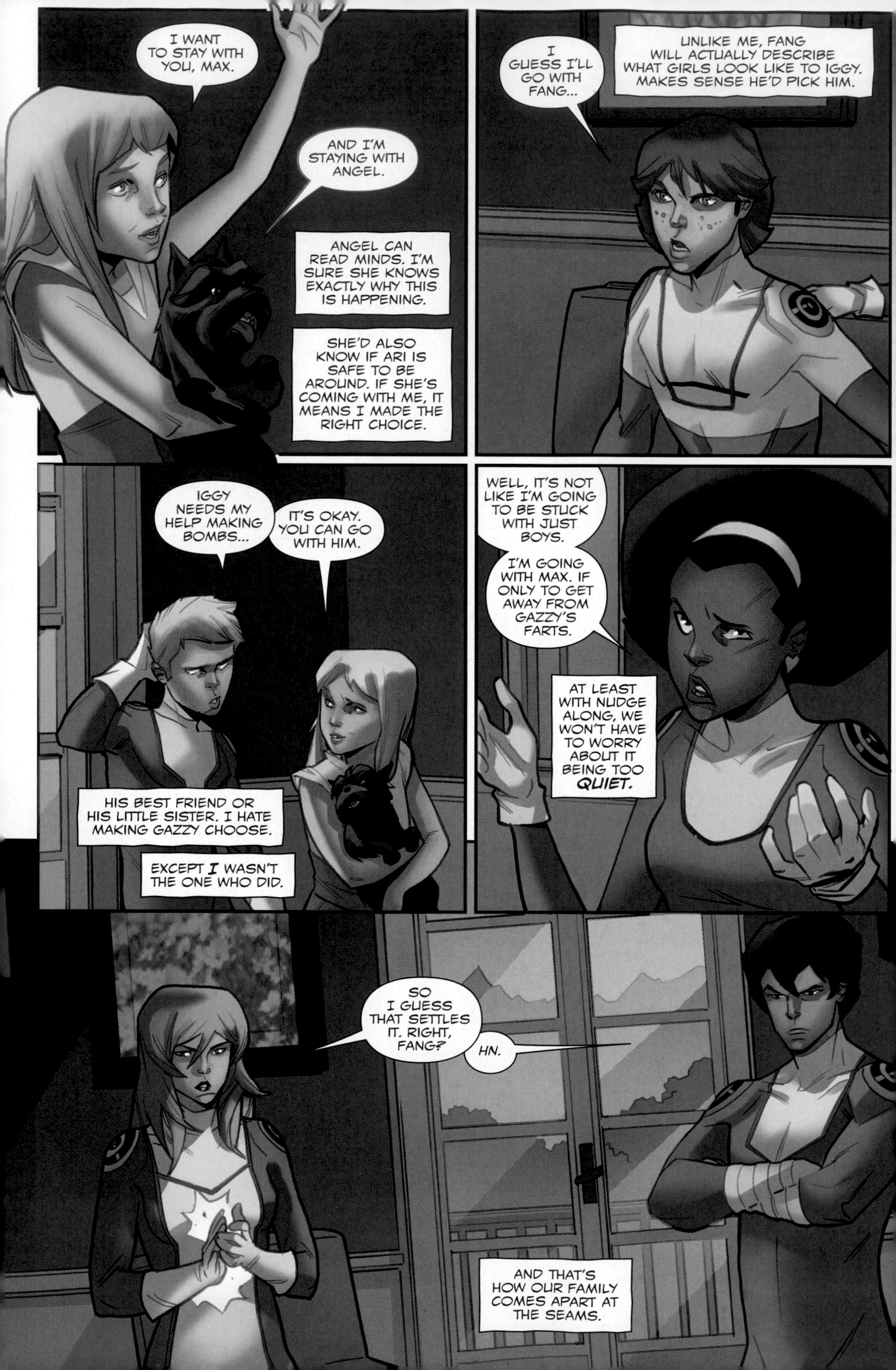
I WANT TO STAY WITH YOU, MAX.
AND I'M STAYING WITH ANGEL.
ANGEL CAN READ MINDS. I'M SURE SHE KNOWS EXACTLY WHY THIS IS HAPPENING.
SHE'D ALSO KNOW IF ARI IS SAFE TO BE AROUND. IF SHE'S COMING WITH ME, IT MEANS I MADE THE RIGHT CHOICE.
I GUESS I'LL GO WITH FANG...
UNLIKE ME, FANG WILL ACTUALLY DESCRIBE WHAT GIRLS LOOK LIKE TO IGGY. MAKES SENSE HE'D PICK HIM.
IGGY NEEDS MY HELP MAKING BOMBS...
IT'S OKAY. YOU CAN GO WITH HIM.
HIS BEST FRIEND OR HIS LITTLE SISTER. I HATE MAKING GAZZY CHOOSE.
EXCEPT *I* WASN'T THE ONE WHO DID.
WELL, IT'S NOT LIKE I'M GOING TO BE STUCK WITH JUST BOYS.
I'M GOING WITH MAX. IF ONLY TO GET AWAY FROM GAZZY'S FARTS.
AT LEAST WITH NUDGE ALONG, WE WON'T HAVE TO WORRY ABOUT IT BEING TOO ***QUIET.***
SO I GUESS THAT SETTLES IT. RIGHT, FANG?
HN.
AND THAT'S HOW OUR FAMILY COMES APART AT THE SEAMS.

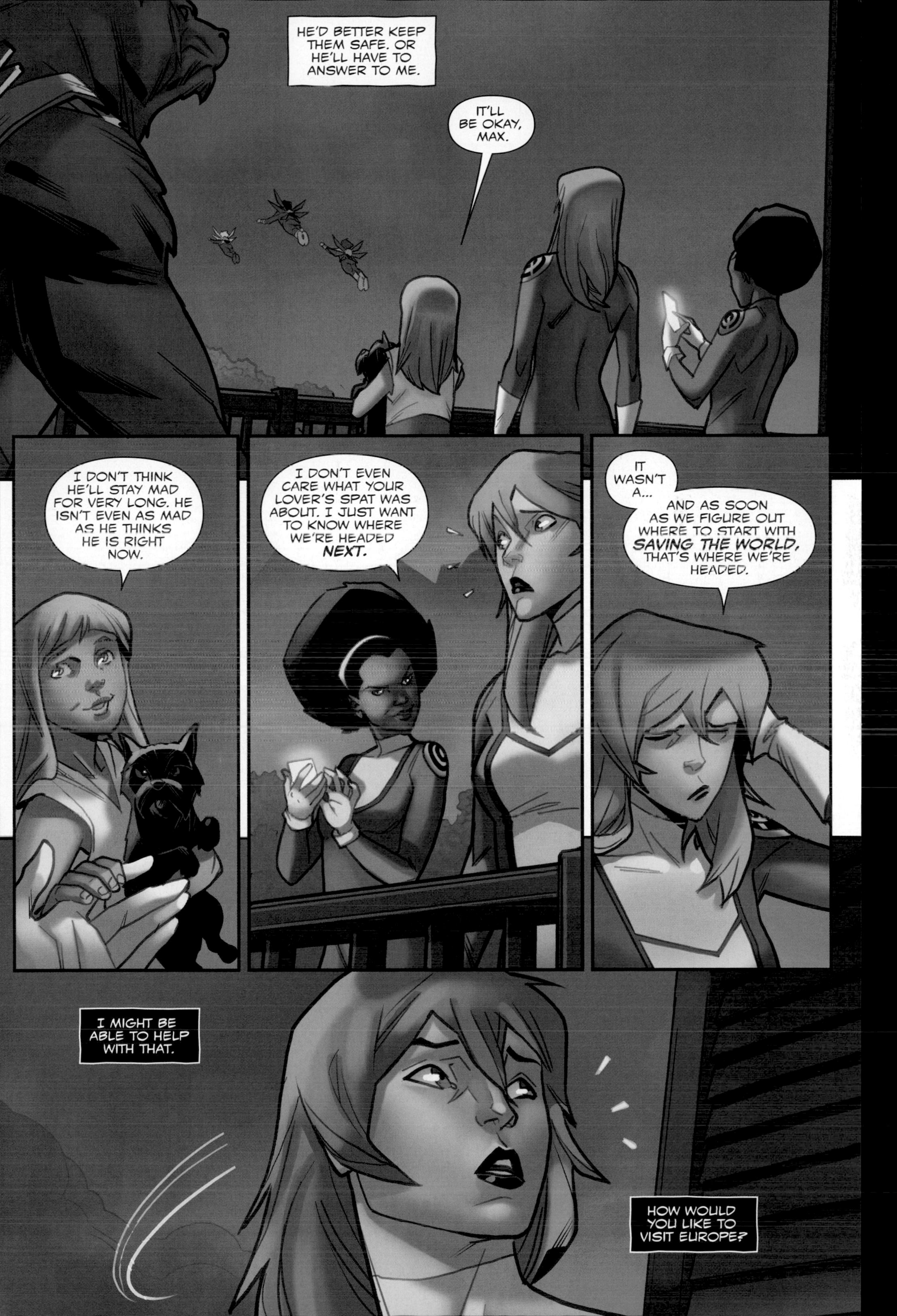
HE'D BETTER KEEP THEM SAFE. OR HE'LL HAVE TO ANSWER TO ME.
IT'LL BE OKAY, MAX.
I DON'T THINK HE'LL STAY MAD FOR VERY LONG. HE ISN'T EVEN AS MAD AS HE THINKS HE IS RIGHT NOW.
I DON'T EVEN CARE WHAT YOUR LOVER'S SPAT WAS ABOUT. I JUST WANT TO KNOW WHERE WE'RE HEADED NEXT.
IT WASN'T A...
AND AS SOON AS WE FIGURE OUT WHERE TO START WITH SAVING THE WORLD, THAT'S WHERE WE'RE HEADED.
I MIGHT BE ABLE TO HELP WITH THAT.
HOW WOULD YOU LIKE TO VISIT EUROPE?

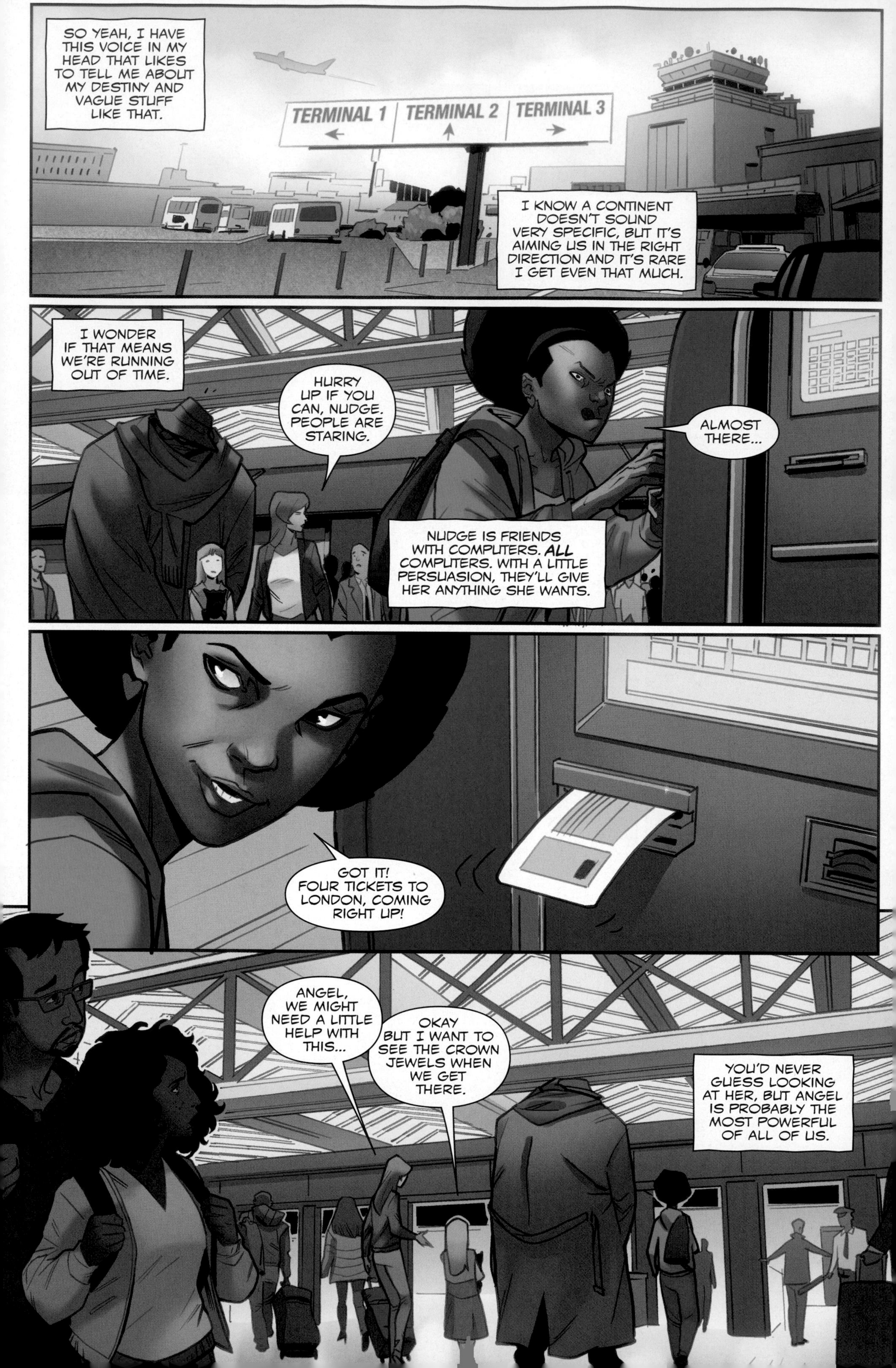
SO YEAH, I HAVE THIS VOICE IN MY HEAD THAT LIKES TO TELL ME ABOUT MY DESTINY AND VAGUE STUFF LIKE THAT.
TERMINAL 1
TERMINAL 2
TERMINAL 3
I KNOW A CONTINENT DOESN'T SOUND VERY SPECIFIC, BUT IT'S AIMING US IN THE RIGHT DIRECTION AND IT'S RARE I GET EVEN THAT MUCH.
I WONDER IF THAT MEANS WE'RE RUNNING OUT OF TIME.
HURRY UP IF YOU CAN, NUDGE. PEOPLE ARE STARING.
ALMOST THERE...
NUDGE IS FRIENDS WITH COMPUTERS. ALL COMPUTERS. WITH A LITTLE PERSUASION, THEY'LL GIVE HER ANYTHING SHE WANTS.
GOT IT! FOUR TICKETS TO LONDON, COMING RIGHT UP!
ANGEL, WE MIGHT NEED A LITTLE HELP WITH THIS...
OKAY BUT I WANT TO SEE THE CROWN JEWELS WHEN WE GET THERE.
YOU'D NEVER GUESS LOOKING AT HER, BUT ANGEL IS PROBABLY THE MOST POWERFUL OF ALL OF US.

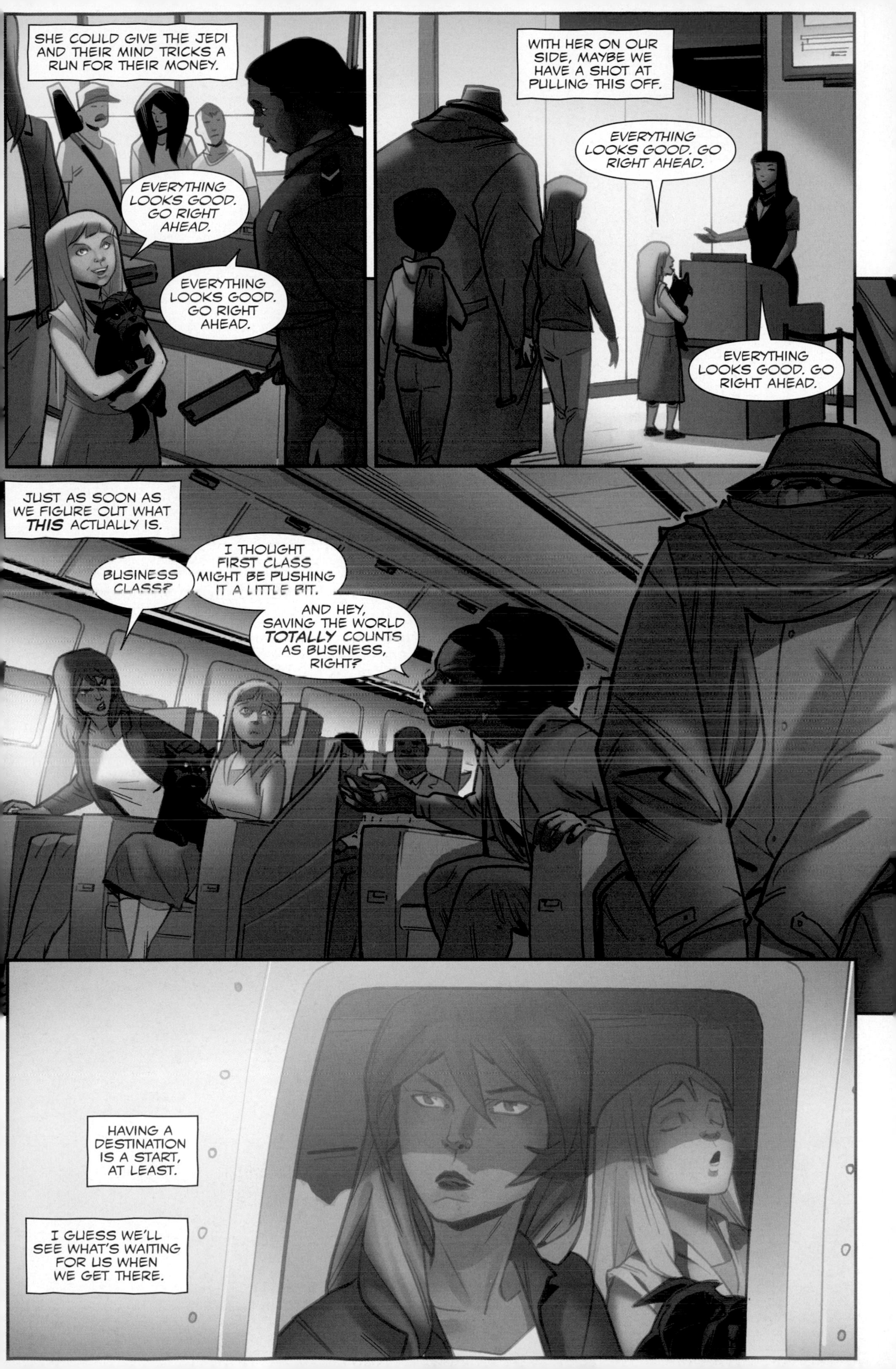

SHE COULD GIVE THE JEDI AND THEIR MIND TRICKS A RUN FOR THEIR MONEY.
EVERYTHING LOOKS GOOD. GO RIGHT AHEAD.
EVERYTHING LOOKS GOOD. GO RIGHT AHEAD.
WITH HER ON OUR SIDE, MAYBE WE HAVE A SHOT AT PULLING THIS OFF.
EVERYTHING LOOKS GOOD. GO RIGHT AHEAD.
EVERYTHING LOOKS GOOD. GO RIGHT AHEAD.
JUST AS SOON AS WE FIGURE OUT WHAT THIS ACTUALLY IS.
BUSINESS CLASS?
I THOUGHT FIRST CLASS MIGHT BE PUSHING IT A LITTLE BIT.
AND HEY, SAVING THE WORLD TOTALLY COUNTS AS BUSINESS, RIGHT?
HAVING A DESTINATION IS A START, AT LEAST.
I GUESS WE'LL SEE WHAT'S WAITING FOR US WHEN WE GET THERE.

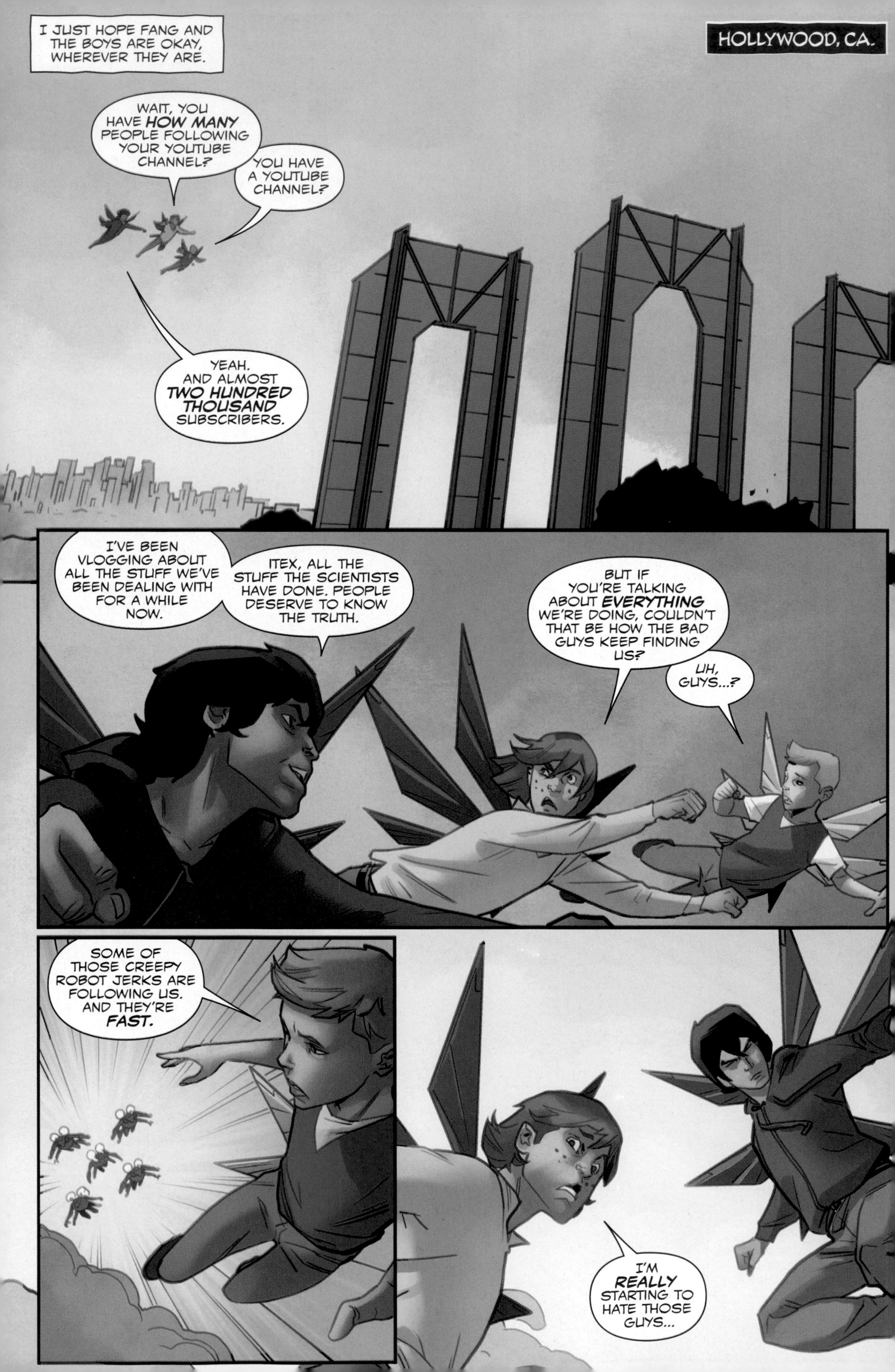
I JUST HOPE FANG AND THE BOYS ARE OKAY, WHEREVER THEY ARE.
HOLLYWOOD, CA.
WAIT, YOU HAVE **HOW MANY** PEOPLE FOLLOWING YOUR YOUTUBE CHANNEL?
YOU HAVE A YOUTUBE CHANNEL?
YEAH. AND ALMOST **TWO HUNDRED THOUSAND** SUBSCRIBERS.
I'VE BEEN VLOGGING ABOUT ALL THE STUFF WE'VE BEEN DEALING WITH FOR A WHILE NOW.
ITEX, ALL THE STUFF THE SCIENTISTS HAVE DONE. PEOPLE DESERVE TO KNOW THE TRUTH.
BUT IF YOU'RE TALKING ABOUT **EVERYTHING** WE'RE DOING, COULDN'T THAT BE HOW THE BAD GUYS KEEP FINDING US?
UH, GUYS...?
SOME OF THOSE CREEPY ROBOT JERKS ARE FOLLOWING US. AND THEY'RE **FAST.**
I'M **REALLY** STARTING TO HATE THOSE GUYS...

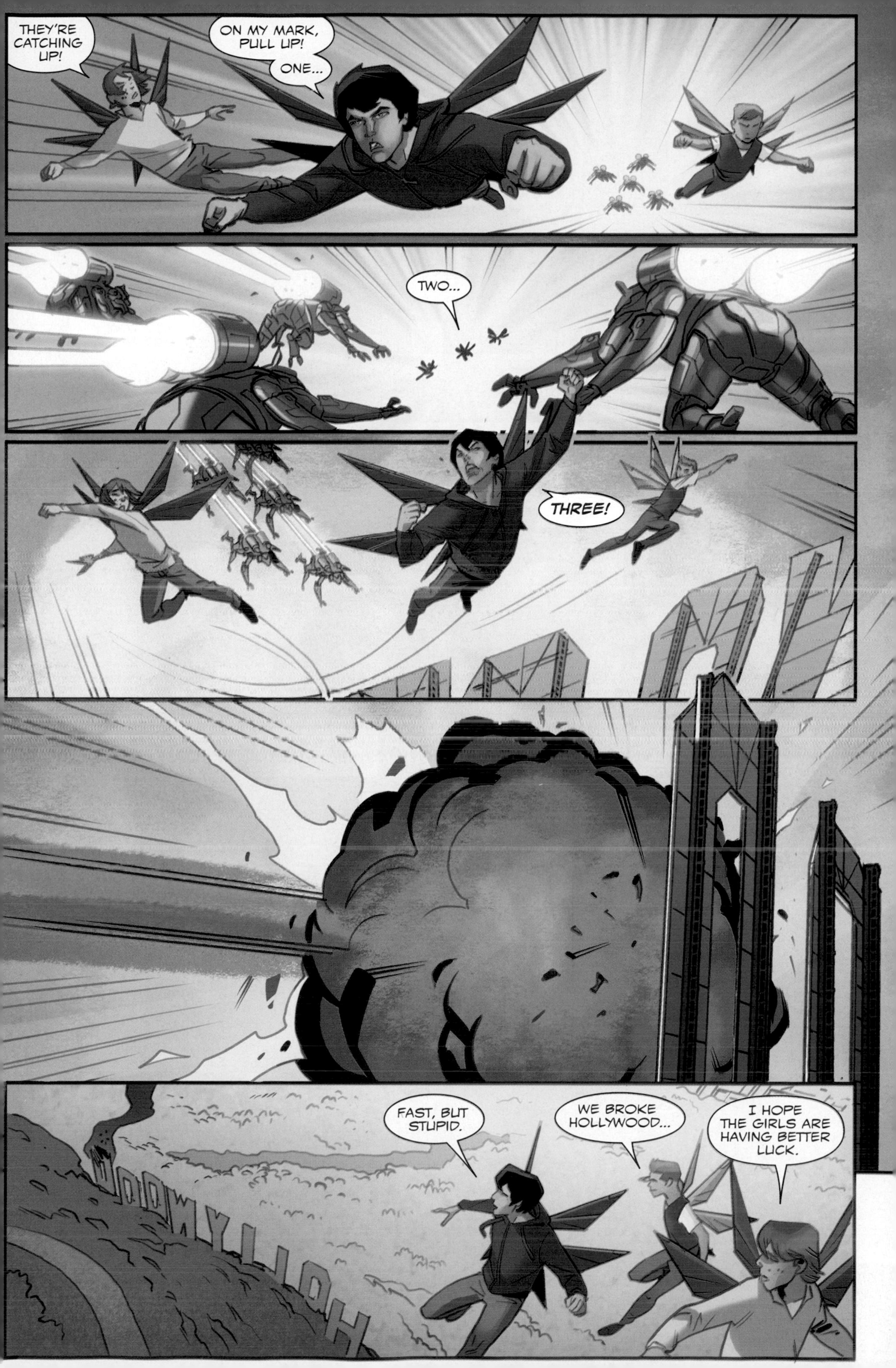
THEY'RE CATCHING UP!
ON MY MARK, PULL UP!
ONE...
TWO...
THREE!
FAST, BUT STUPID.
WE BROKE HOLLYWOOD...
I HOPE THE GIRLS ARE HAVING BETTER LUCK.

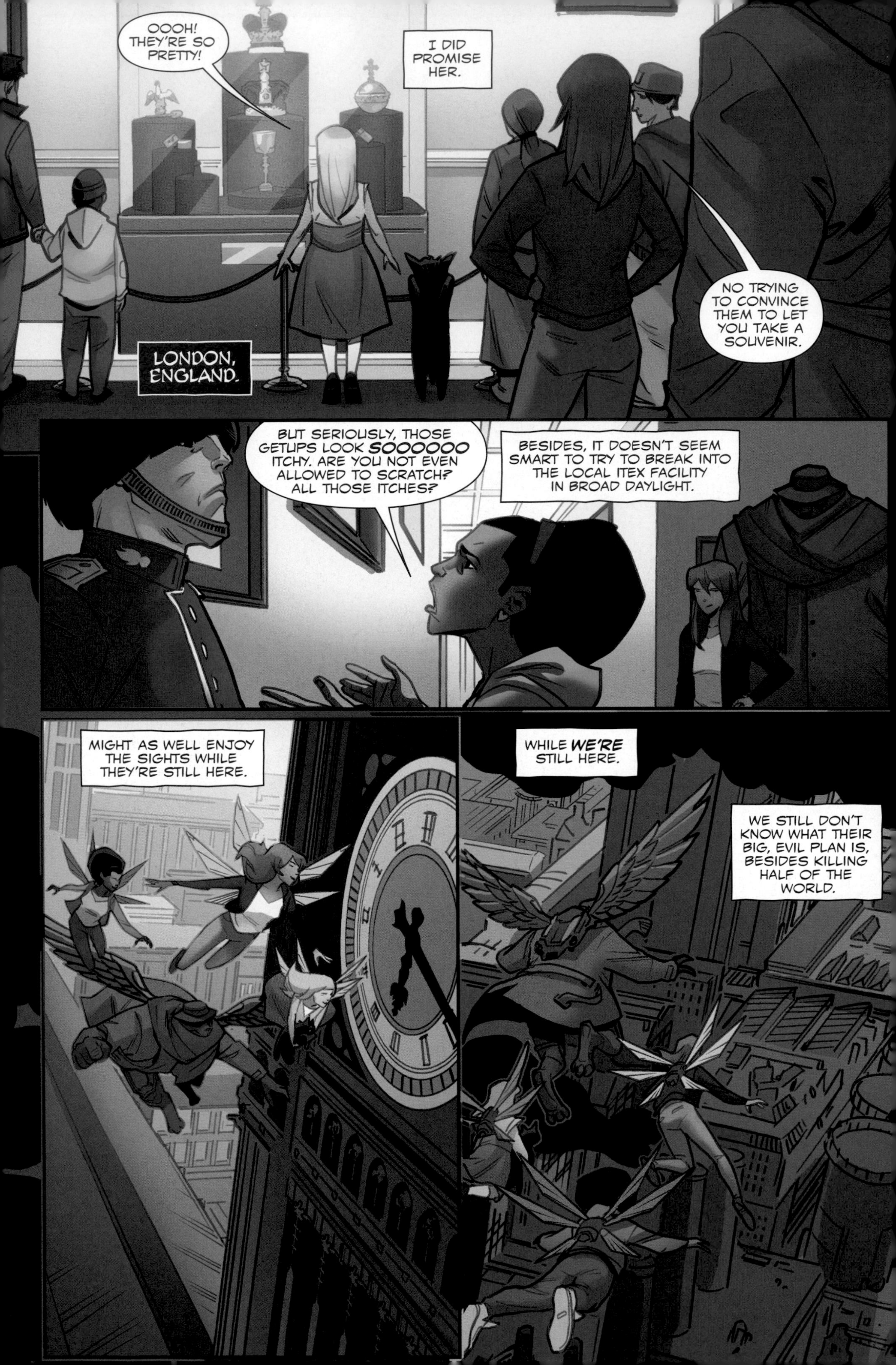
OOOH! THEY'RE SO PRETTY!
I DID PROMISE HER.
NO TRYING TO CONVINCE THEM TO LET YOU TAKE A SOUVENIR.
LONDON, ENGLAND.
BUT SERIOUSLY, THOSE GETUPS LOOK SOOOOOO ITCHY. ARE YOU NOT EVEN ALLOWED TO SCRATCH? ALL THOSE ITCHES?
BESIDES, IT DOESN'T SEEM SMART TO TRY TO BREAK INTO THE LOCAL ITEX FACILITY IN BROAD DAYLIGHT.
MIGHT AS WELL ENJOY THE SIGHTS WHILE THEY'RE STILL HERE.
WHILE WE'RE STILL HERE.
WE STILL DON'T KNOW WHAT THEIR BIG, EVIL PLAN IS, BESIDES KILLING HALF OF THE WORLD.

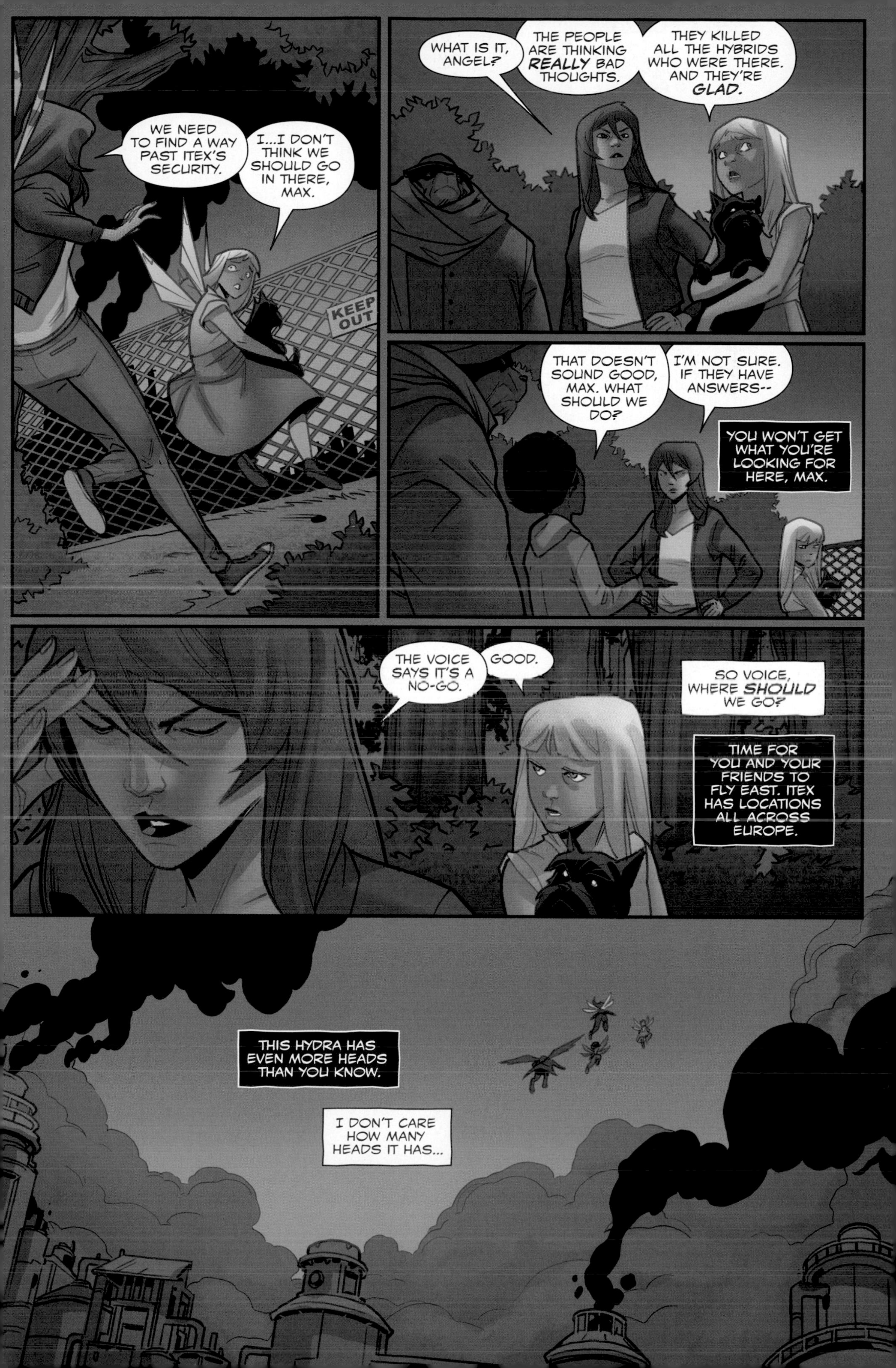
WE NEED TO FIND A WAY PAST ITEX'S SECURITY.
I...I DON'T THINK WE SHOULD GO IN THERE, MAX.
KEEP OUT
WHAT IS IT, ANGEL?
THE PEOPLE ARE THINKING REALLY BAD THOUGHTS.
THEY KILLED ALL THE HYBRIDS WHO WERE THERE. AND THEY'RE GLAD.
THAT DOESN'T SOUND GOOD, MAX. WHAT SHOULD WE DO?
I'M NOT SURE. IF THEY HAVE ANSWERS--
YOU WON'T GET WHAT YOU'RE LOOKING FOR HERE, MAX.
THE VOICE SAYS IT'S A NO-GO.
GOOD.
SO VOICE, WHERE SHOULD WE GO?
TIME FOR YOU AND YOUR FRIENDS TO FLY EAST. ITEX HAS LOCATIONS ALL ACROSS EUROPE.
THIS HYDRA HAS EVEN MORE HEADS THAN YOU KNOW.
I DON'T CARE HOW MANY HEADS IT HAS...

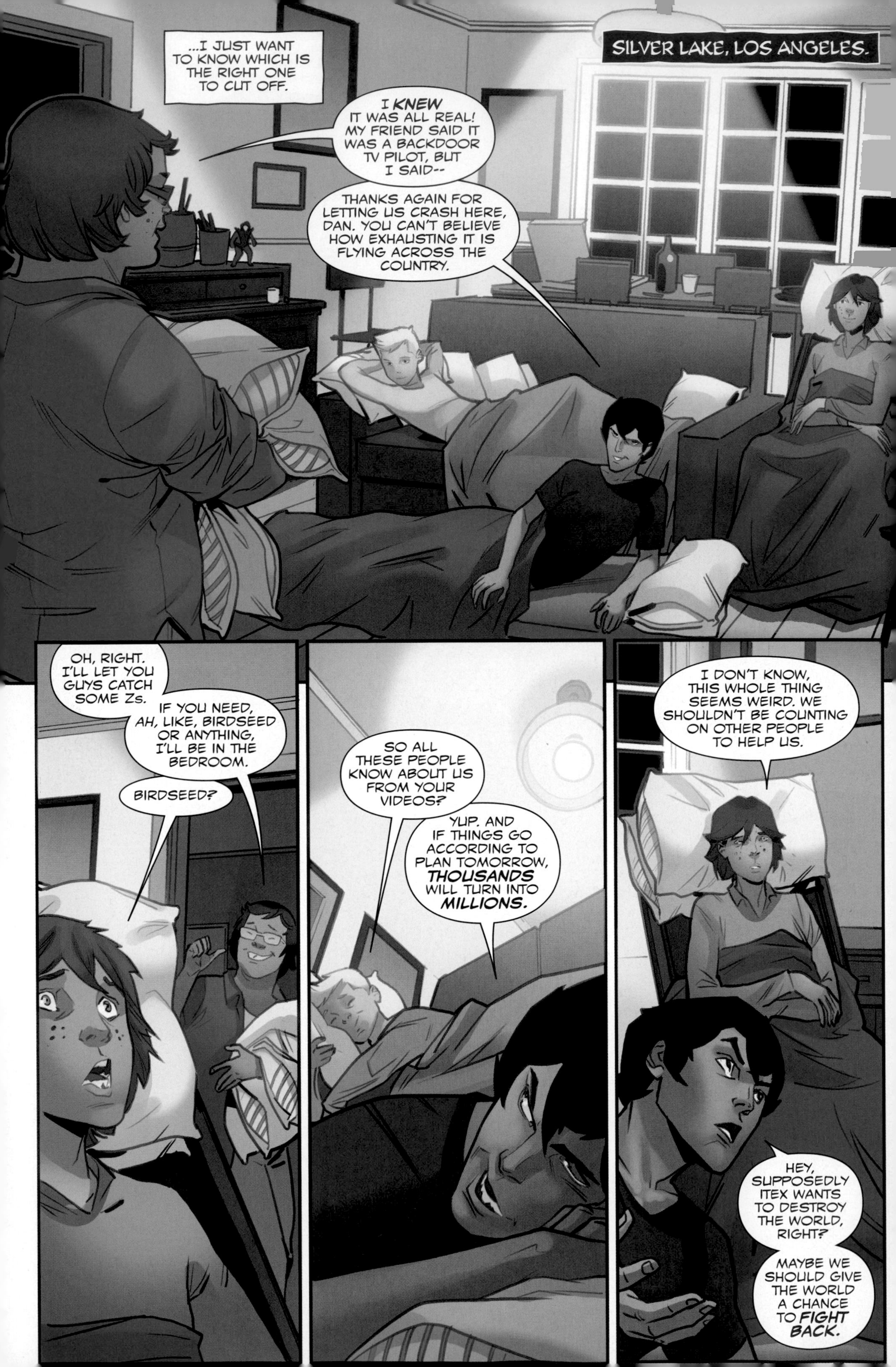

SILVER LAKE, LOS ANGELES.
...I JUST WANT TO KNOW WHICH IS THE RIGHT ONE TO CUT OFF.
I KNEW IT WAS ALL REAL! MY FRIEND SAID IT WAS A BACKDOOR TV PILOT, BUT I SAID--
THANKS AGAIN FOR LETTING US CRASH HERE, DAN. YOU CAN'T BELIEVE HOW EXHAUSTING IT IS FLYING ACROSS THE COUNTRY.
OH, RIGHT. I'LL LET YOU GUYS CATCH SOME Zs.
IF YOU NEED, AH, LIKE, BIRDSEED OR ANYTHING, I'LL BE IN THE BEDROOM.
BIRDSEED?
SO ALL THESE PEOPLE KNOW ABOUT US FROM YOUR VIDEOS?
YUP. AND IF THINGS GO ACCORDING TO PLAN TOMORROW, THOUSANDS WILL TURN INTO MILLIONS.
I DON'T KNOW, THIS WHOLE THING SEEMS WEIRD. WE SHOULDN'T BE COUNTING ON OTHER PEOPLE TO HELP US.
HEY, SUPPOSEDLY ITEX WANTS TO DESTROY THE WORLD, RIGHT?
MAYBE WE SHOULD GIVE THE WORLD A CHANCE TO FIGHT BACK.

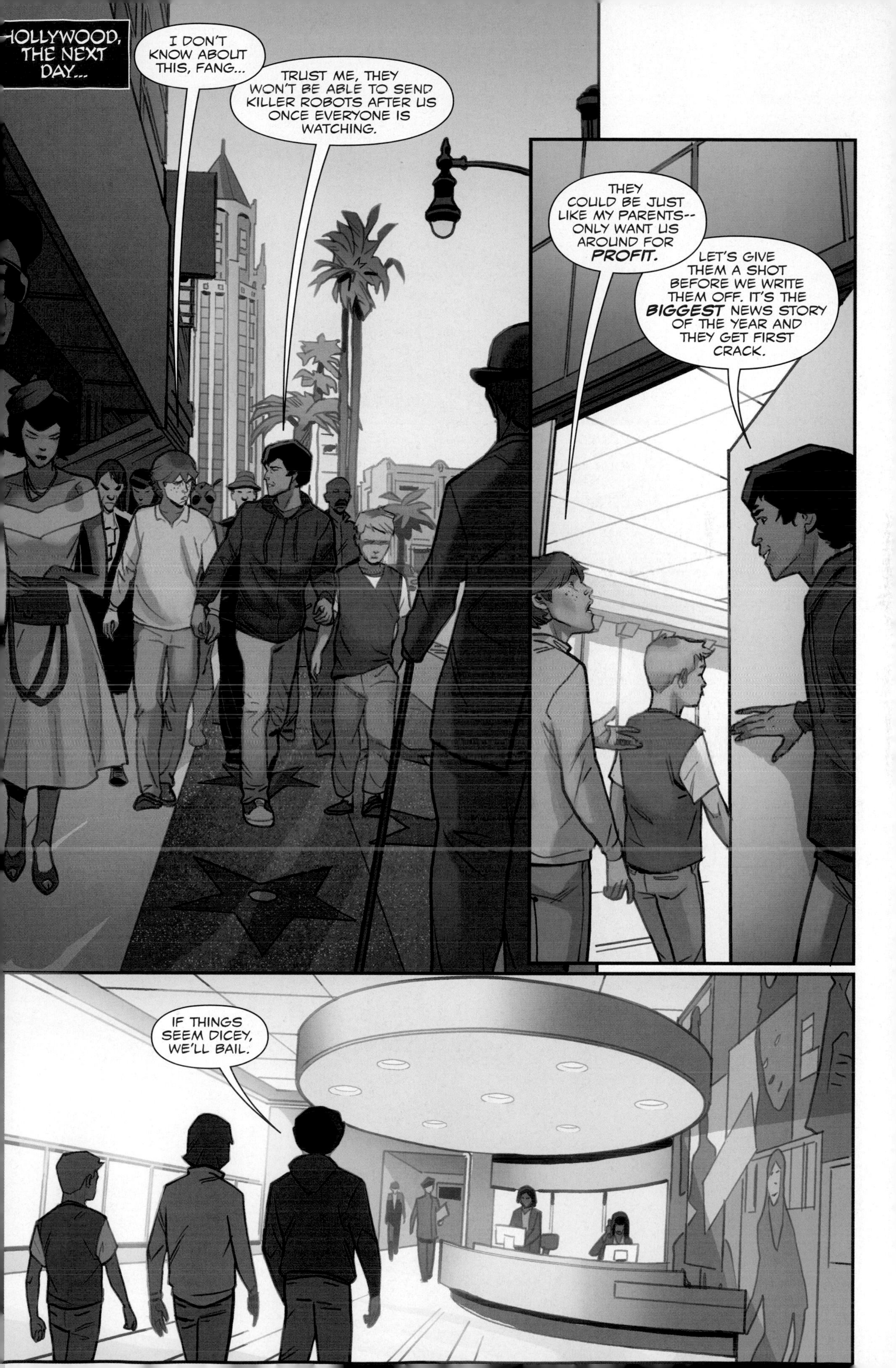
HOLLYWOOD, THE NEXT DAY...
I DON'T KNOW ABOUT THIS, FANG...
TRUST ME, THEY WON'T BE ABLE TO SEND KILLER ROBOTS AFTER US ONCE EVERYONE IS WATCHING.
THEY COULD BE JUST LIKE MY PARENTS--ONLY WANT US AROUND FOR PROFIT.
LET'S GIVE THEM A SHOT BEFORE WE WRITE THEM OFF. IT'S THE BIGGEST NEWS STORY OF THE YEAR AND THEY GET FIRST CRACK.
IF THINGS SEEM DICEY, WE'LL BAIL.

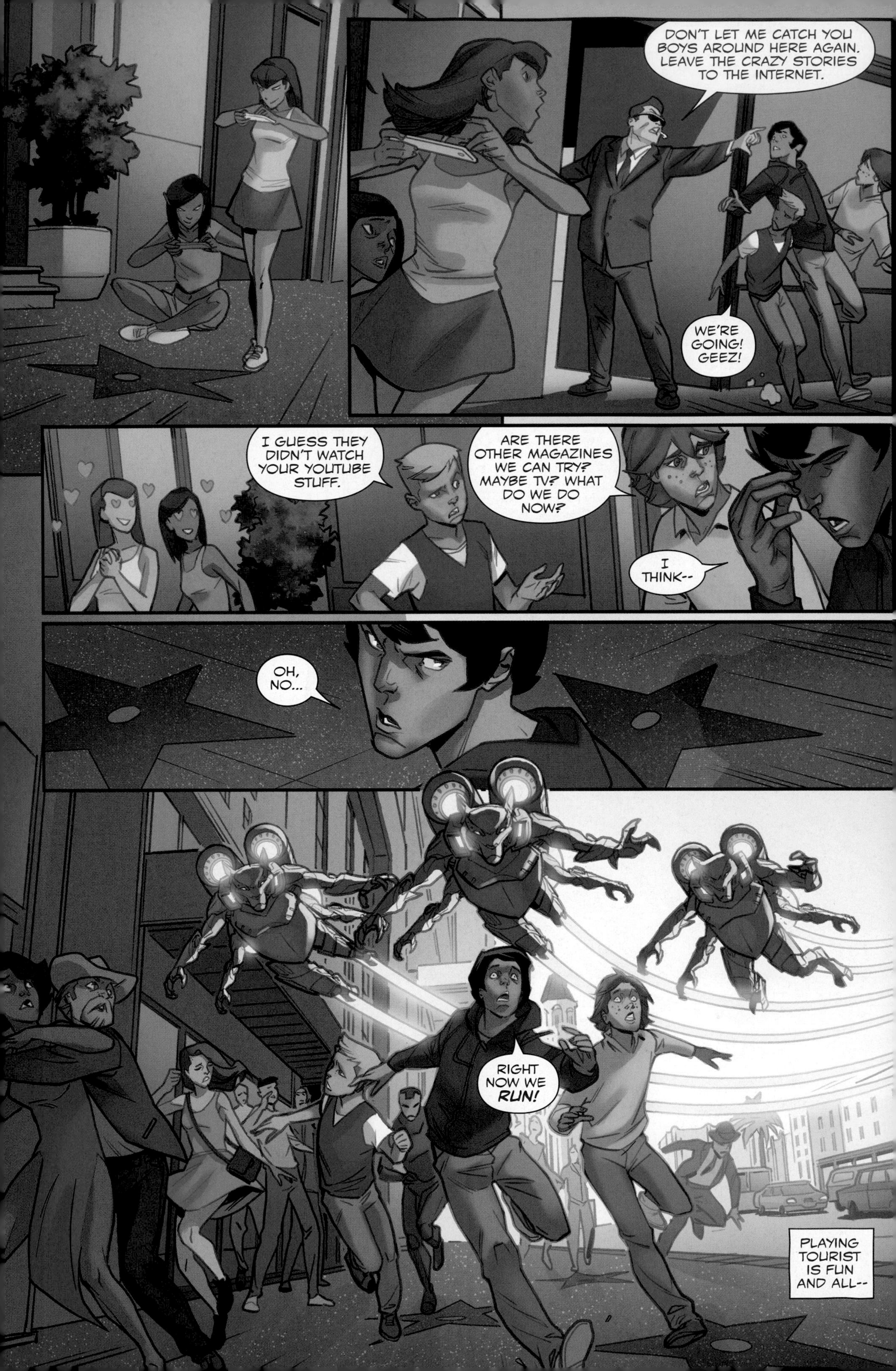
DON'T LET ME CATCH YOU BOYS AROUND HERE AGAIN. LEAVE THE CRAZY STORIES TO THE INTERNET.
WE'RE GOING! GEEZ!
I GUESS THEY DIDN'T WATCH YOUR YOUTUBE STUFF.
ARE THERE OTHER MAGAZINES WE CAN TRY? MAYBE TV? WHAT DO WE DO NOW?
I THINK--
OH, NO...
RIGHT NOW WE RUN!
PLAYING TOURIST IS FUN AND ALL--

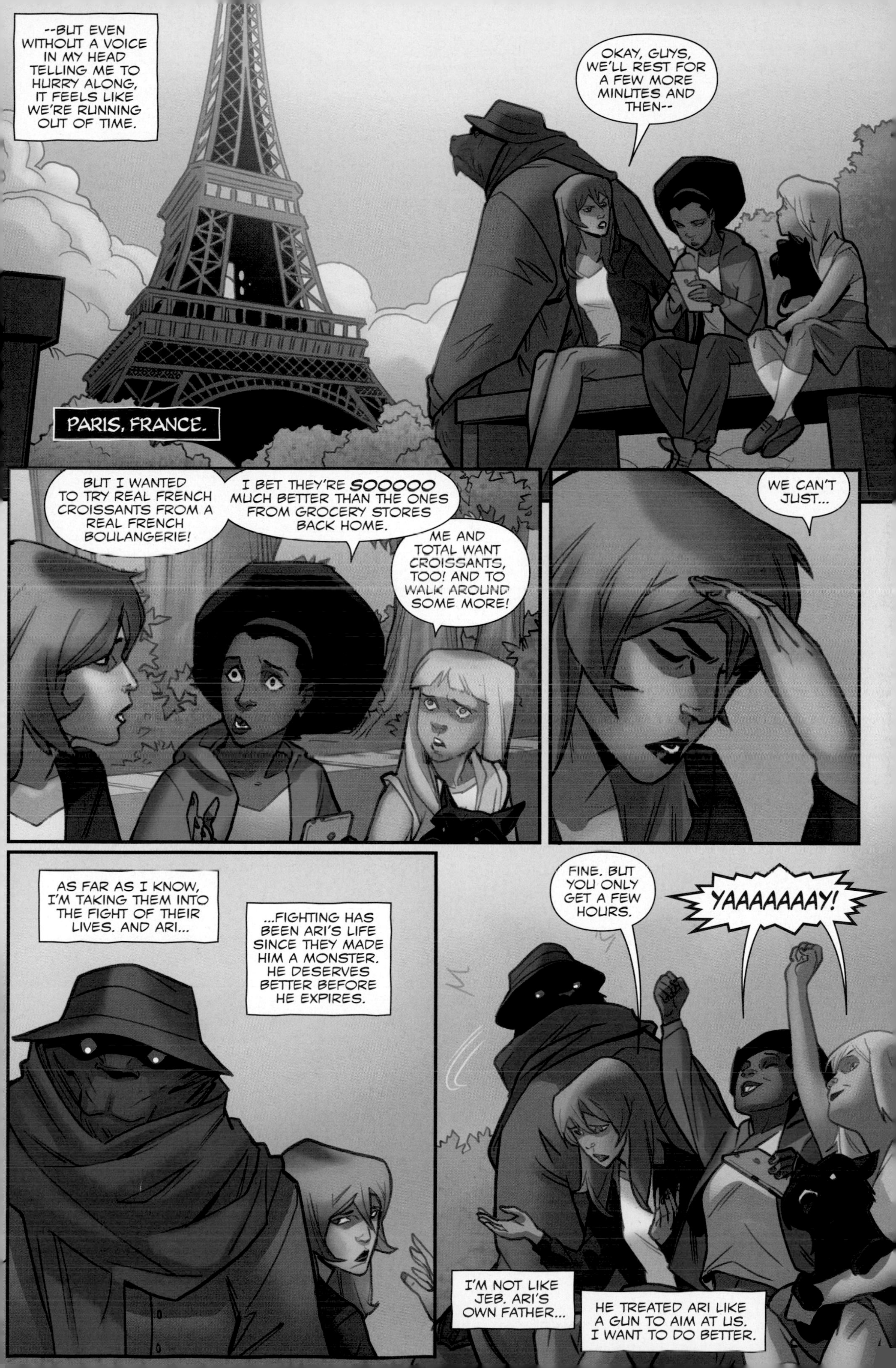
--BUT EVEN WITHOUT A VOICE IN MY HEAD TELLING ME TO HURRY ALONG, IT FEELS LIKE WE'RE RUNNING OUT OF TIME.
PARIS, FRANCE.
OKAY, GUYS, WE'LL REST FOR A FEW MORE MINUTES AND THEN--
BUT I WANTED TO TRY REAL FRENCH CROISSANTS FROM A REAL FRENCH BOULANGERIE!
I BET THEY'RE SOOOOO MUCH BETTER THAN THE ONES FROM GROCERY STORES BACK HOME.
ME AND TOTAL WANT CROISSANTS, TOO! AND TO WALK AROUND SOME MORE!
WE CAN'T JUST...
AS FAR AS I KNOW, I'M TAKING THEM INTO THE FIGHT OF THEIR LIVES. AND ARI...
...FIGHTING HAS BEEN ARI'S LIFE SINCE THEY MADE HIM A MONSTER. HE DESERVES BETTER BEFORE HE EXPIRES.
FINE. BUT YOU ONLY GET A FEW HOURS.
YAAAAAAAY!
I'M NOT LIKE JEB. ARI'S OWN FATHER...
HE TREATED ARI LIKE A GUN TO AIM AT US. I WANT TO DO BETTER.

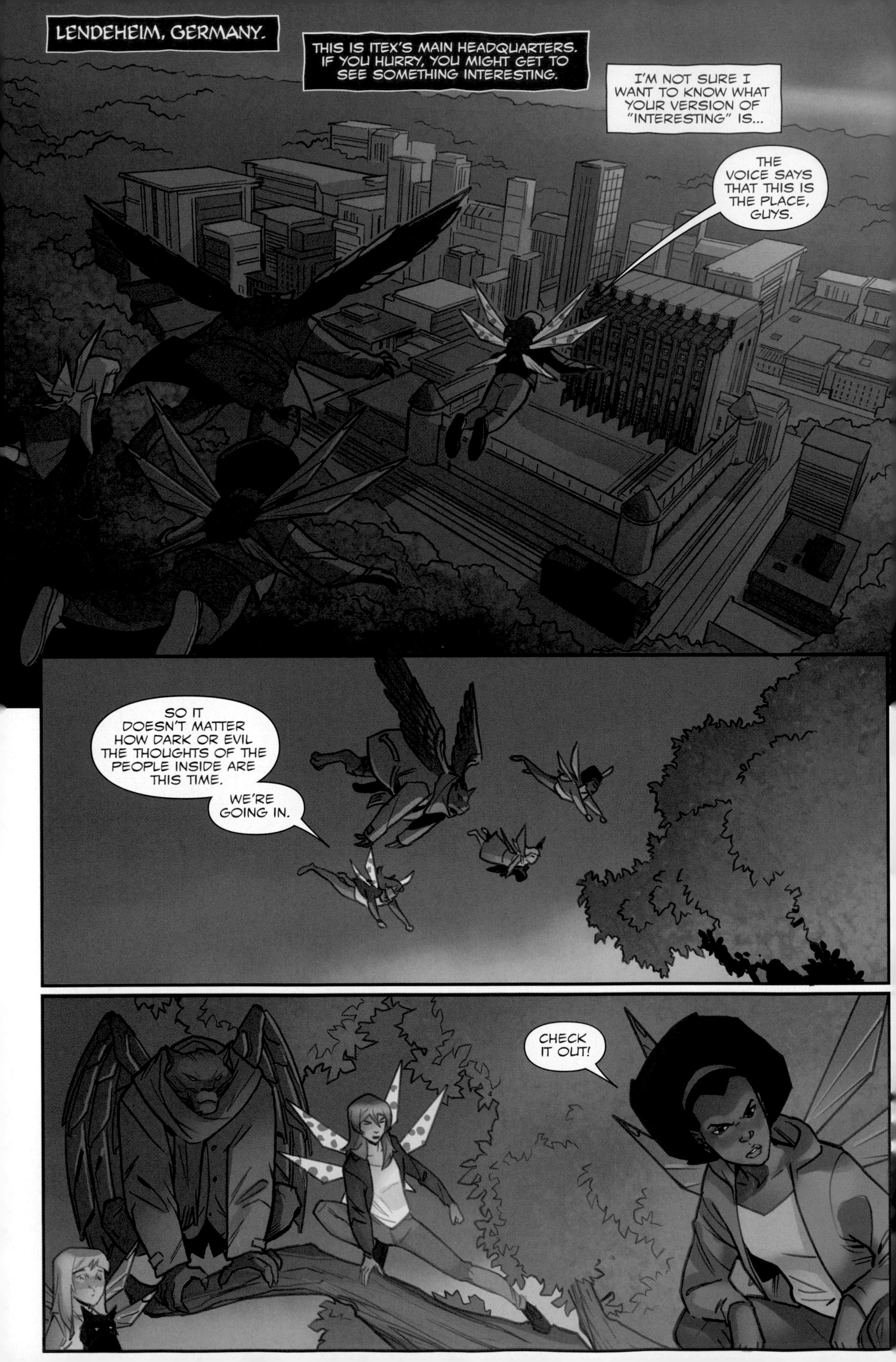
LENDEHEIM, GERMANY.
THIS IS ITEX'S MAIN HEADQUARTERS. IF YOU HURRY, YOU MIGHT GET TO SEE SOMETHING INTERESTING.
I'M NOT SURE I WANT TO KNOW WHAT YOUR VERSION OF "INTERESTING" IS...
THE VOICE SAYS THAT THIS IS THE PLACE, GUYS.
SO IT DOESN'T MATTER HOW DARK OR EVIL THE THOUGHTS OF THE PEOPLE INSIDE ARE THIS TIME.
WE'RE GOING IN.
CHECK IT OUT!

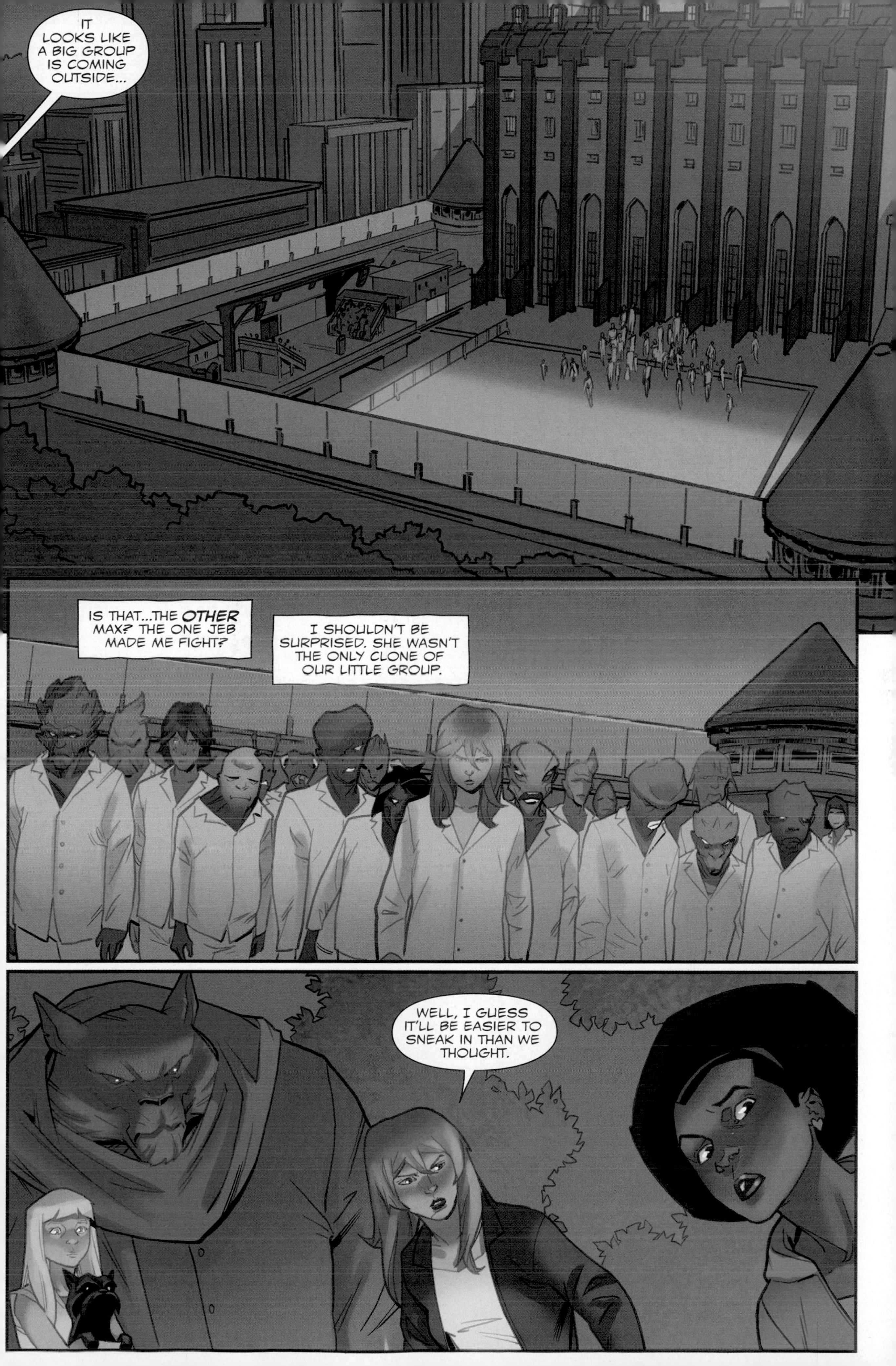
IT LOOKS LIKE A BIG GROUP IS COMING OUTSIDE...
IS THAT...THE OTHER MAX? THE ONE JEB MADE ME FIGHT?
I SHOULDN'T BE SURPRISED. SHE WASN'T THE ONLY CLONE OF OUR LITTLE GROUP.
WELL, I GUESS IT'LL BE EASIER TO SNEAK IN THAN WE THOUGHT.

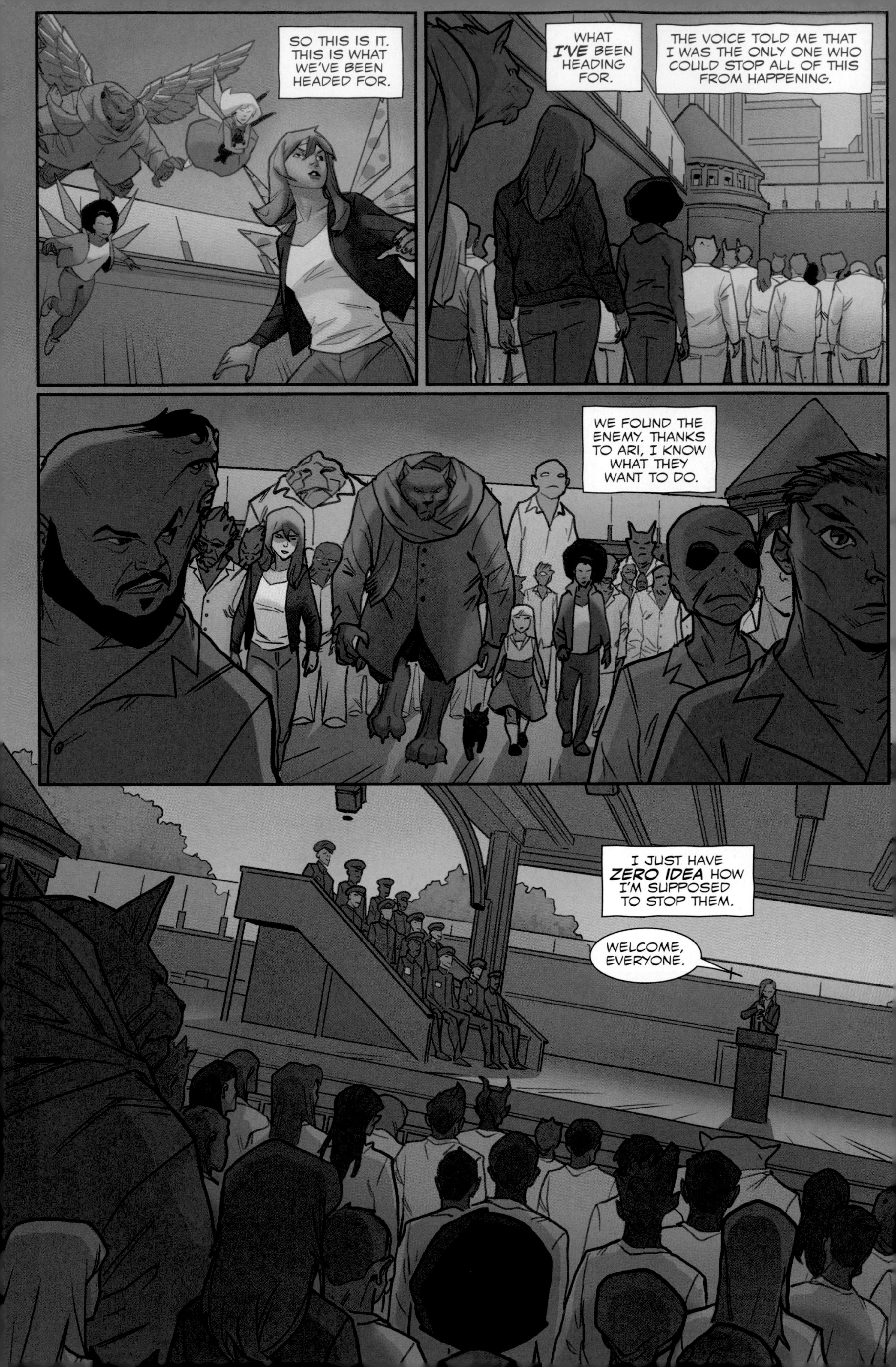
SO THIS IS IT. THIS IS WHAT WE'VE BEEN HEADED FOR.
WHAT I'VE BEEN HEADING FOR.
THE VOICE TOLD ME THAT I WAS THE ONLY ONE WHO COULD STOP ALL OF THIS FROM HAPPENING.
WE FOUND THE ENEMY. THANKS TO ARI, I KNOW WHAT THEY WANT TO DO.
I JUST HAVE ZERO IDEA HOW I'M SUPPOSED TO STOP THEM.
WELCOME, EVERYONE.

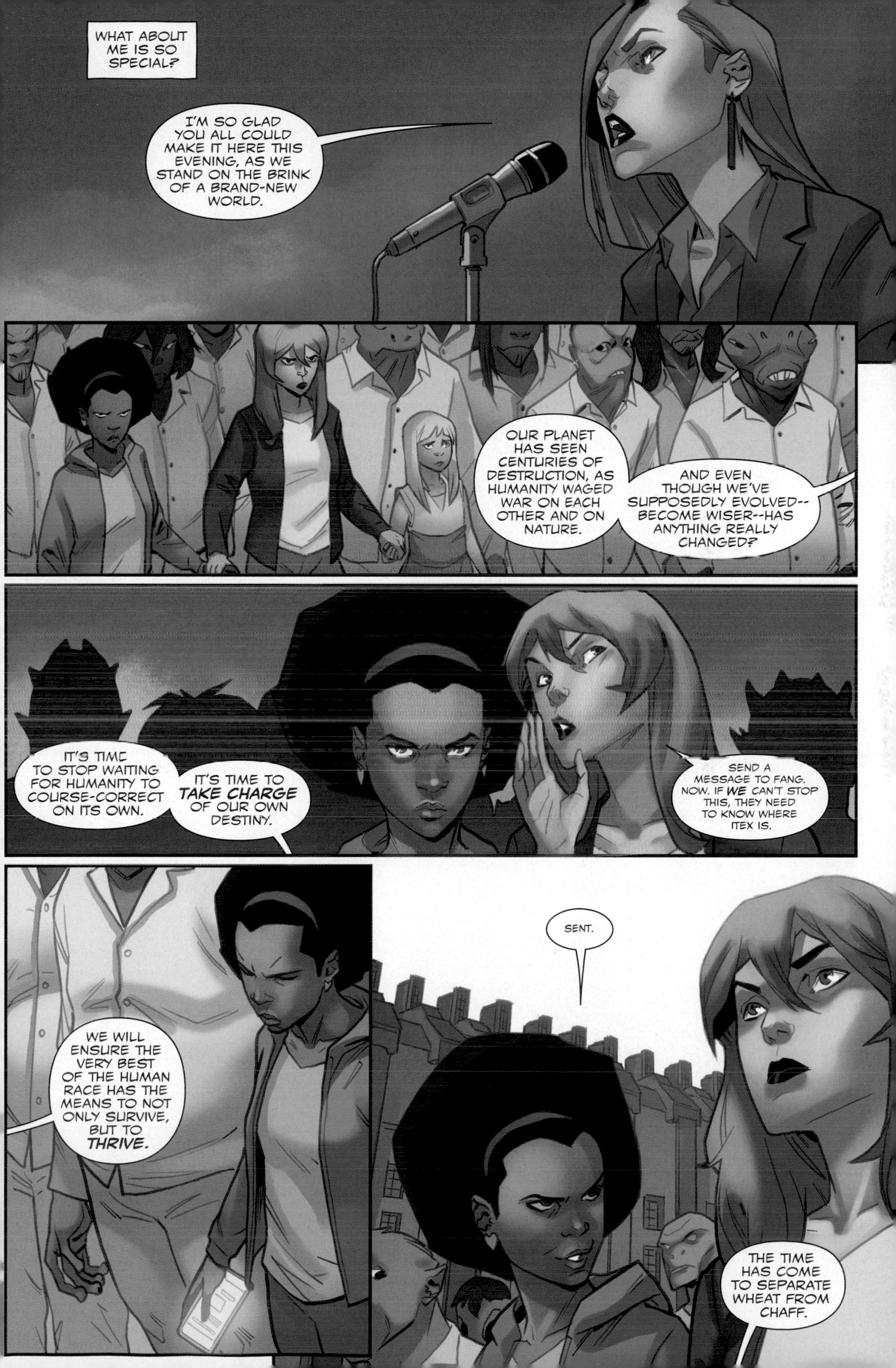
WHAT ABOUT ME IS SO SPECIAL?
I'M SO GLAD YOU ALL COULD MAKE IT HERE THIS EVENING, AS WE STAND ON THE BRINK OF A BRAND-NEW WORLD.
OUR PLANET HAS SEEN CENTURIES OF DESTRUCTION, AS HUMANITY WAGED WAR ON EACH OTHER AND ON NATURE.
AND EVEN THOUGH WE'VE SUPPOSEDLY EVOLVED--BECOME WISER--HAS ANYTHING REALLY CHANGED?
IT'S TIME TO STOP WAITING FOR HUMANITY TO COURSE-CORRECT ON ITS OWN.
IT'S TIME TO TAKE CHARGE OF OUR OWN DESTINY.
SEND A MESSAGE TO FANG. NOW. IF WE CAN'T STOP THIS, THEY NEED TO KNOW WHERE ITEX IS.
WE WILL ENSURE THE VERY BEST OF THE HUMAN RACE HAS THE MEANS TO NOT ONLY SURVIVE, BUT TO THRIVE.
SENT.
THE TIME HAS COME TO SEPARATE WHEAT FROM CHAFF.

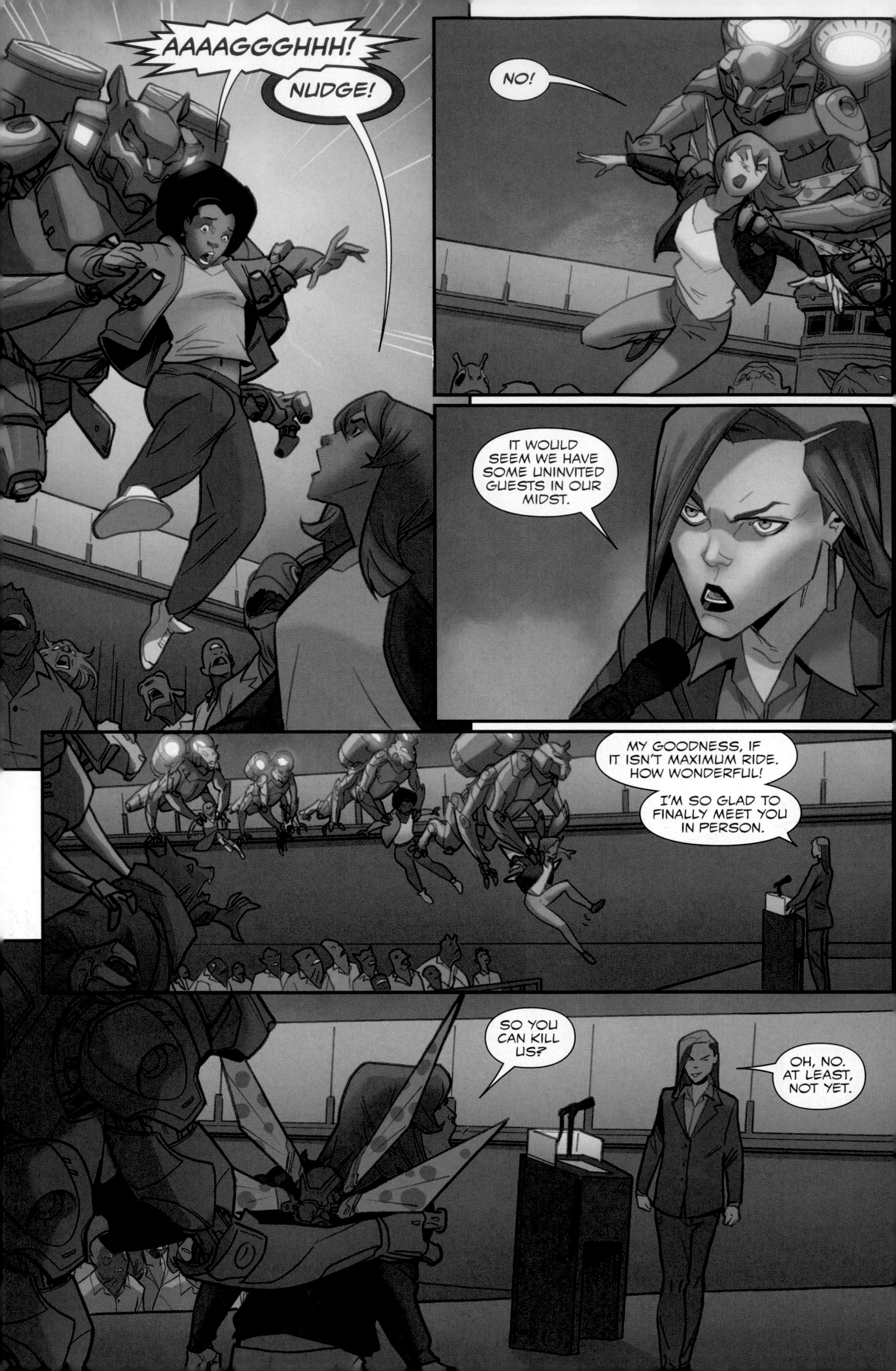
AAAAGGGHHH!
NUDGE!
NO!
IT WOULD SEEM WE HAVE SOME UNINVITED GUESTS IN OUR MIDST.
MY GOODNESS, IF IT ISN'T MAXIMUM RIDE. HOW WONDERFUL!
I'M SO GLAD TO FINALLY MEET YOU IN PERSON.
SO YOU CAN KILL US?
OH, NO. AT LEAST, NOT YET.

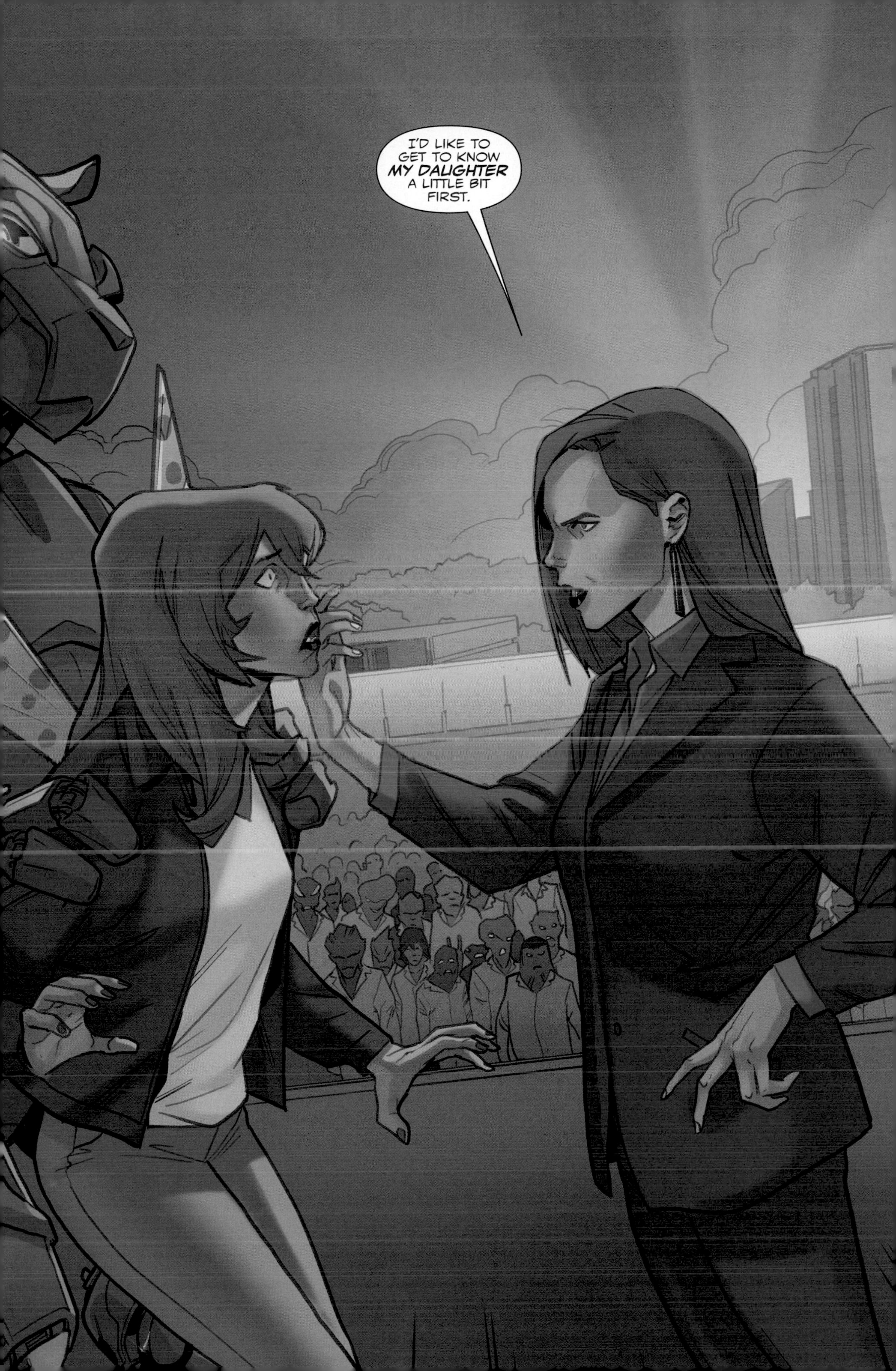
I'D LIKE TO GET TO KNOW **MY DAUGHTER** A LITTLE BIT FIRST.

CHAPTER 4

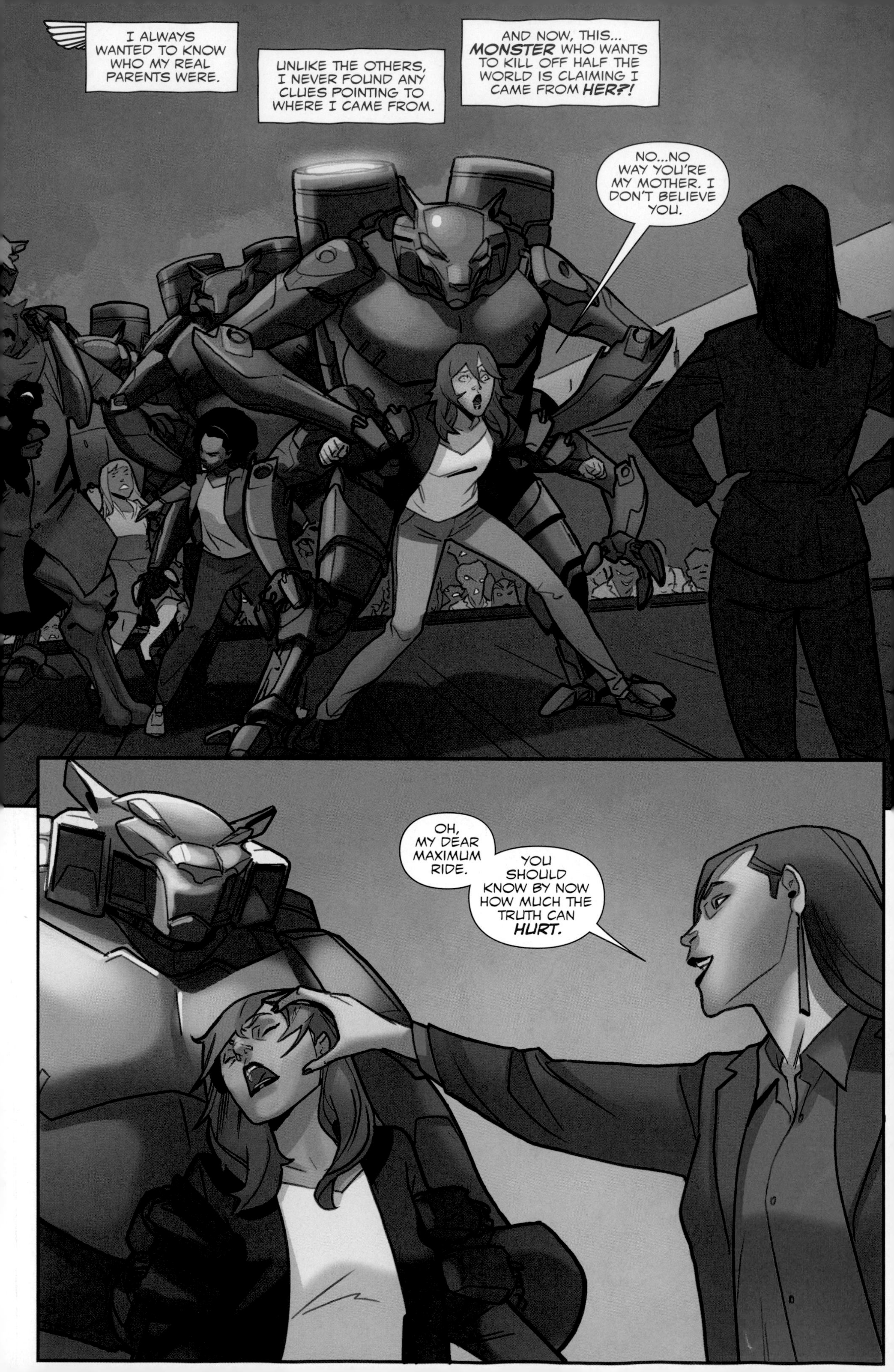
I ALWAYS WANTED TO KNOW WHO MY REAL PARENTS WERE.
UNLIKE THE OTHERS, I NEVER FOUND ANY CLUES POINTING TO WHERE I CAME FROM.
AND NOW, THIS... **MONSTER** WHO WANTS TO KILL OFF HALF THE WORLD IS CLAIMING I CAME FROM **HER?!**
NO...NO WAY YOU'RE MY MOTHER. I DON'T BELIEVE YOU.
OH, MY DEAR MAXIMUM RIDE.
YOU SHOULD KNOW BY NOW HOW MUCH THE TRUTH CAN **HURT.**

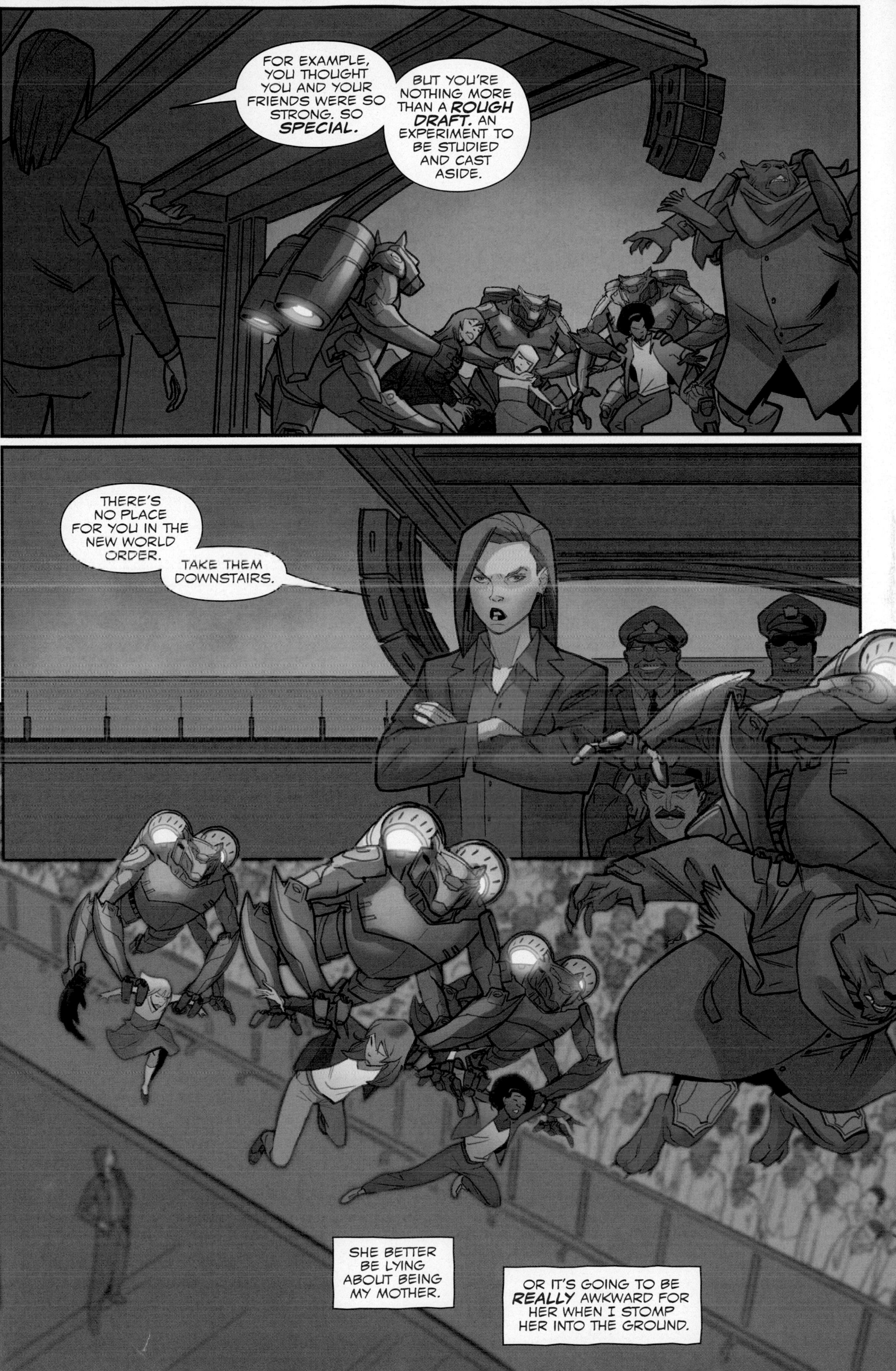
FOR EXAMPLE, YOU THOUGHT YOU AND YOUR FRIENDS WERE SO STRONG. SO SPECIAL.
BUT YOU'RE NOTHING MORE THAN A ROUGH DRAFT. AN EXPERIMENT TO BE STUDIED AND CAST ASIDE.
THERE'S NO PLACE FOR YOU IN THE NEW WORLD ORDER.
TAKE THEM DOWNSTAIRS.
SHE BETTER BE LYING ABOUT BEING MY MOTHER.
OR IT'S GOING TO BE REALLY AWKWARD FOR HER WHEN I STOMP HER INTO THE GROUND.

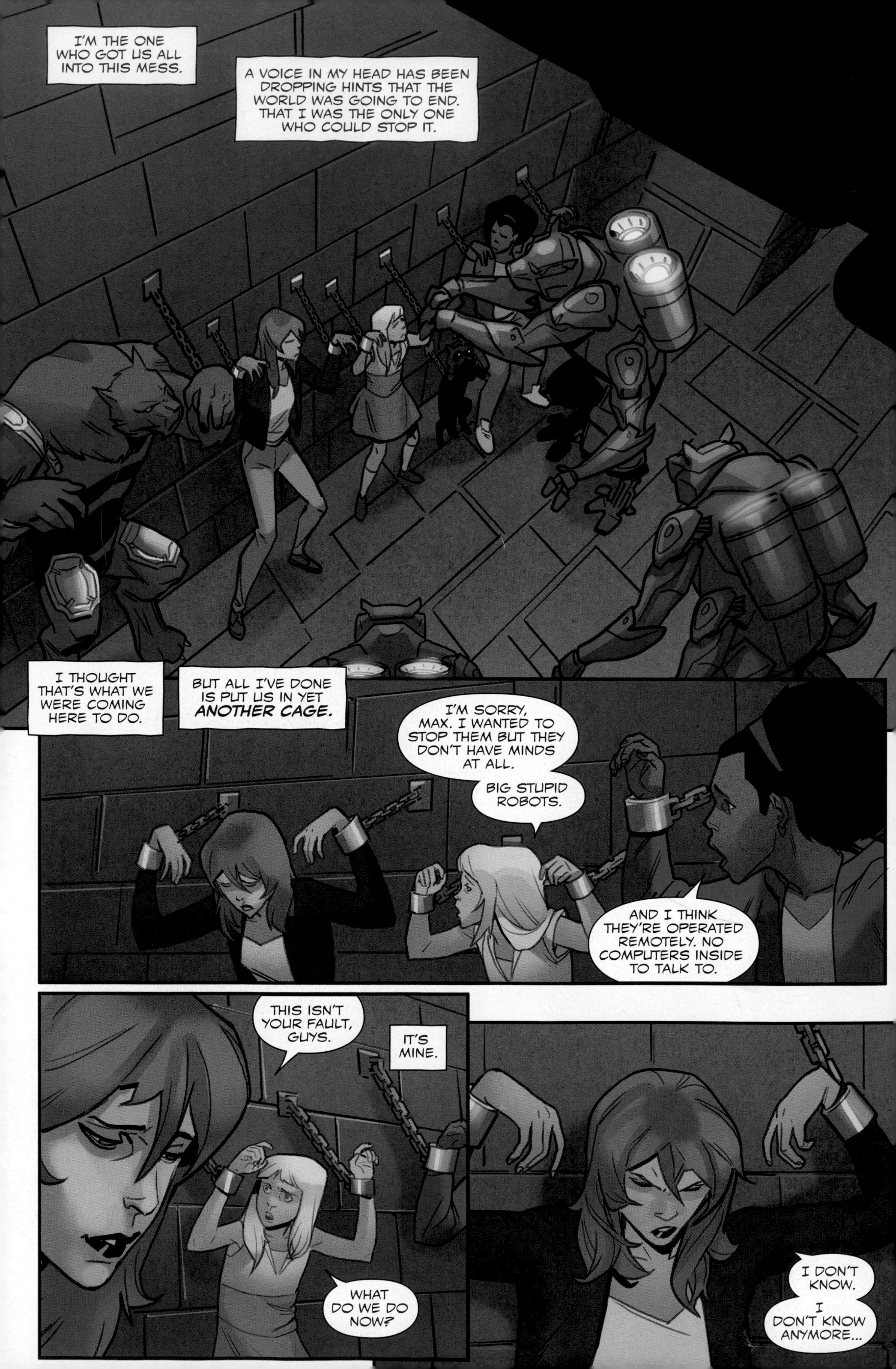
I'M THE ONE WHO GOT US ALL INTO THIS MESS.
A VOICE IN MY HEAD HAS BEEN DROPPING HINTS THAT THE WORLD WAS GOING TO END. THAT I WAS THE ONLY ONE WHO COULD STOP IT.
I THOUGHT THAT'S WHAT WE WERE COMING HERE TO DO.
BUT ALL I'VE DONE IS PUT US IN YET ***ANOTHER CAGE.***
I'M SORRY, MAX. I WANTED TO STOP THEM BUT THEY DON'T HAVE MINDS AT ALL.
BIG STUPID ROBOTS.
AND I THINK THEY'RE OPERATED REMOTELY. NO COMPUTERS INSIDE TO TALK TO.
THIS ISN'T YOUR FAULT, GUYS.
IT'S MINE.
WHAT DO WE DO NOW?
I DON'T KNOW.
I DON'T KNOW ANYMORE...

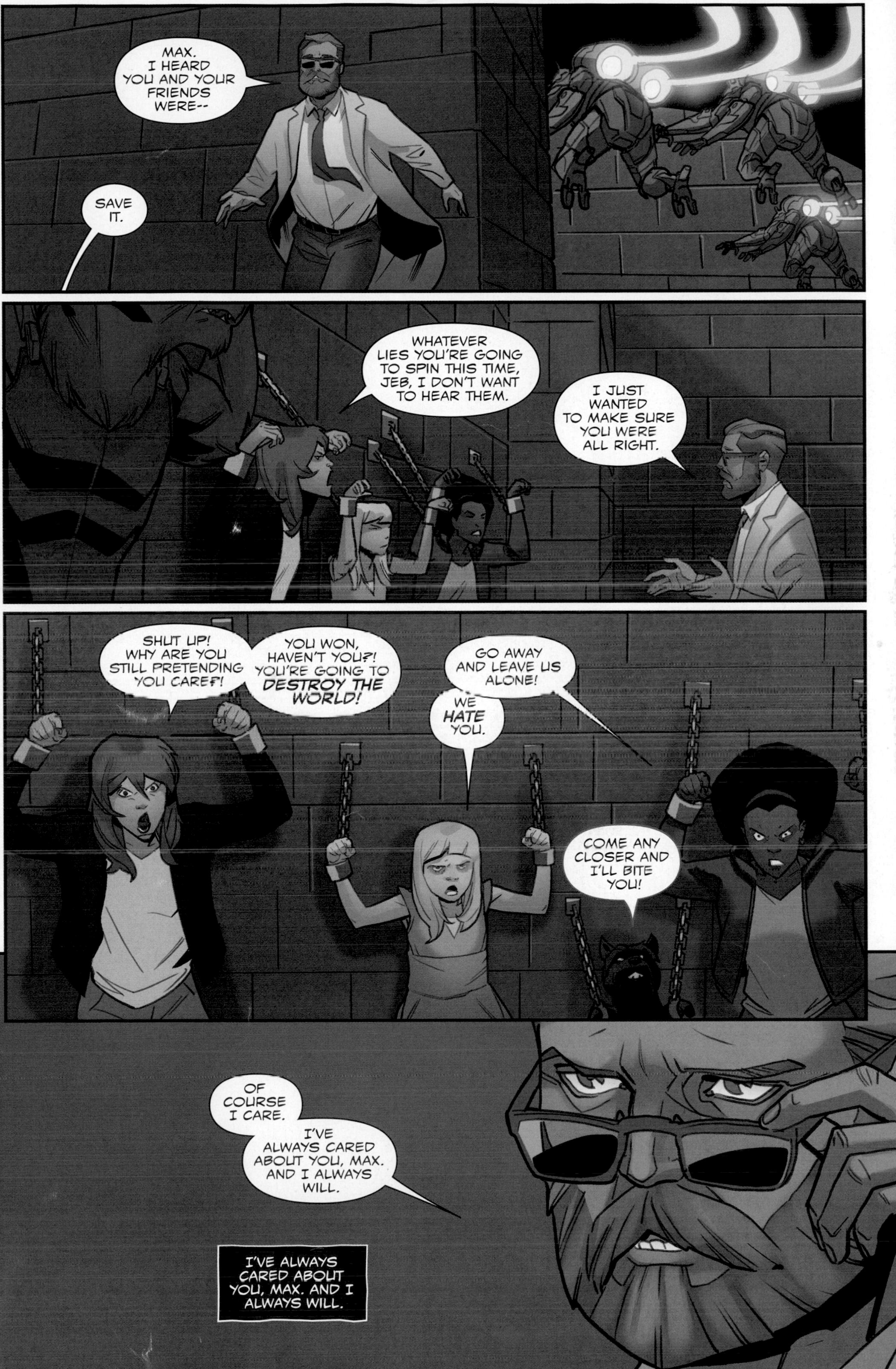

MAX. I HEARD YOU AND YOUR FRIENDS WERE--
SAVE IT.
WHATEVER LIES YOU'RE GOING TO SPIN THIS TIME, JEB, I DON'T WANT TO HEAR THEM.
I JUST WANTED TO MAKE SURE YOU WERE ALL RIGHT.
SHUT UP! WHY ARE YOU STILL PRETENDING YOU CARE?!
YOU WON, HAVEN'T YOU?! YOU'RE GOING TO DESTROY THE WORLD!
GO AWAY AND LEAVE US ALONE!
WE HATE YOU.
COME ANY CLOSER AND I'LL BITE YOU!
OF COURSE I CARE.
I'VE ALWAYS CARED ABOUT YOU, MAX. AND I ALWAYS WILL.
I'VE ALWAYS CARED ABOUT YOU, MAX. AND I ALWAYS WILL.

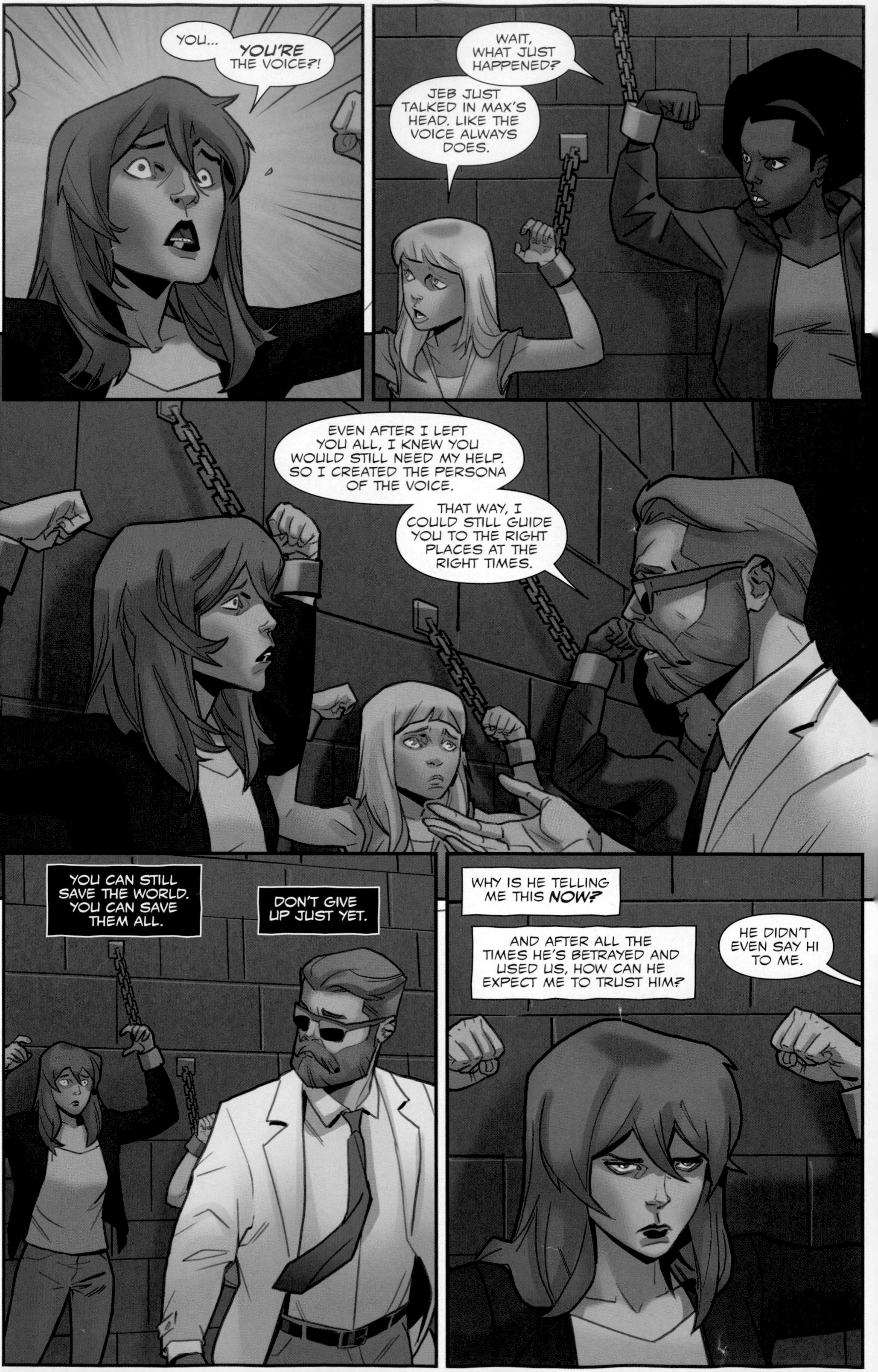
YOU... YOU'RE THE VOICE?!
WAIT, WHAT JUST HAPPENED?
JEB JUST TALKED IN MAX'S HEAD. LIKE THE VOICE ALWAYS DOES.
EVEN AFTER I LEFT YOU ALL, I KNEW YOU WOULD STILL NEED MY HELP. SO I CREATED THE PERSONA OF THE VOICE.
THAT WAY, I COULD STILL GUIDE YOU TO THE RIGHT PLACES AT THE RIGHT TIMES.
YOU CAN STILL SAVE THE WORLD. YOU CAN SAVE THEM ALL.
DON'T GIVE UP JUST YET.
WHY IS HE TELLING ME THIS NOW?
AND AFTER ALL THE TIMES HE'S BETRAYED AND USED US, HOW CAN HE EXPECT ME TO TRUST HIM?
HE DIDN'T EVEN SAY HI TO ME.

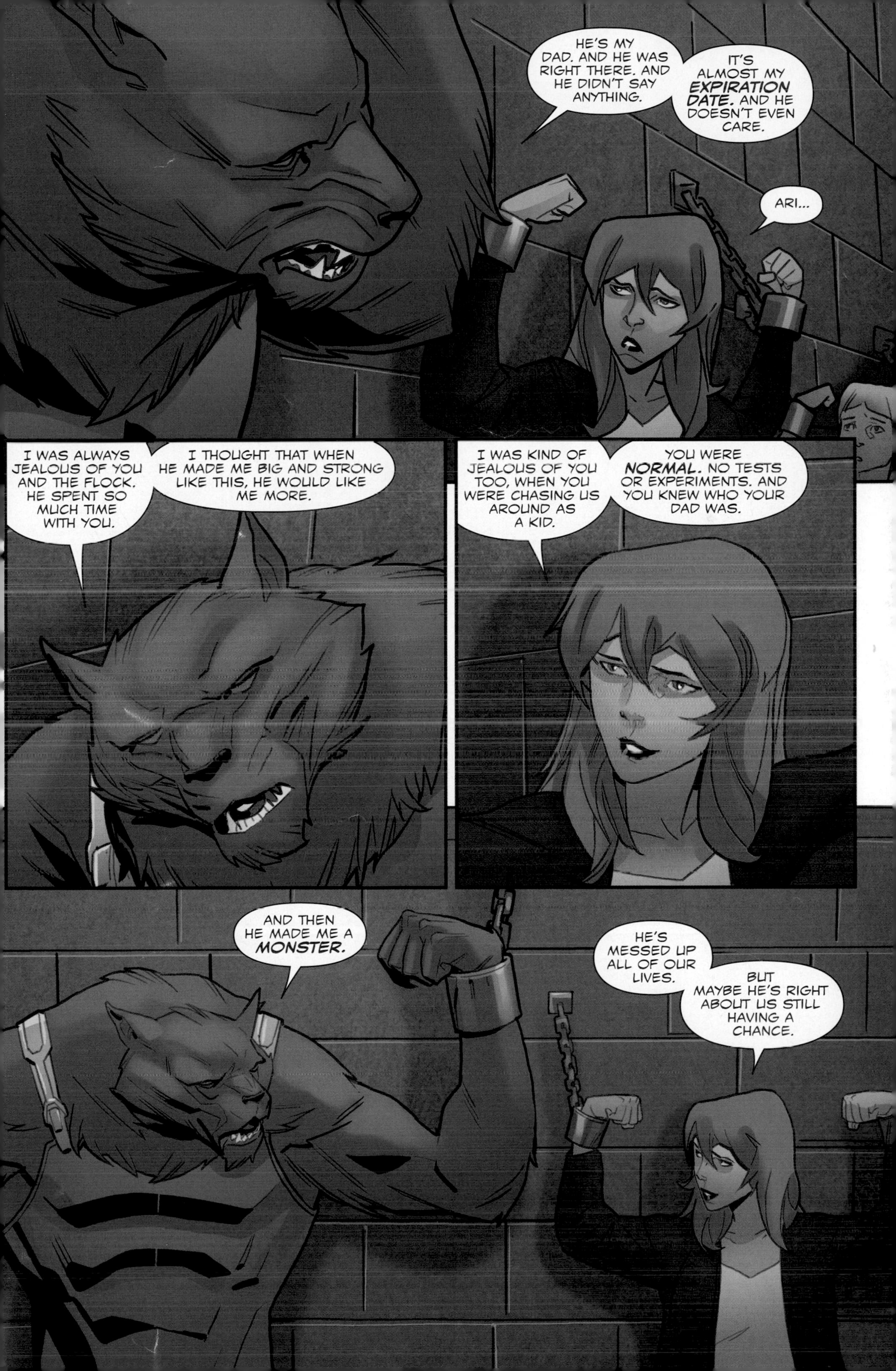
HE'S MY DAD. AND HE WAS RIGHT THERE. AND HE DIDN'T SAY ANYTHING.
IT'S ALMOST MY EXPIRATION DATE. AND HE DOESN'T EVEN CARE.
ARI...
I WAS ALWAYS JEALOUS OF YOU AND THE FLOCK. HE SPENT SO MUCH TIME WITH YOU.
I THOUGHT THAT WHEN HE MADE ME BIG AND STRONG LIKE THIS, HE WOULD LIKE ME MORE.
I WAS KIND OF JEALOUS OF YOU TOO, WHEN YOU WERE CHASING US AROUND AS A KID.
YOU WERE NORMAL. NO TESTS OR EXPERIMENTS. AND YOU KNEW WHO YOUR DAD WAS.
AND THEN HE MADE ME A MONSTER.
HE'S MESSED UP ALL OF OUR LIVES.
BUT MAYBE HE'S RIGHT ABOUT US STILL HAVING A CHANCE.

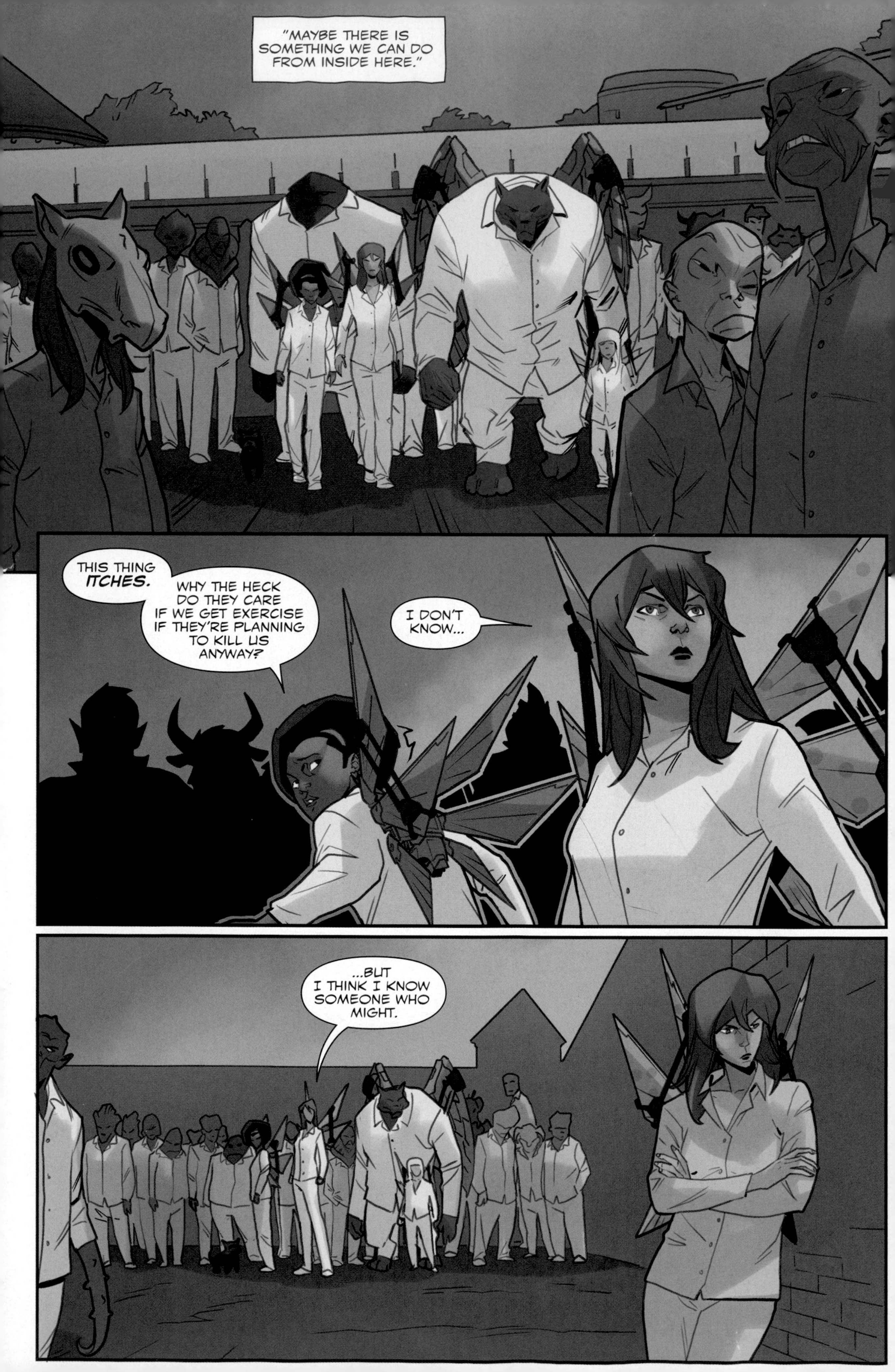
"MAYBE THERE IS SOMETHING WE CAN DO FROM INSIDE HERE."
THIS THING ITCHES.
WHY THE HECK DO THEY CARE IF WE GET EXERCISE IF THEY'RE PLANNING TO KILL US ANYWAY?
I DON'T KNOW...
...BUT I THINK I KNOW SOMEONE WHO MIGHT.

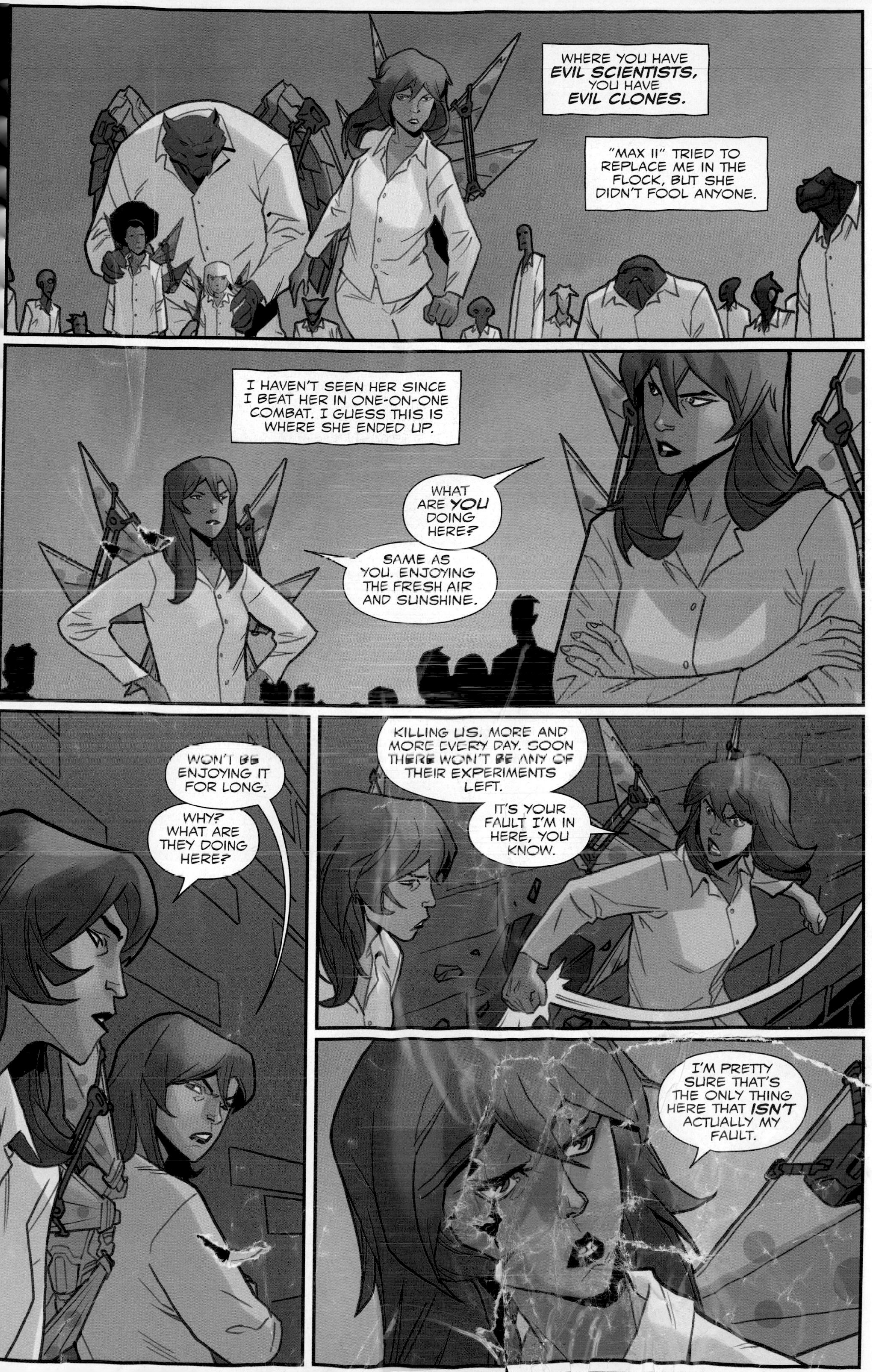

WHERE YOU HAVE EVIL SCIENTISTS, YOU HAVE EVIL CLONES.
"MAX II" TRIED TO REPLACE ME IN THE FLOCK, BUT SHE DIDN'T FOOL ANYONE.
I HAVEN'T SEEN HER SINCE I BEAT HER IN ONE-ON-ONE COMBAT. I GUESS THIS IS WHERE SHE ENDED UP.
WHAT ARE YOU DOING HERE?
SAME AS YOU. ENJOYING THE FRESH AIR AND SUNSHINE.
WON'T BE ENJOYING IT FOR LONG.
WHY? WHAT ARE THEY DOING HERE?
KILLING US. MORE AND MORE EVERY DAY. SOON THERE WON'T BE ANY OF THEIR EXPERIMENTS LEFT.
IT'S YOUR FAULT I'M IN HERE, YOU KNOW.
I'M PRETTY SURE THAT'S THE ONLY THING HERE THAT ISN'T ACTUALLY MY FAULT.

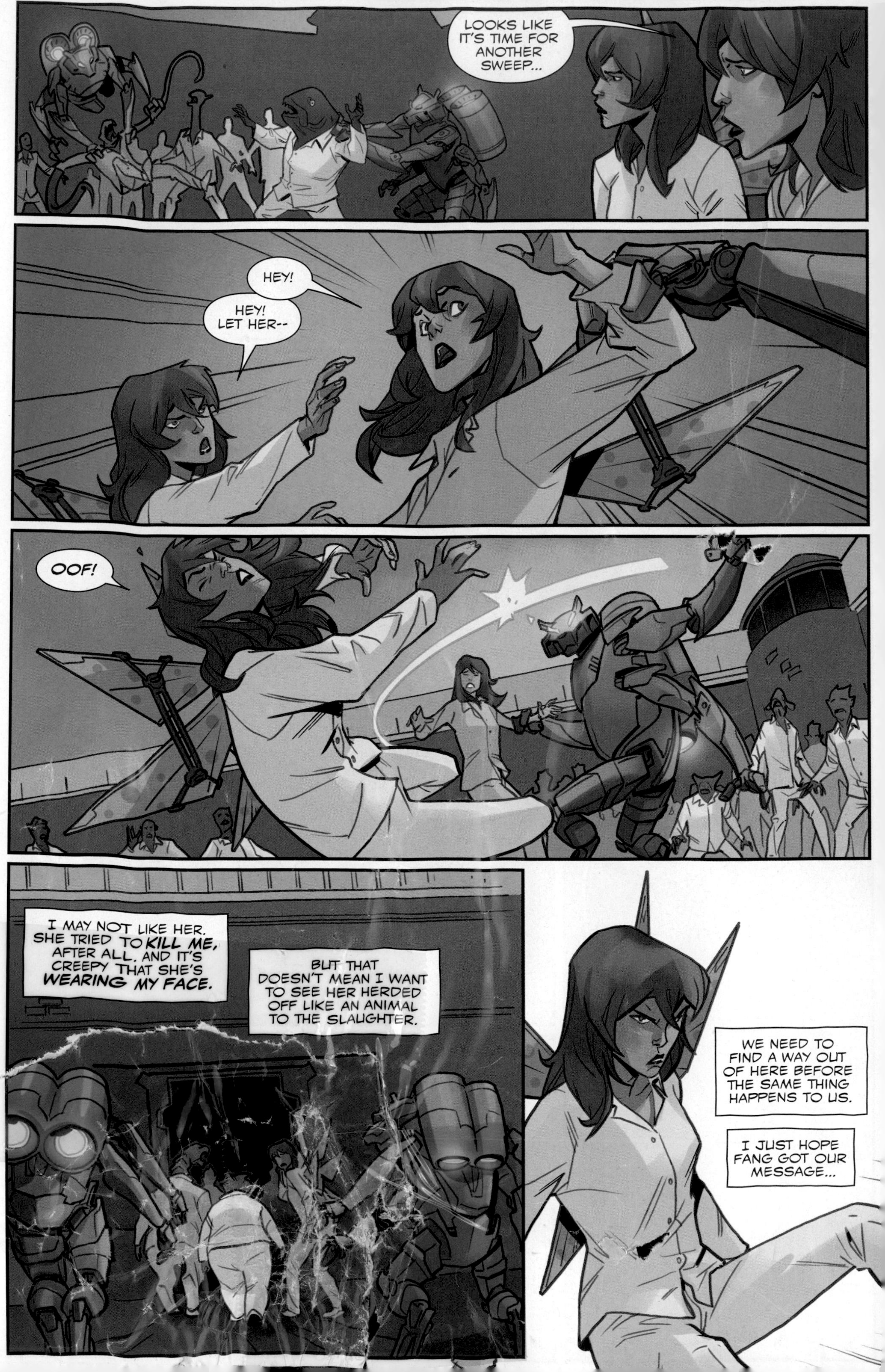

LOOKS LIKE IT'S TIME FOR ANOTHER SWEEP...
HEY!
HEY! LET HER--
OOF!
I MAY NOT LIKE HER. SHE TRIED TO KILL ME, AFTER ALL. AND IT'S CREEPY THAT SHE'S WEARING MY FACE.
BUT THAT DOESN'T MEAN I WANT TO SEE HER HERDED OFF LIKE AN ANIMAL TO THE SLAUGHTER.
WE NEED TO FIND A WAY OUT OF HERE BEFORE THE SAME THING HAPPENS TO US.
I JUST HOPE FANG GOT OUR MESSAGE...

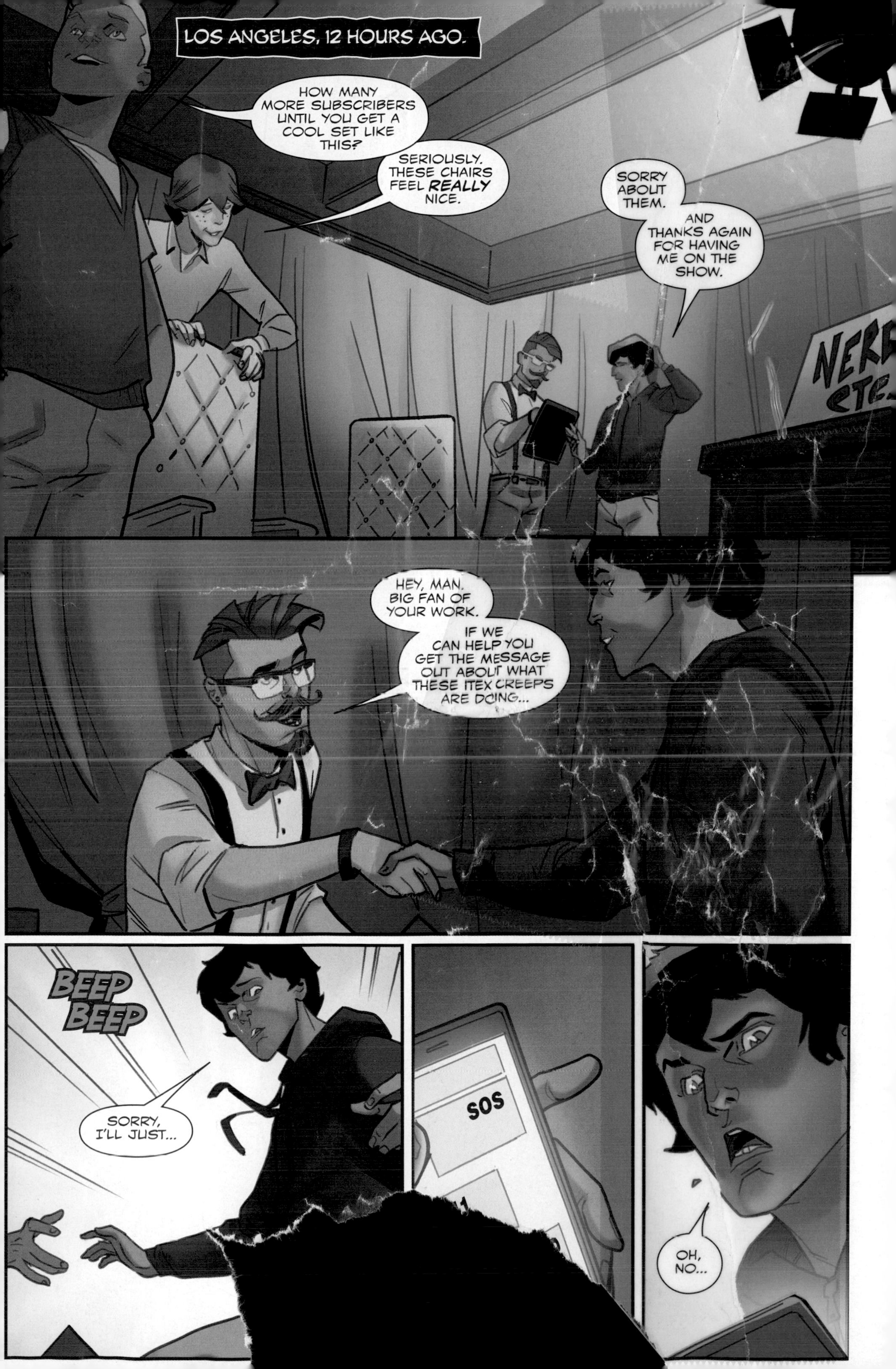
LOS ANGELES, 12 HOURS AGO.
HOW MANY MORE SUBSCRIBERS UNTIL YOU GET A COOL SET LIKE THIS?
SERIOUSLY. THESE CHAIRS FEEL REALLY NICE.
SORRY ABOUT THEM.
AND THANKS AGAIN FOR HAVING ME ON THE SHOW.
HEY, MAN. BIG FAN OF YOUR WORK.
IF WE CAN HELP YOU GET THE MESSAGE OUT ABOUT WHAT THESE ITEX CREEPS ARE DOING...
BEEP BEEP
SORRY, I'LL JUST...
SOS
OH, NO...

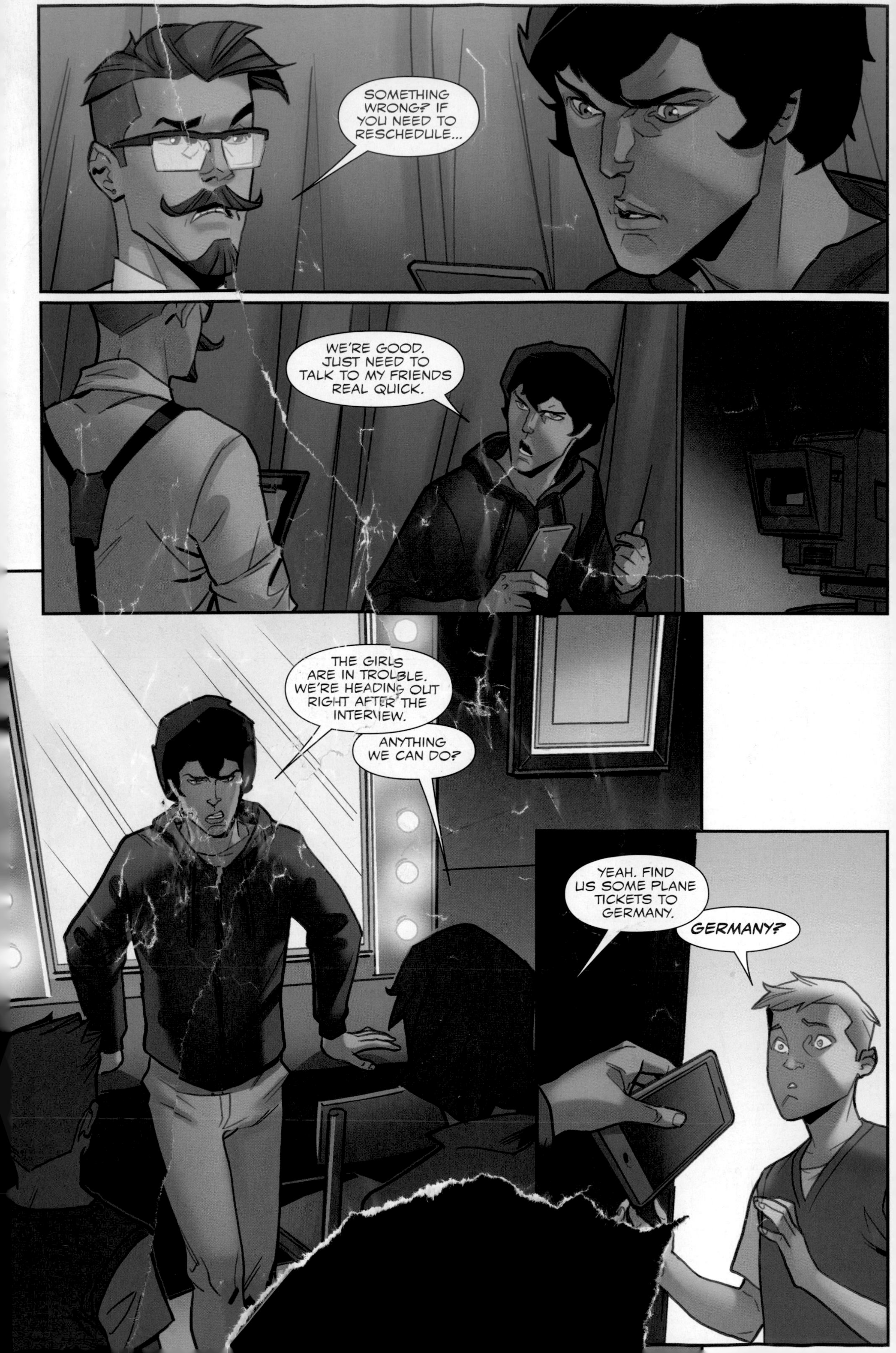
SOMETHING WRONG? IF YOU NEED TO RESCHEDULE...
WE'RE GOOD. JUST NEED TO TALK TO MY FRIENDS REAL QUICK.
THE GIRLS ARE IN TROUBLE. WE'RE HEADING OUT RIGHT AFTER THE INTERVIEW.
ANYTHING WE CAN DO?
YEAH. FIND US SOME PLANE TICKETS TO GERMANY.
GERMANY?

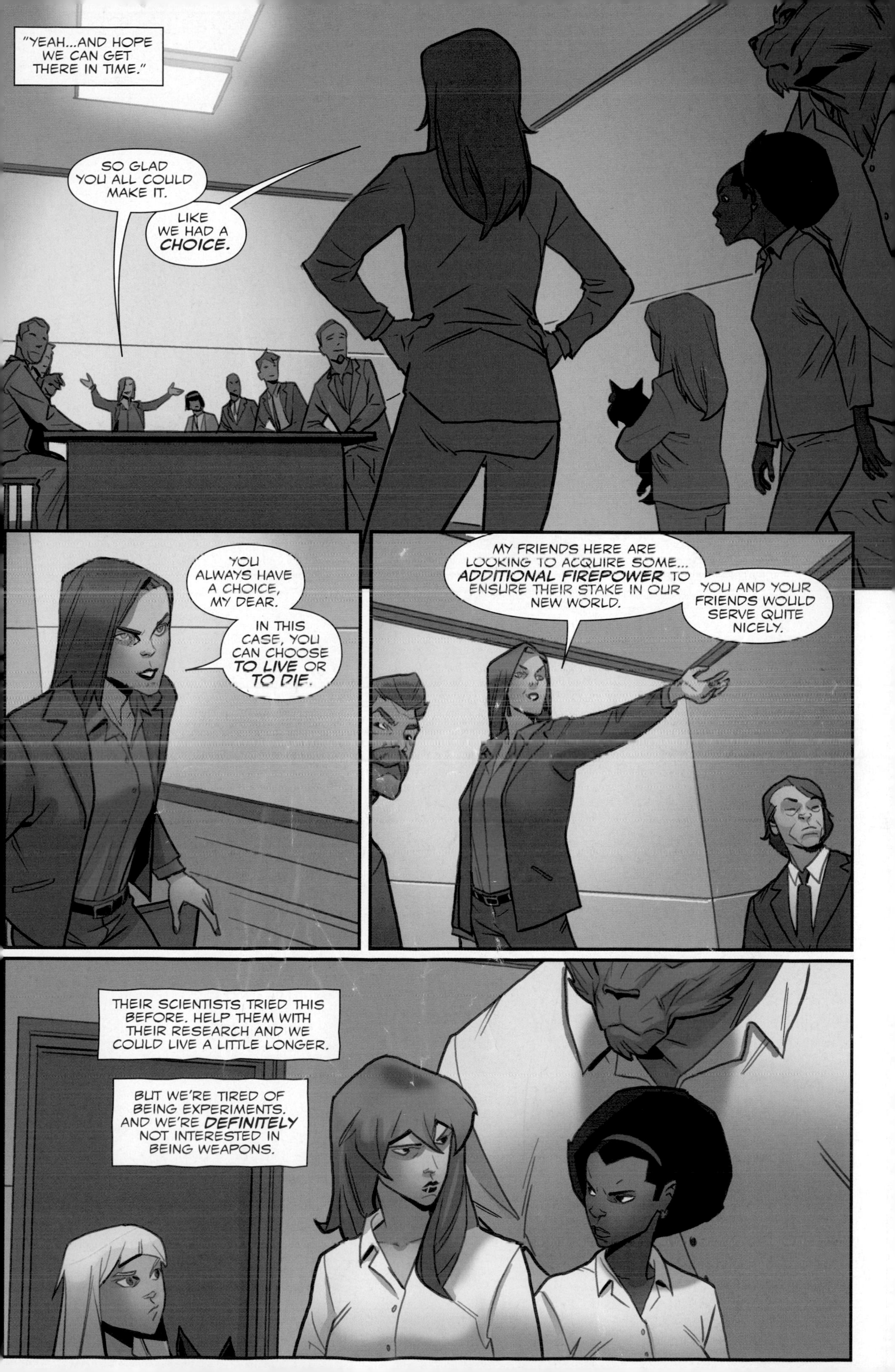
"YEAH...AND HOPE WE CAN GET THERE IN TIME."
SO GLAD YOU ALL COULD MAKE IT.
LIKE WE HAD A CHOICE.
YOU ALWAYS HAVE A CHOICE, MY DEAR.
IN THIS CASE, YOU CAN CHOOSE TO LIVE OR TO DIE.
MY FRIENDS HERE ARE LOOKING TO ACQUIRE SOME... ADDITIONAL FIREPOWER TO ENSURE THEIR STAKE IN OUR NEW WORLD.
YOU AND YOUR FRIENDS WOULD SERVE QUITE NICELY.
THEIR SCIENTISTS TRIED THIS BEFORE. HELP THEM WITH THEIR RESEARCH AND WE COULD LIVE A LITTLE LONGER.
BUT WE'RE TIRED OF BEING EXPERIMENTS. AND WE'RE DEFINITELY NOT INTERESTED IN BEING WEAPONS.

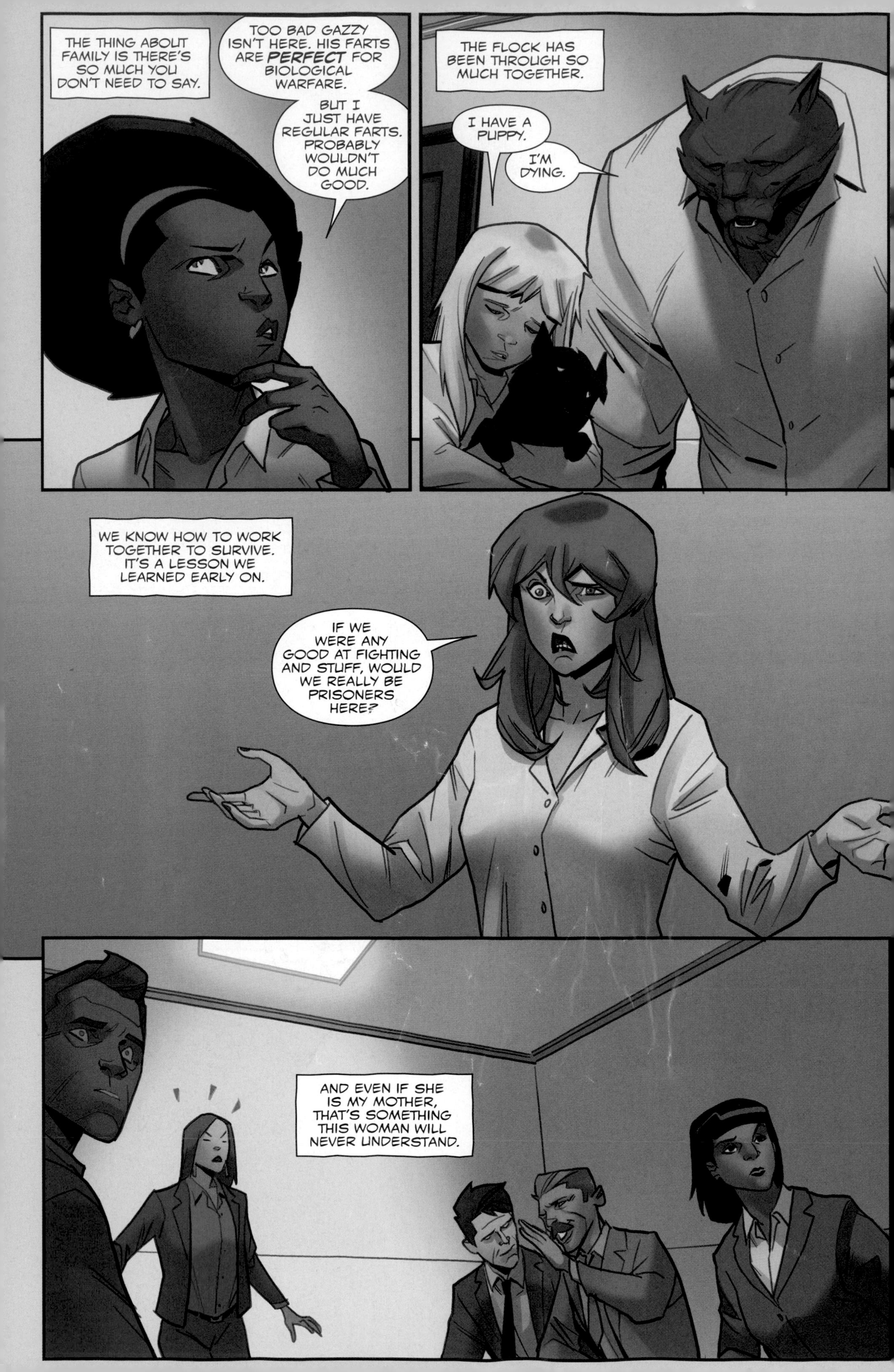
THE THING ABOUT FAMILY IS THERE'S SO MUCH YOU DON'T NEED TO SAY.
TOO BAD GAZZY ISN'T HERE. HIS FARTS ARE PERFECT FOR BIOLOGICAL WARFARE.
BUT I JUST HAVE REGULAR FARTS. PROBABLY WOULDN'T DO MUCH GOOD.
THE FLOCK HAS BEEN THROUGH SO MUCH TOGETHER.
I HAVE A PUPPY.
I'M DYING.
WE KNOW HOW TO WORK TOGETHER TO SURVIVE. IT'S A LESSON WE LEARNED EARLY ON.
IF WE WERE ANY GOOD AT FIGHTING AND STUFF, WOULD WE REALLY BE PRISONERS HERE?
AND EVEN IF SHE IS MY MOTHER, THAT'S SOMETHING THIS WOMAN WILL NEVER UNDERSTAND.

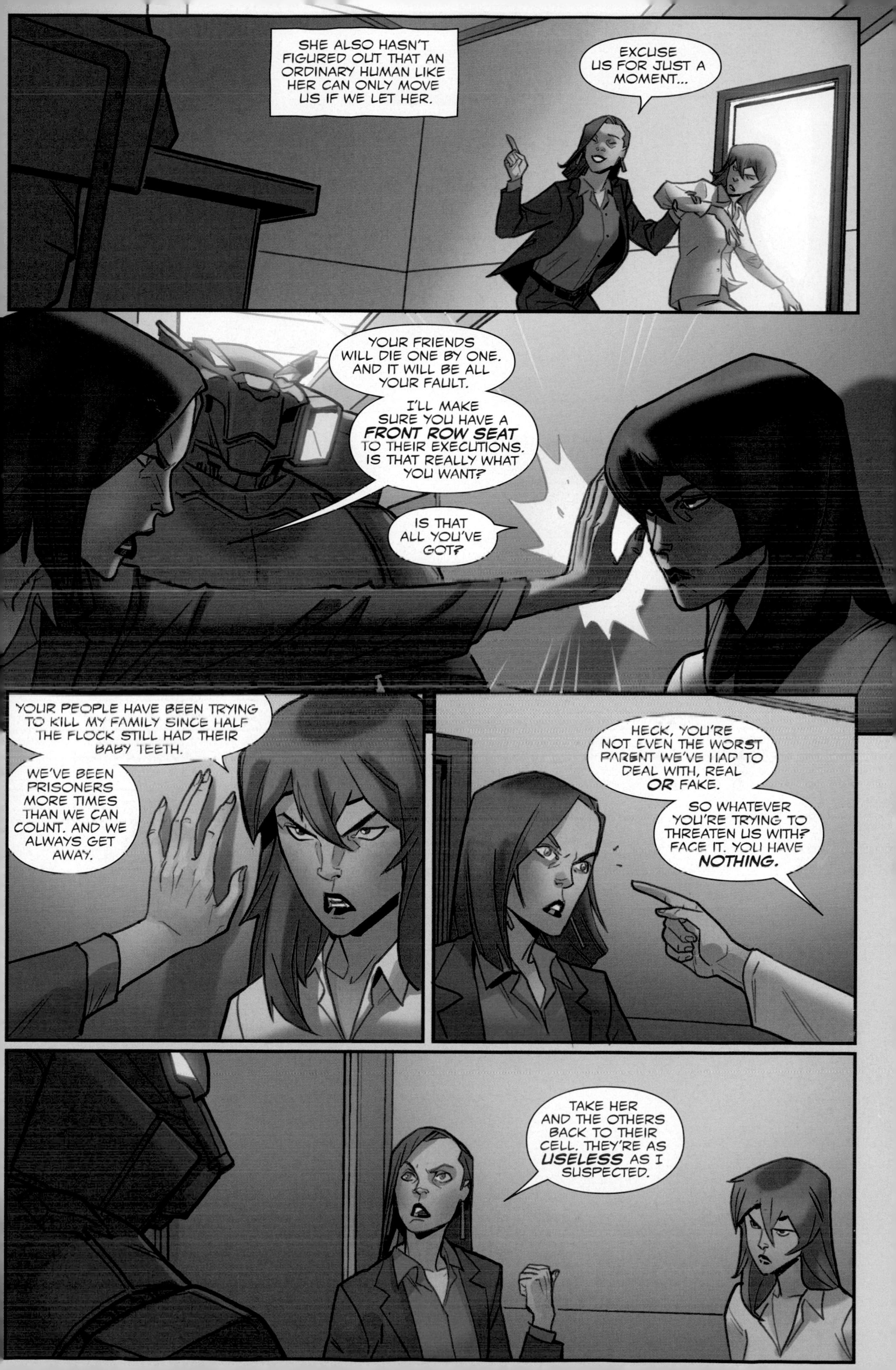
SHE ALSO HASN'T FIGURED OUT THAT AN ORDINARY HUMAN LIKE HER CAN ONLY MOVE US IF WE LET HER.
EXCUSE US FOR JUST A MOMENT...
YOUR FRIENDS WILL DIE ONE BY ONE. AND IT WILL BE ALL YOUR FAULT.
I'LL MAKE SURE YOU HAVE A FRONT ROW SEAT TO THEIR EXECUTIONS. IS THAT REALLY WHAT YOU WANT?
IS THAT ALL YOU'VE GOT?
YOUR PEOPLE HAVE BEEN TRYING TO KILL MY FAMILY SINCE HALF THE FLOCK STILL HAD THEIR BABY TEETH.
WE'VE BEEN PRISONERS MORE TIMES THAN WE CAN COUNT. AND WE ALWAYS GET AWAY.
HECK, YOU'RE NOT EVEN THE WORST PARENT WE'VE HAD TO DEAL WITH, REAL OR FAKE.
SO WHATEVER YOU'RE TRYING TO THREATEN US WITH? FACE IT. YOU HAVE NOTHING.
TAKE HER AND THE OTHERS BACK TO THEIR CELL. THEY'RE AS USELESS AS I SUSPECTED.

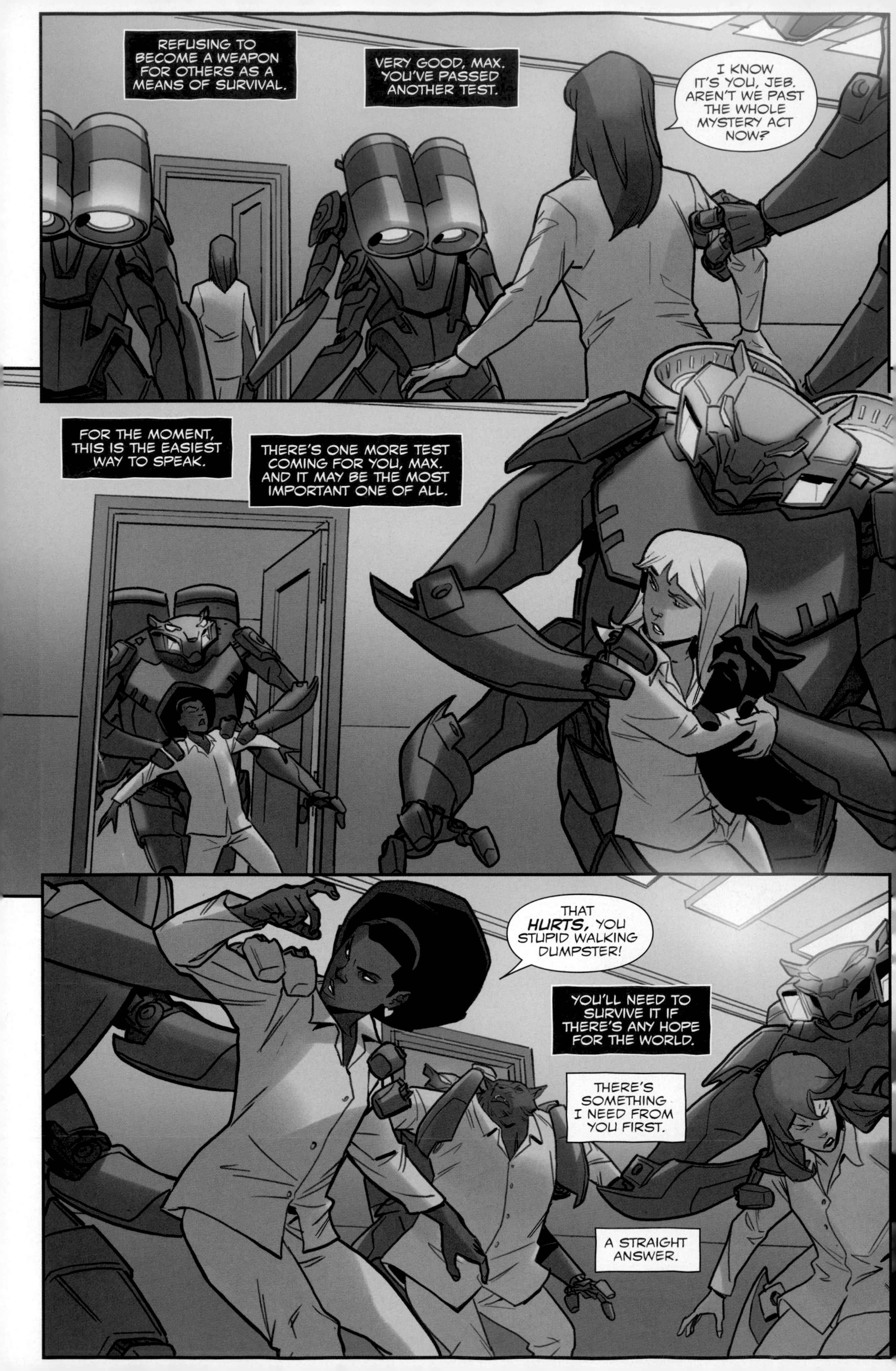
REFUSING TO BECOME A WEAPON FOR OTHERS AS A MEANS OF SURVIVAL.
VERY GOOD, MAX. YOU'VE PASSED ANOTHER TEST.
I KNOW IT'S YOU, JEB. AREN'T WE PAST THE WHOLE MYSTERY ACT NOW?
FOR THE MOMENT, THIS IS THE EASIEST WAY TO SPEAK.
THERE'S ONE MORE TEST COMING FOR YOU, MAX. AND IT MAY BE THE MOST IMPORTANT ONE OF ALL.
THAT HURTS, YOU STUPID WALKING DUMPSTER!
YOU'LL NEED TO SURVIVE IT IF THERE'S ANY HOPE FOR THE WORLD.
THERE'S SOMETHING I NEED FROM YOU FIRST.
A STRAIGHT ANSWER.

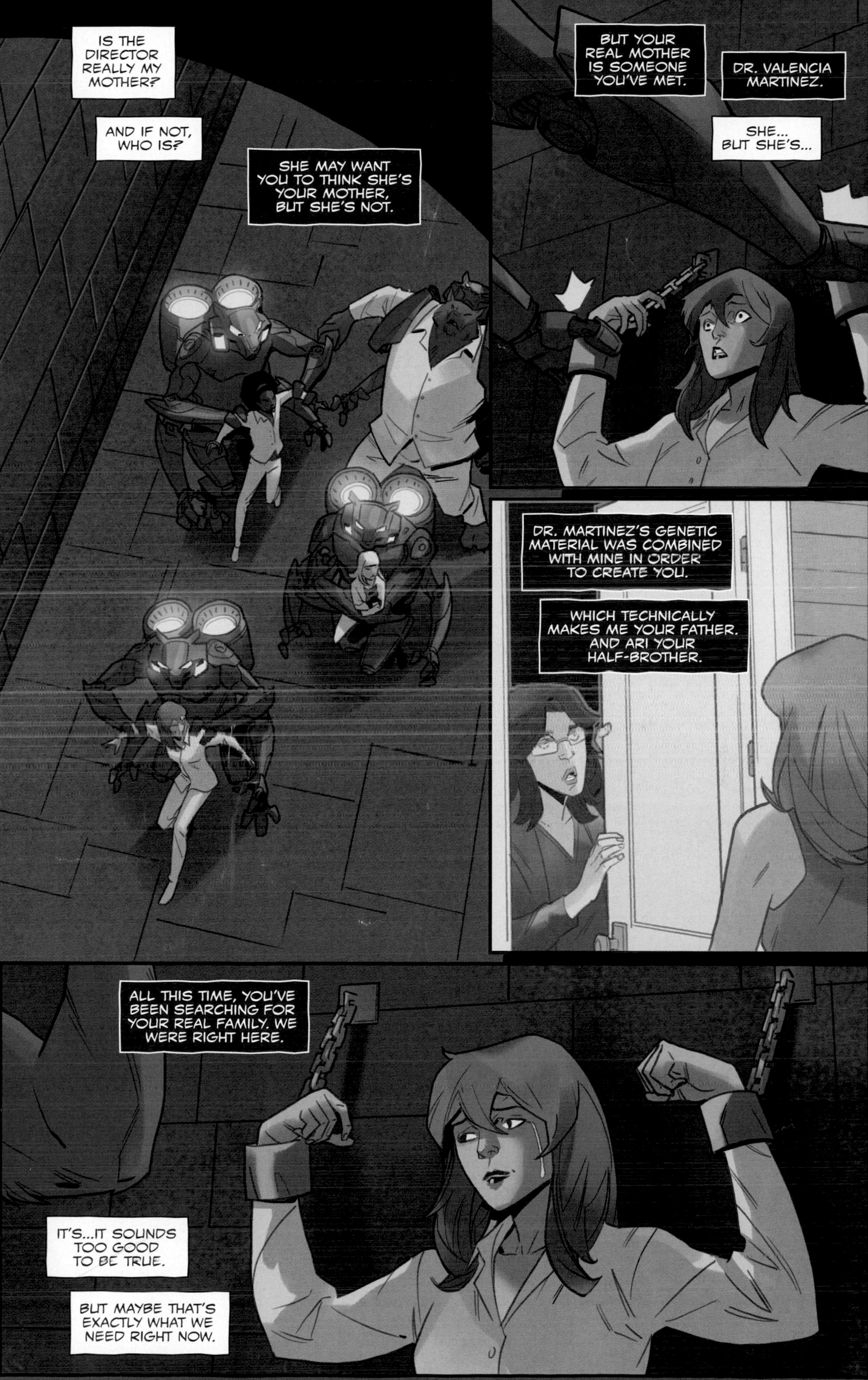
IS THE DIRECTOR REALLY MY MOTHER?
AND IF NOT, WHO IS?
SHE MAY WANT YOU TO THINK SHE'S YOUR MOTHER, BUT SHE'S NOT.
BUT YOUR REAL MOTHER IS SOMEONE YOU'VE MET.
DR. VALENCIA MARTINEZ.
SHE... BUT SHE'S...
DR. MARTINEZ'S GENETIC MATERIAL WAS COMBINED WITH MINE IN ORDER TO CREATE YOU.
WHICH TECHNICALLY MAKES ME YOUR FATHER. AND ARI YOUR HALF-BROTHER.
ALL THIS TIME, YOU'VE BEEN SEARCHING FOR YOUR REAL FAMILY. WE WERE RIGHT HERE.
IT'S...IT SOUNDS TOO GOOD TO BE TRUE.
BUT MAYBE THAT'S EXACTLY WHAT WE NEED RIGHT NOW.

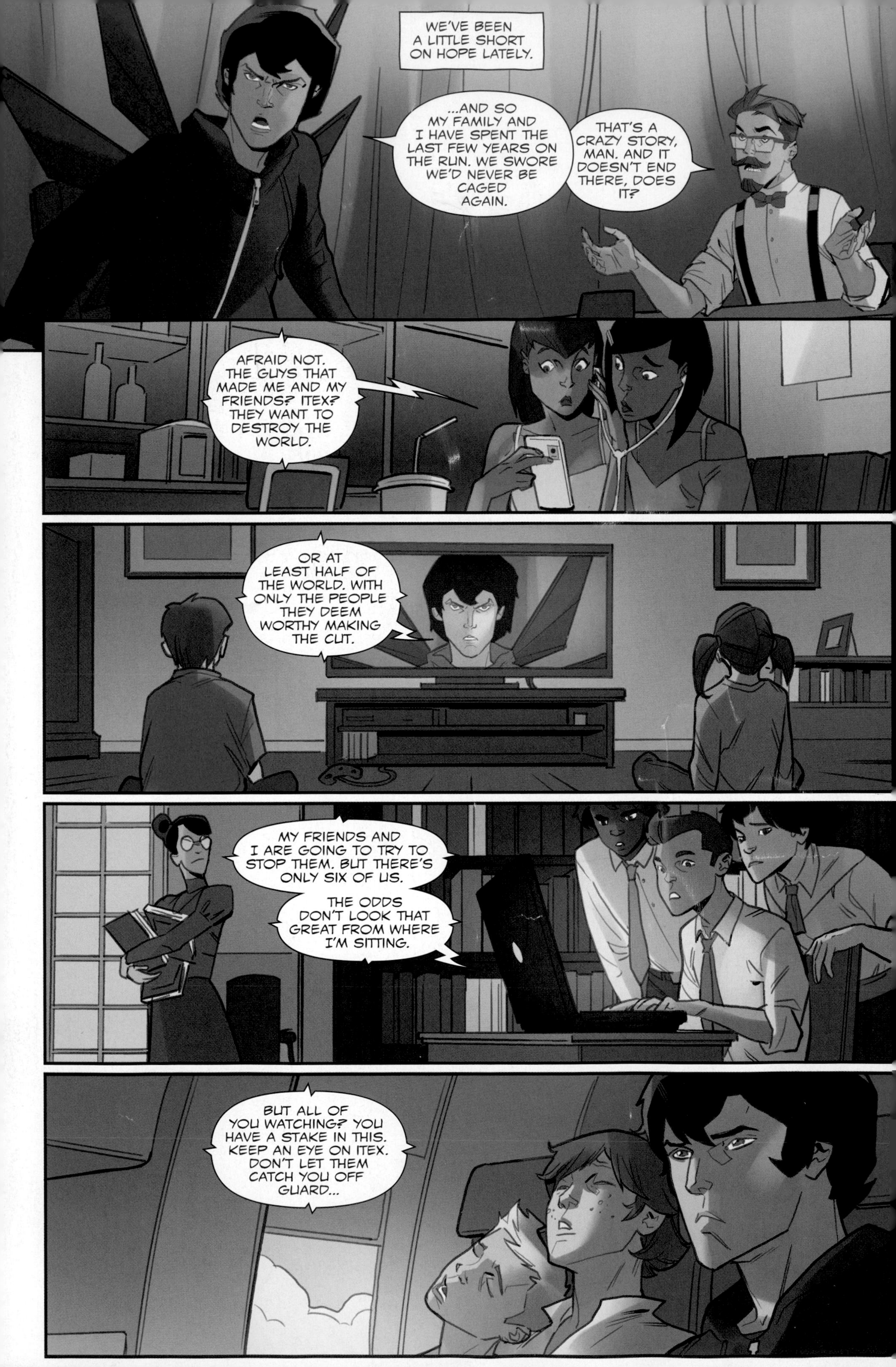
WE'VE BEEN A LITTLE SHORT ON HOPE LATELY.
...AND SO MY FAMILY AND I HAVE SPENT THE LAST FEW YEARS ON THE RUN. WE SWORE WE'D NEVER BE CAGED AGAIN.
THAT'S A CRAZY STORY, MAN. AND IT DOESN'T END THERE, DOES IT?
AFRAID NOT. THE GUYS THAT MADE ME AND MY FRIENDS? ITEX? THEY WANT TO DESTROY THE WORLD.
OR AT LEAST HALF OF THE WORLD. WITH ONLY THE PEOPLE THEY DEEM WORTHY MAKING THE CUT.
MY FRIENDS AND I ARE GOING TO TRY TO STOP THEM. BUT THERE'S ONLY SIX OF US.
THE ODDS DON'T LOOK THAT GREAT FROM WHERE I'M SITTING.
BUT ALL OF YOU WATCHING? YOU HAVE A STAKE IN THIS. KEEP AN EYE ON ITEX. DON'T LET THEM CATCH YOU OFF GUARD...

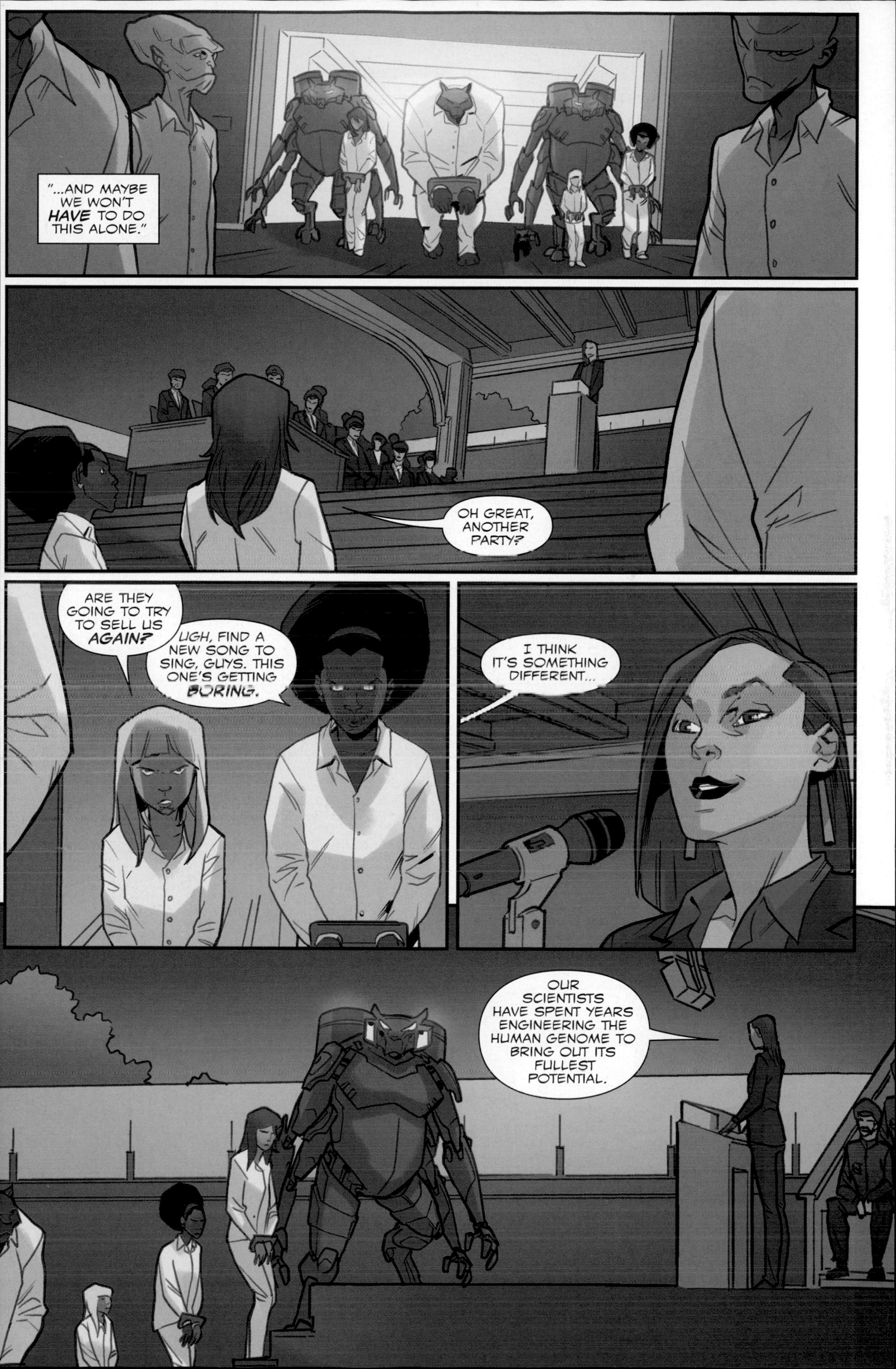
"...AND MAYBE WE WON'T HAVE TO DO THIS ALONE."
OH GREAT, ANOTHER PARTY?
ARE THEY GOING TO TRY TO SELL US AGAIN?
UGH, FIND A NEW SONG TO SING, GUYS. THIS ONE'S GETTING BORING.
I THINK IT'S SOMETHING DIFFERENT...
OUR SCIENTISTS HAVE SPENT YEARS ENGINEERING THE HUMAN GENOME TO BRING OUT ITS FULLEST POTENTIAL.

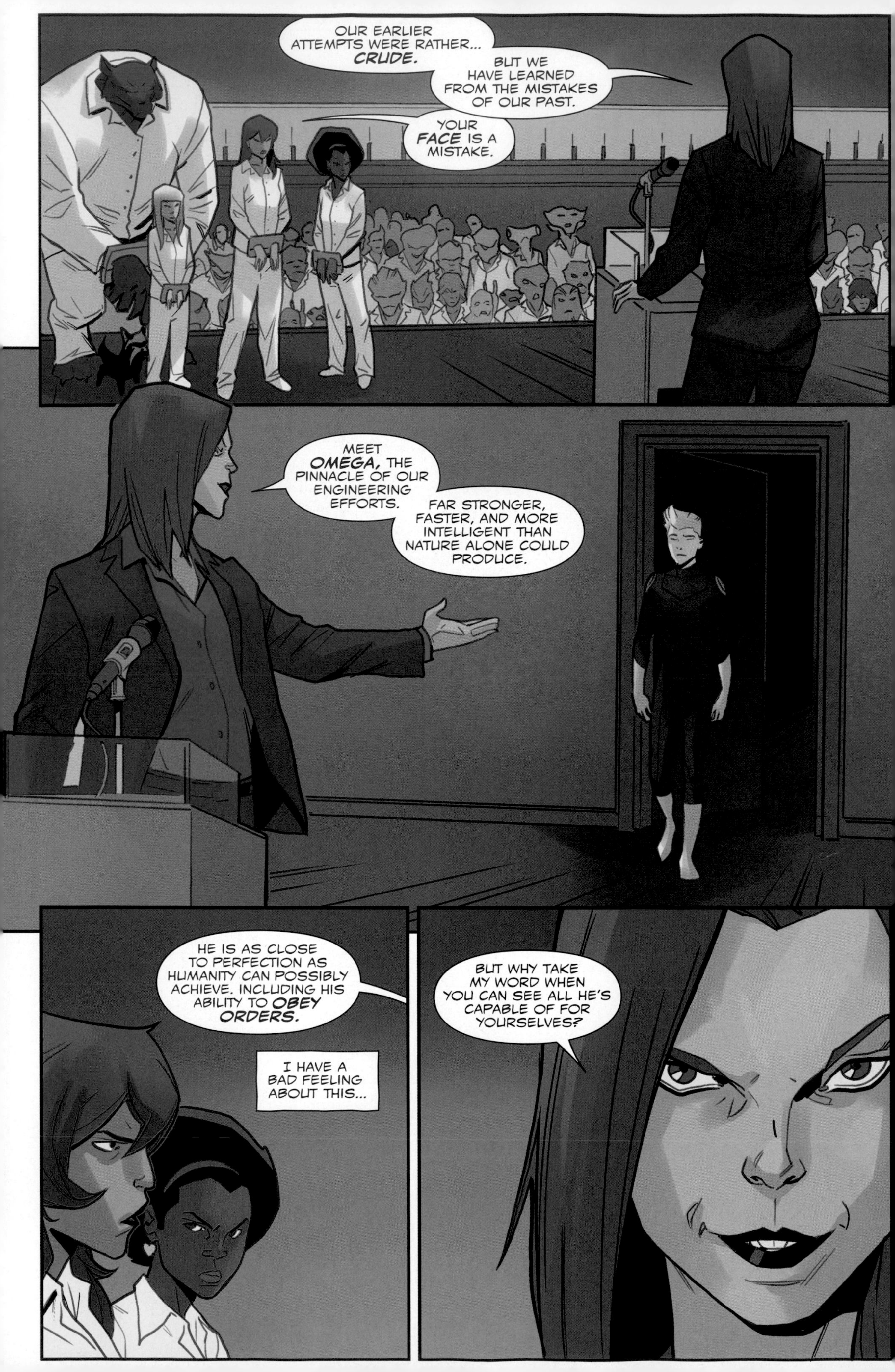
OUR EARLIER ATTEMPTS WERE RATHER... CRUDE.
BUT WE HAVE LEARNED FROM THE MISTAKES OF OUR PAST.
YOUR FACE IS A MISTAKE.
MEET OMEGA, THE PINNACLE OF OUR ENGINEERING EFFORTS.
FAR STRONGER, FASTER, AND MORE INTELLIGENT THAN NATURE ALONE COULD PRODUCE.
HE IS AS CLOSE TO PERFECTION AS HUMANITY CAN POSSIBLY ACHIEVE. INCLUDING HIS ABILITY TO OBEY ORDERS.
I HAVE A BAD FEELING ABOUT THIS...
BUT WHY TAKE MY WORD WHEN YOU CAN SEE ALL HE'S CAPABLE OF FOR YOURSELVES?

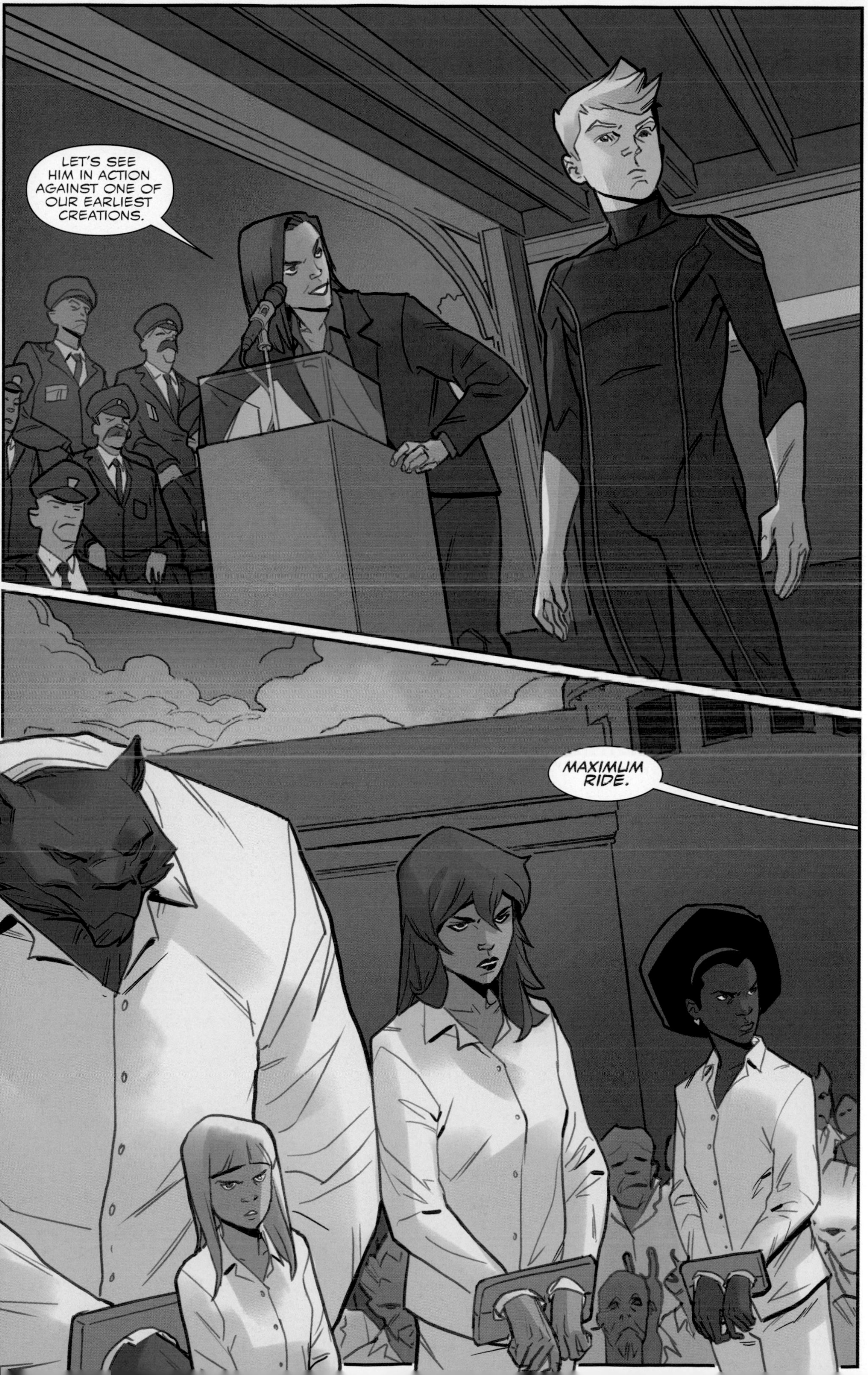
LET'S SEE HIM IN ACTION AGAINST ONE OF OUR EARLIEST CREATIONS.
MAXIMUM RIDE.

CHAPTER 5

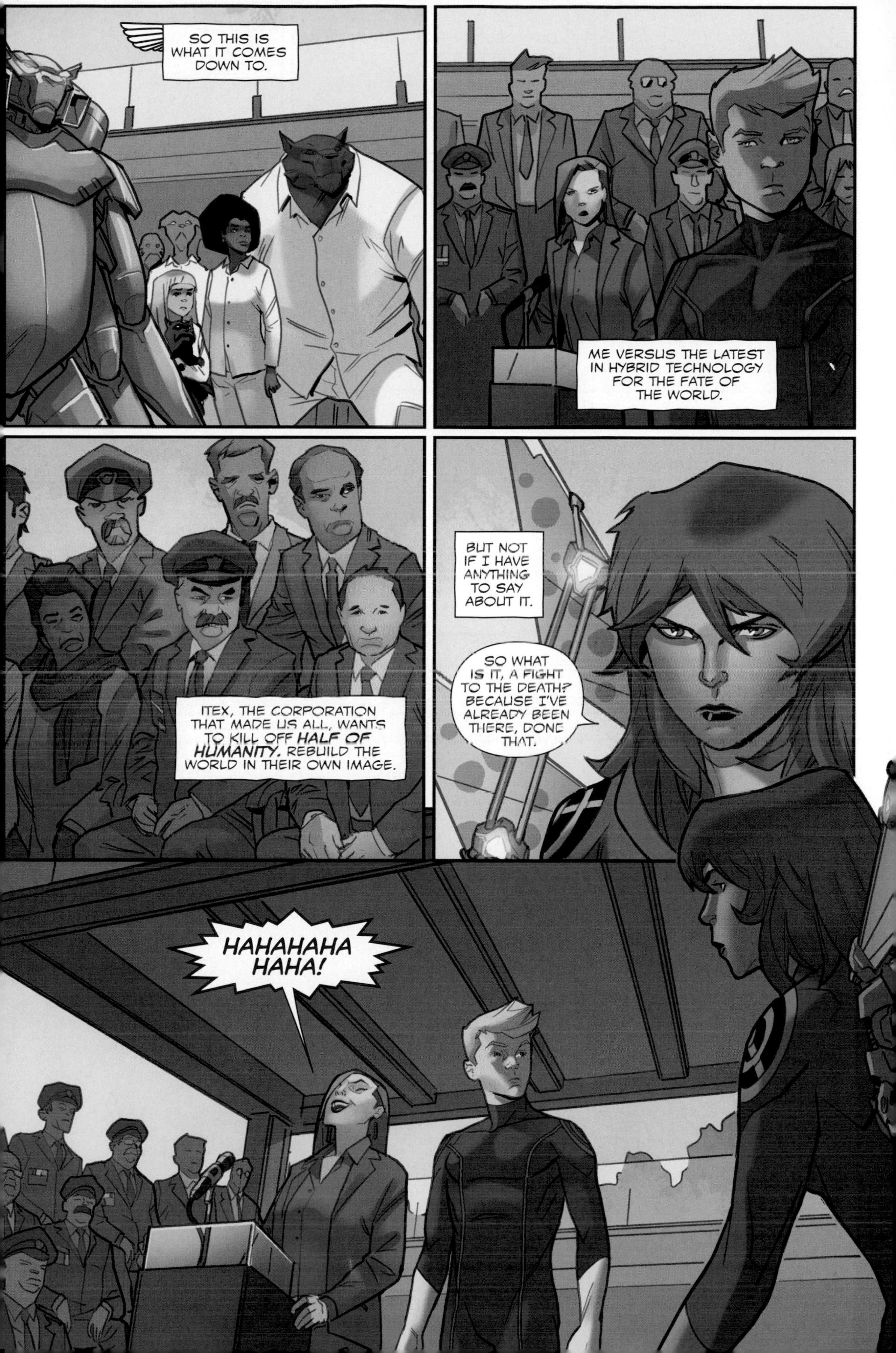

SO THIS IS WHAT IT COMES DOWN TO.
ME VERSUS THE LATEST IN HYBRID TECHNOLOGY FOR THE FATE OF THE WORLD.
ITEX, THE CORPORATION THAT MADE US ALL, WANTS TO KILL OFF HALF OF HUMANITY. REBUILD THE WORLD IN THEIR OWN IMAGE.
BUT NOT IF I HAVE ANYTHING TO SAY ABOUT IT.
SO WHAT IS IT, A FIGHT TO THE DEATH? BECAUSE I'VE ALREADY BEEN THERE, DONE THAT.
HAHAHAHA HAHA!

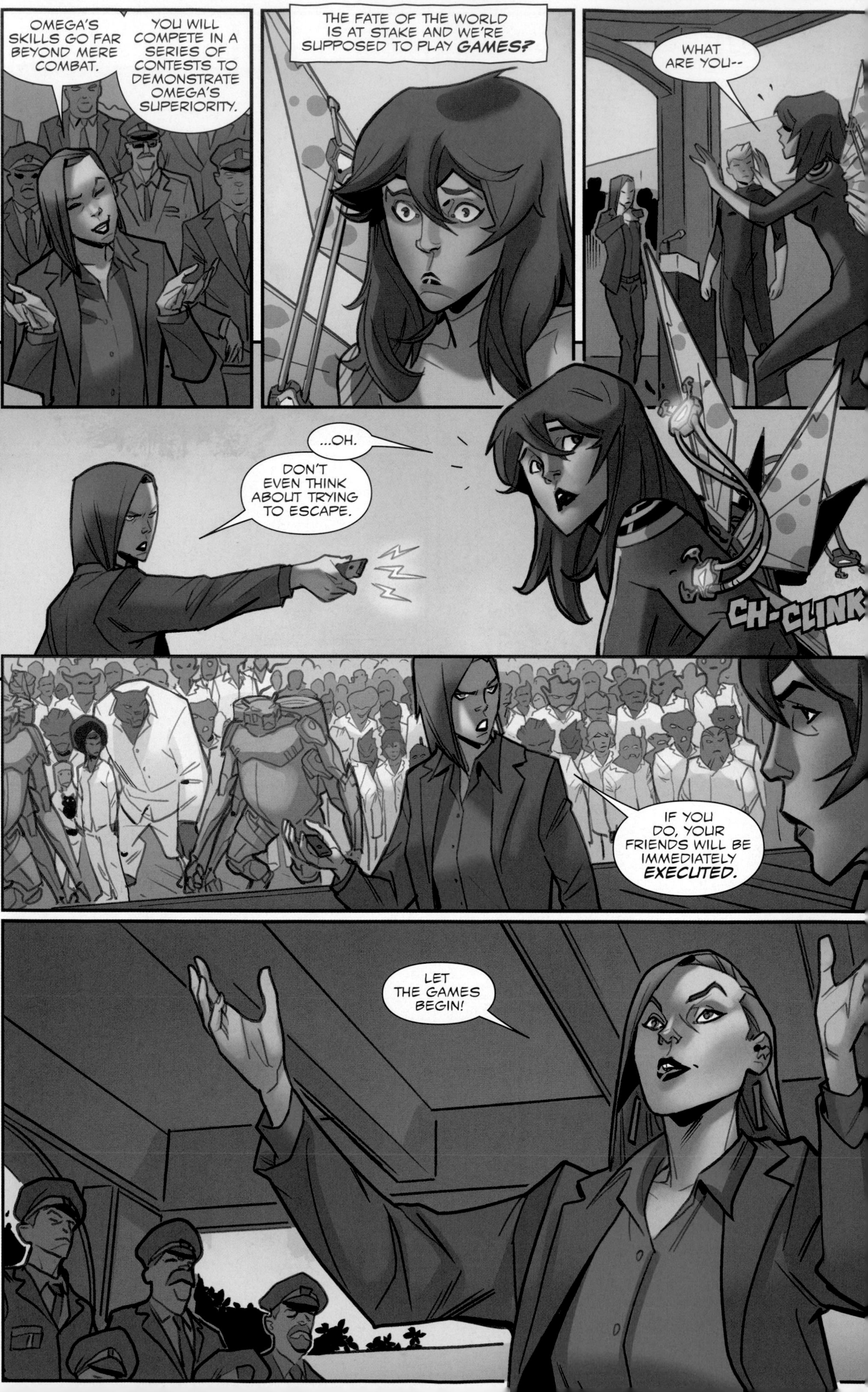
OMEGA'S SKILLS GO FAR BEYOND MERE COMBAT.
YOU WILL COMPETE IN A SERIES OF CONTESTS TO DEMONSTRATE OMEGA'S SUPERIORITY.
THE FATE OF THE WORLD IS AT STAKE AND WE'RE SUPPOSED TO PLAY GAMES?
WHAT ARE YOU--
...OH.
DON'T EVEN THINK ABOUT TRYING TO ESCAPE.
CH-CLINK
IF YOU DO, YOUR FRIENDS WILL BE IMMEDIATELY EXECUTED.
LET THE GAMES BEGIN!

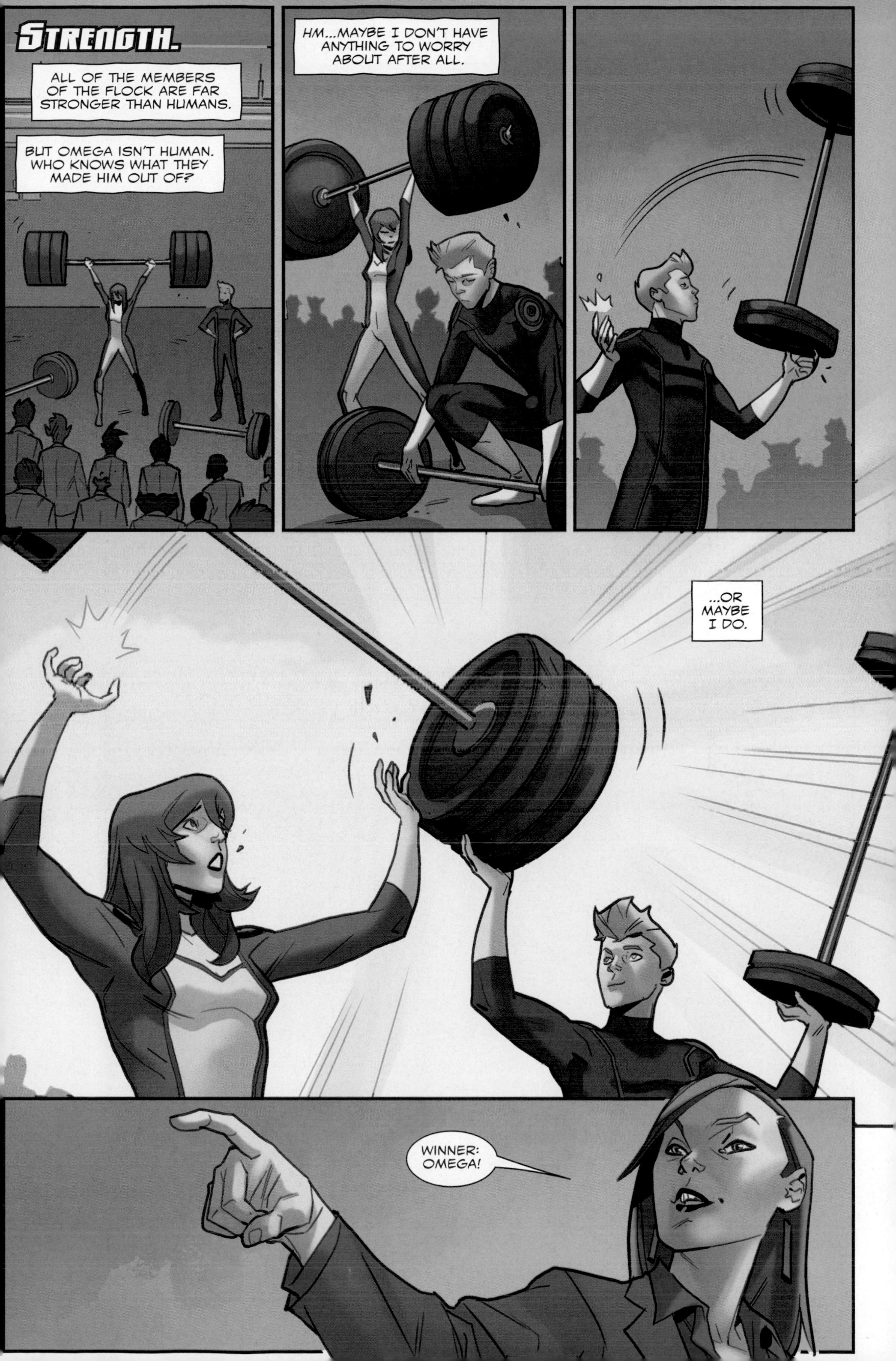
STRENGTH.
ALL OF THE MEMBERS OF THE FLOCK ARE FAR STRONGER THAN HUMANS.
BUT OMEGA ISN'T HUMAN. WHO KNOWS WHAT THEY MADE HIM OUT OF?
HM...MAYBE I DON'T HAVE ANYTHING TO WORRY ABOUT AFTER ALL.
...OR MAYBE I DO.
WINNER: OMEGA!

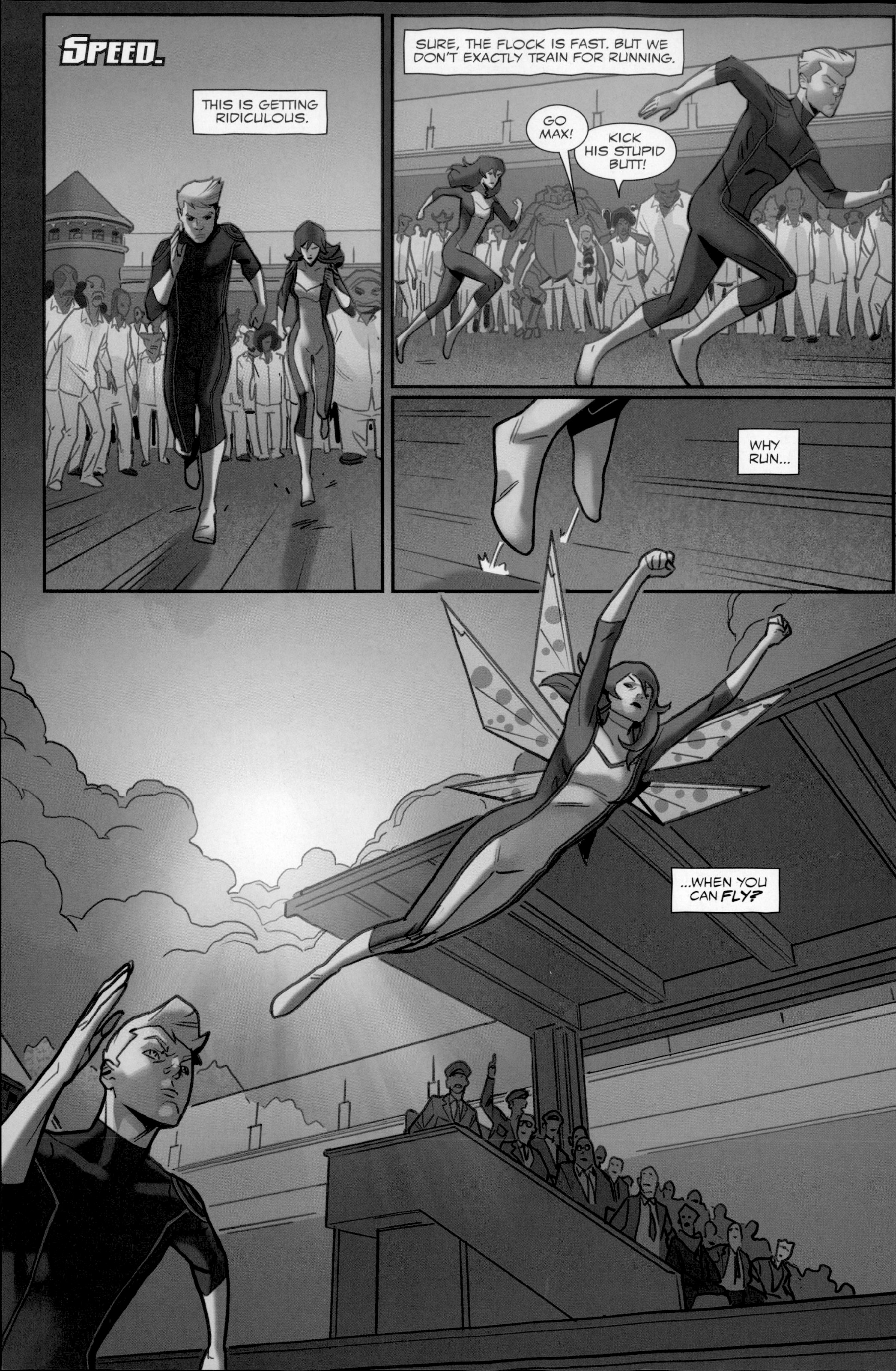
SPEED.
THIS IS GETTING RIDICULOUS.
SURE, THE FLOCK IS FAST. BUT WE DON'T EXACTLY TRAIN FOR RUNNING.
GO MAX!
KICK HIS STUPID BUTT!
WHY RUN...
...WHEN YOU CAN FLY?

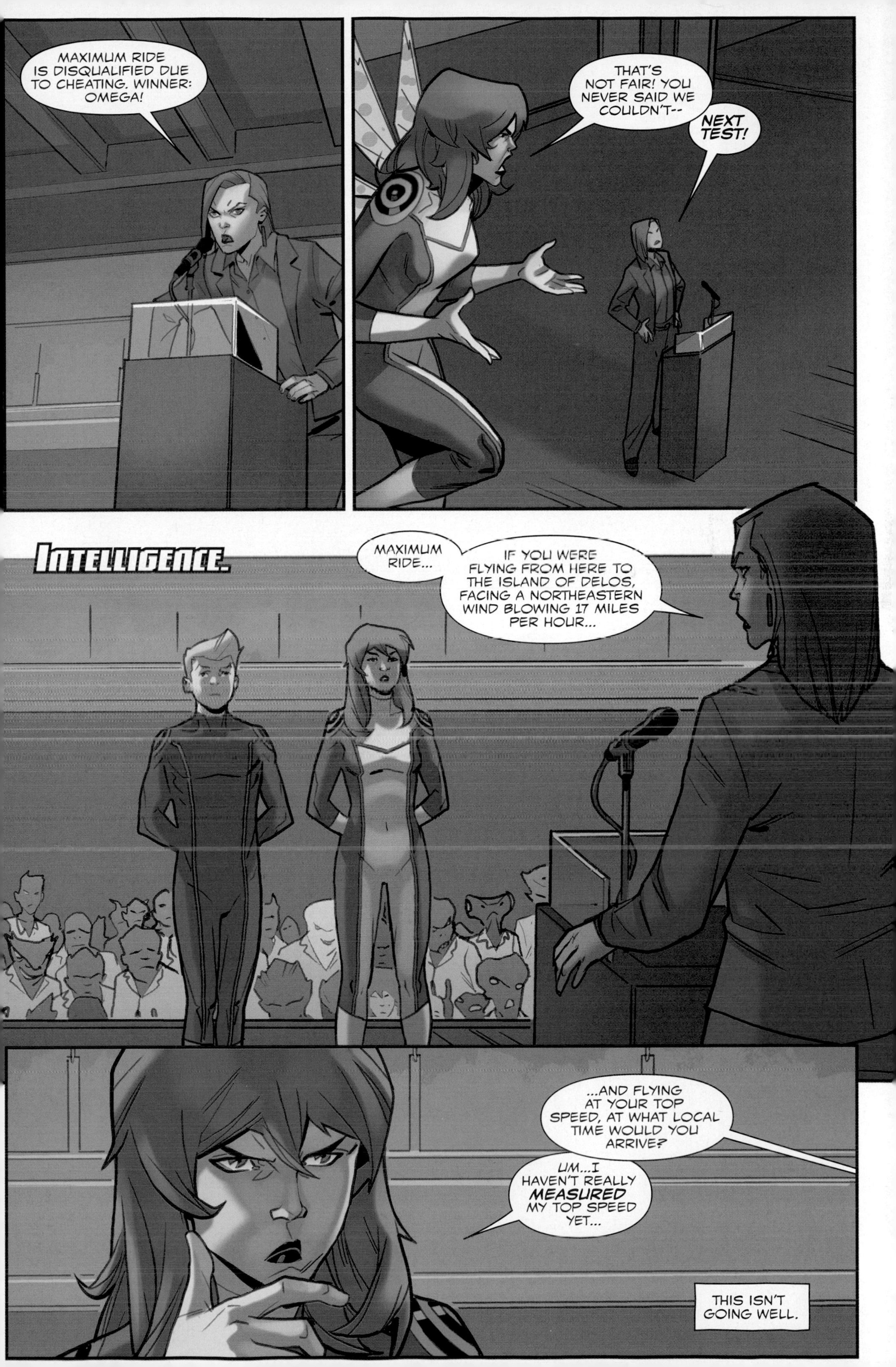
MAXIMUM RIDE IS DISQUALIFIED DUE TO CHEATING. WINNER: OMEGA!
THAT'S NOT FAIR! YOU NEVER SAID WE COULDN'T--
NEXT TEST!
INTELLIGENCE.
MAXIMUM RIDE...
IF YOU WERE FLYING FROM HERE TO THE ISLAND OF DELOS, FACING A NORTHEASTERN WIND BLOWING 17 MILES PER HOUR...
...AND FLYING AT YOUR TOP SPEED, AT WHAT LOCAL TIME WOULD YOU ARRIVE?
UM...I HAVEN'T REALLY MEASURED MY TOP SPEED YET...
THIS ISN'T GOING WELL.

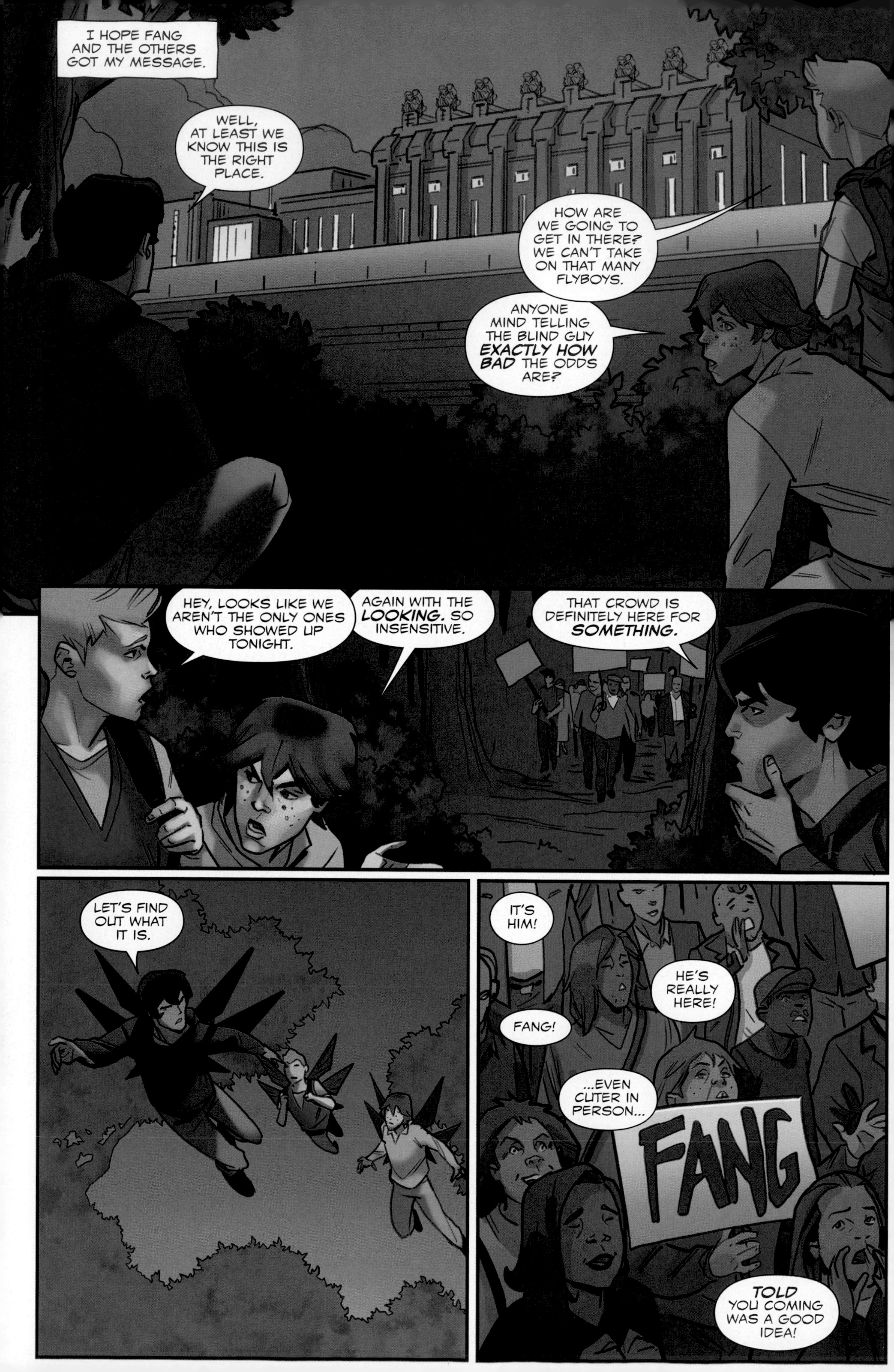
I HOPE FANG AND THE OTHERS GOT MY MESSAGE.
WELL, AT LEAST WE KNOW THIS IS THE RIGHT PLACE.
HOW ARE WE GOING TO GET IN THERE? WE CAN'T TAKE ON THAT MANY FLYBOYS.
ANYONE MIND TELLING THE BLIND GUY EXACTLY HOW BAD THE ODDS ARE?
HEY, LOOKS LIKE WE AREN'T THE ONLY ONES WHO SHOWED UP TONIGHT.
AGAIN WITH THE LOOKING. SO INSENSITIVE.
THAT CROWD IS DEFINITELY HERE FOR SOMETHING.
LET'S FIND OUT WHAT IT IS.
IT'S HIM!
HE'S REALLY HERE!
FANG!
...EVEN CUTER IN PERSON...
FANG
TOLD YOU COMING WAS A GOOD IDEA!

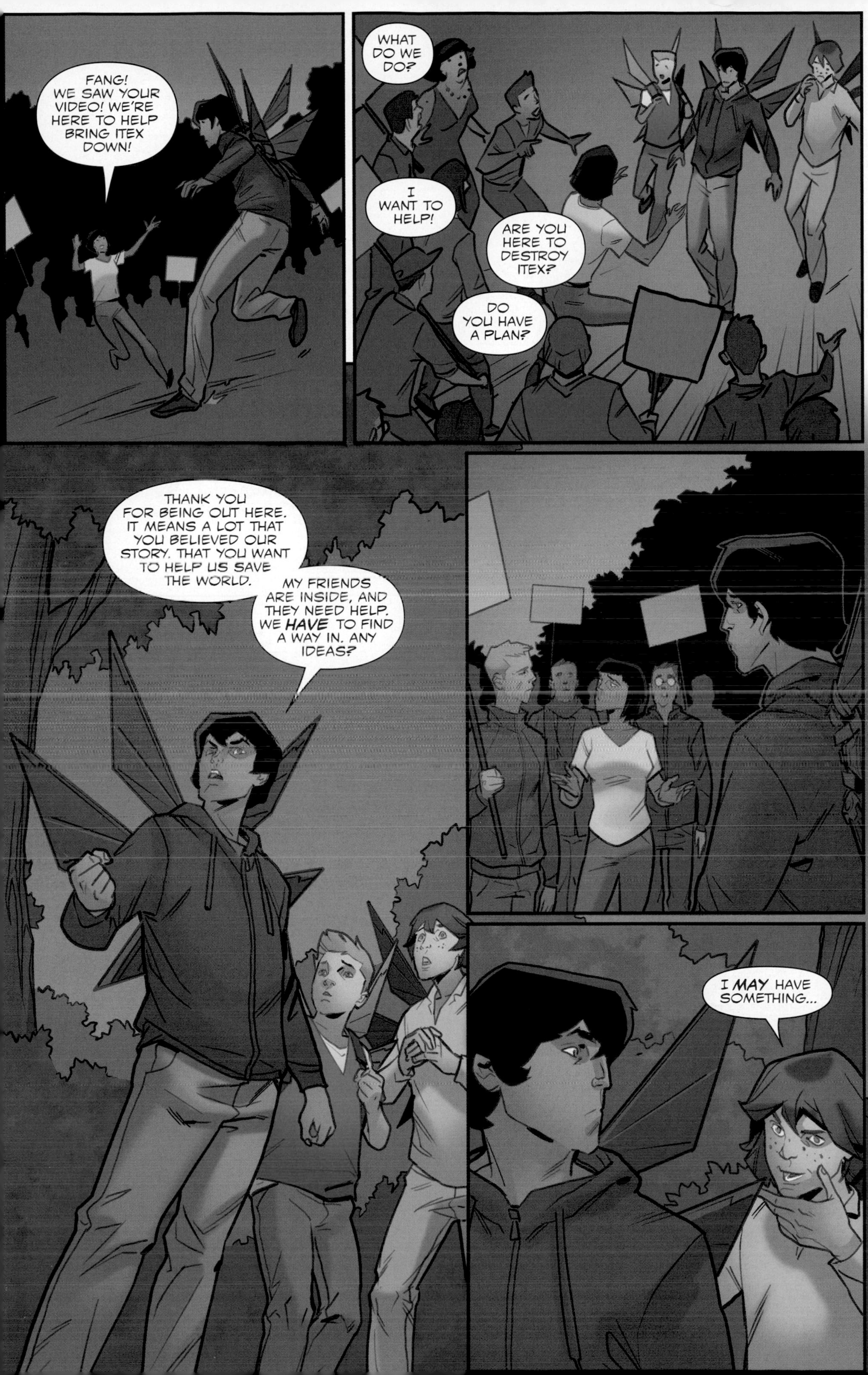
FANG! WE SAW YOUR VIDEO! WE'RE HERE TO HELP BRING ITEX DOWN!
WHAT DO WE DO?
I WANT TO HELP!
ARE YOU HERE TO DESTROY ITEX?
DO YOU HAVE A PLAN?
THANK YOU FOR BEING OUT HERE. IT MEANS A LOT THAT YOU BELIEVED OUR STORY. THAT YOU WANT TO HELP US SAVE THE WORLD.
MY FRIENDS ARE INSIDE, AND THEY NEED HELP. WE HAVE TO FIND A WAY IN. ANY IDEAS?
I MAY HAVE SOMETHING...

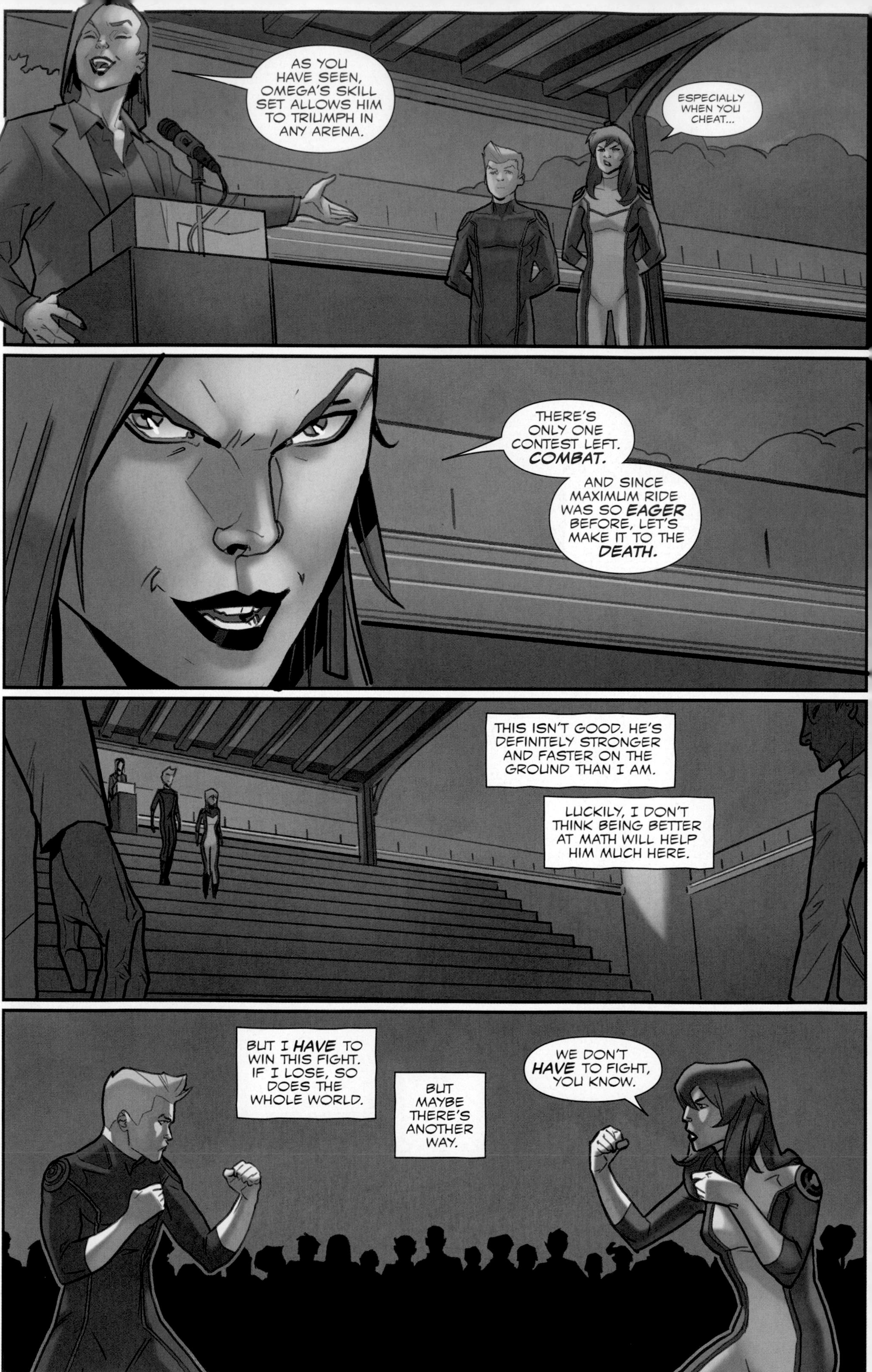
AS YOU HAVE SEEN, OMEGA'S SKILL SET ALLOWS HIM TO TRIUMPH IN ANY ARENA.
ESPECIALLY WHEN YOU CHEAT...
THERE'S ONLY ONE CONTEST LEFT. COMBAT.
AND SINCE MAXIMUM RIDE WAS SO EAGER BEFORE, LET'S MAKE IT TO THE DEATH.
THIS ISN'T GOOD. HE'S DEFINITELY STRONGER AND FASTER ON THE GROUND THAN I AM.
LUCKILY, I DON'T THINK BEING BETTER AT MATH WILL HELP HIM MUCH HERE.
BUT I HAVE TO WIN THIS FIGHT. IF I LOSE, SO DOES THE WHOLE WORLD.
BUT MAYBE THERE'S ANOTHER WAY.
WE DON'T HAVE TO FIGHT, YOU KNOW.

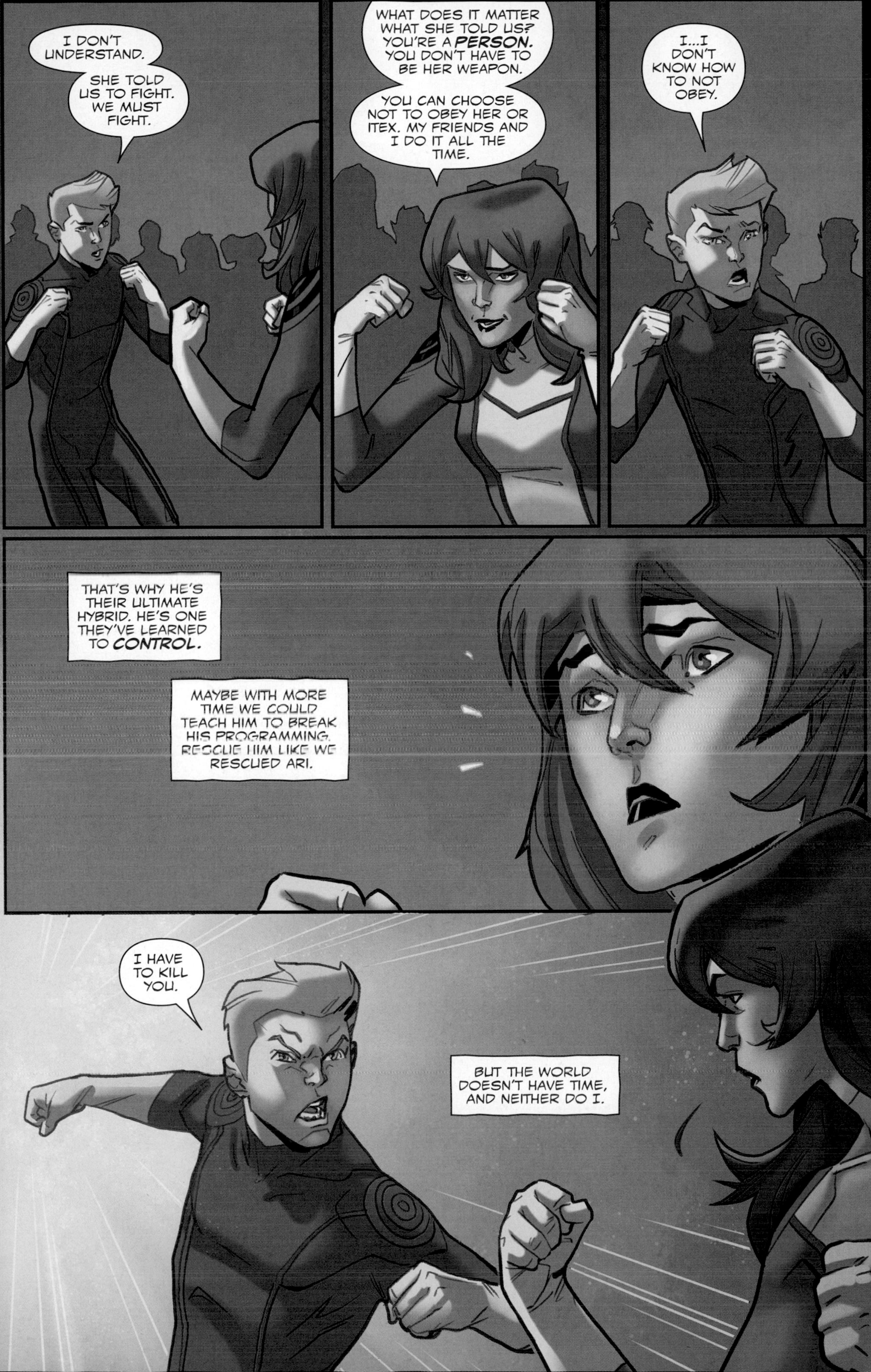

I DON'T UNDERSTAND.
SHE TOLD US TO FIGHT. WE MUST FIGHT.
WHAT DOES IT MATTER WHAT SHE TOLD US? YOU'RE A **PERSON.** YOU DON'T HAVE TO BE HER WEAPON.
YOU CAN CHOOSE NOT TO OBEY HER OR ITEX. MY FRIENDS AND I DO IT ALL THE TIME.
I...I DON'T KNOW HOW TO NOT OBEY.
THAT'S WHY HE'S THEIR ULTIMATE HYBRID. HE'S ONE THEY'VE LEARNED TO **CONTROL.**
MAYBE WITH MORE TIME WE COULD TEACH HIM TO BREAK HIS PROGRAMMING. RESCUE HIM LIKE WE RESCUED ARI.
I HAVE TO KILL YOU.
BUT THE WORLD DOESN'T HAVE TIME, AND NEITHER DO I.

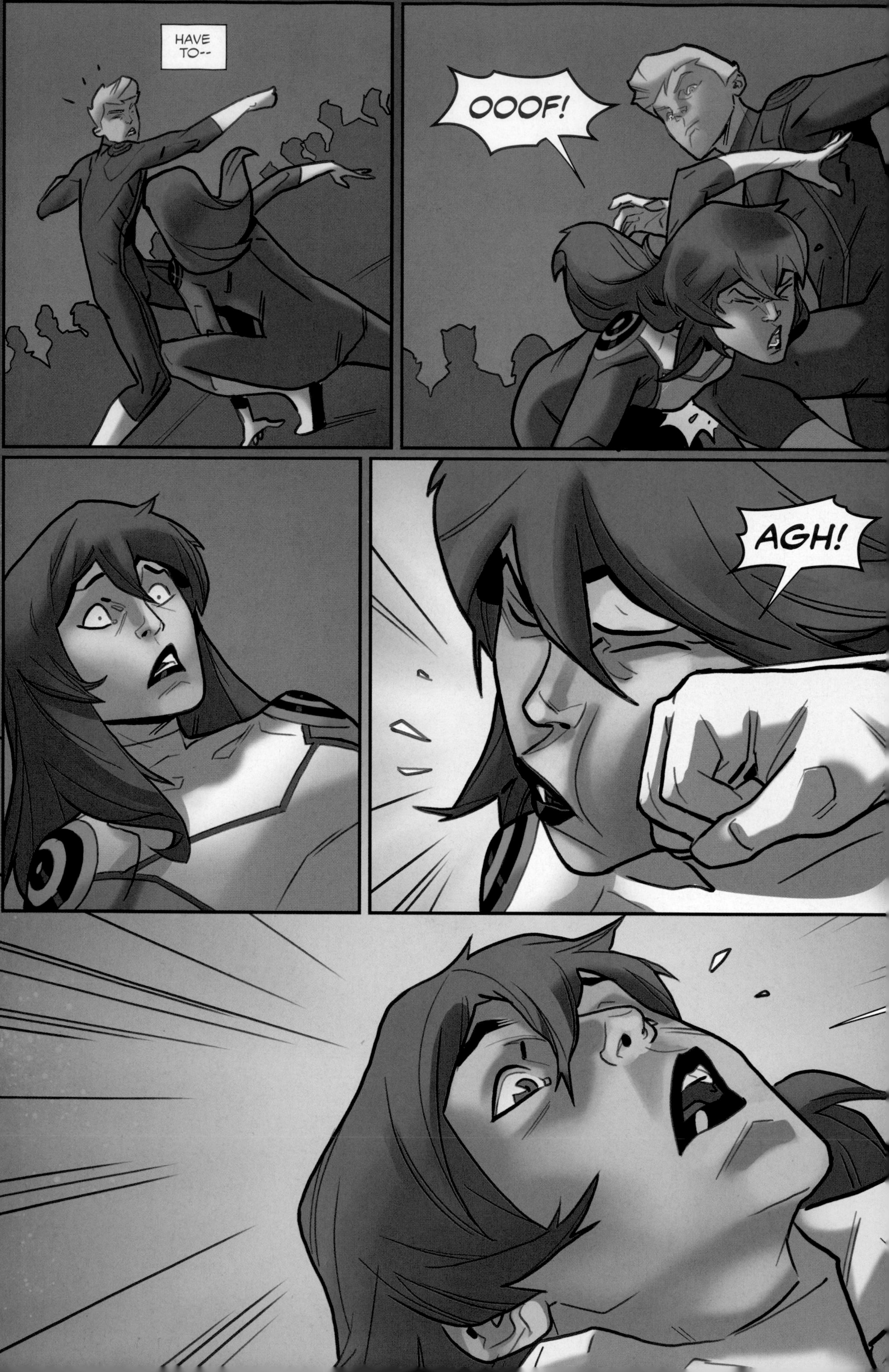
HAVE TO--
OOOF!
AGH!

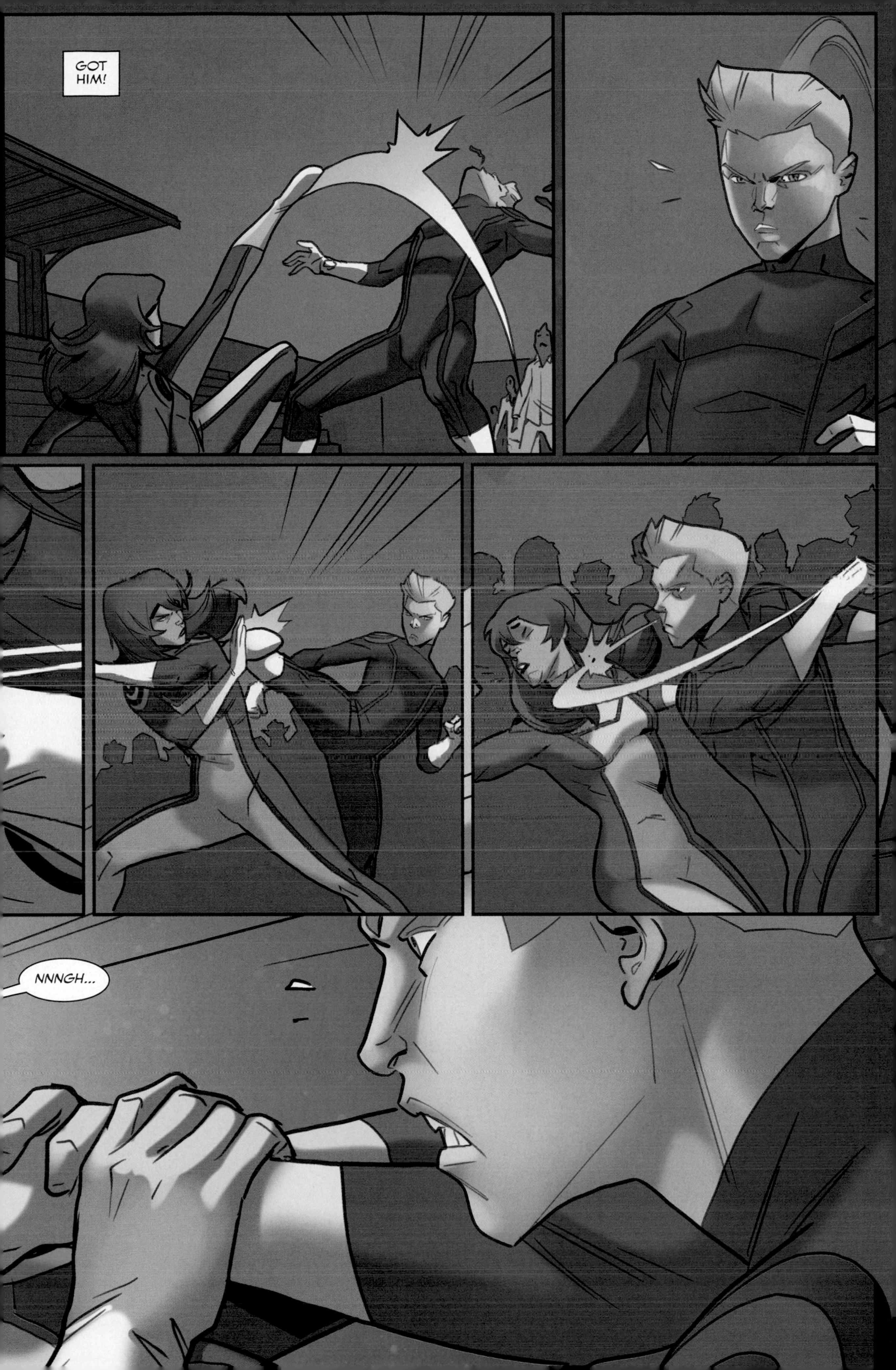
GOT HIM!
NNNGH...

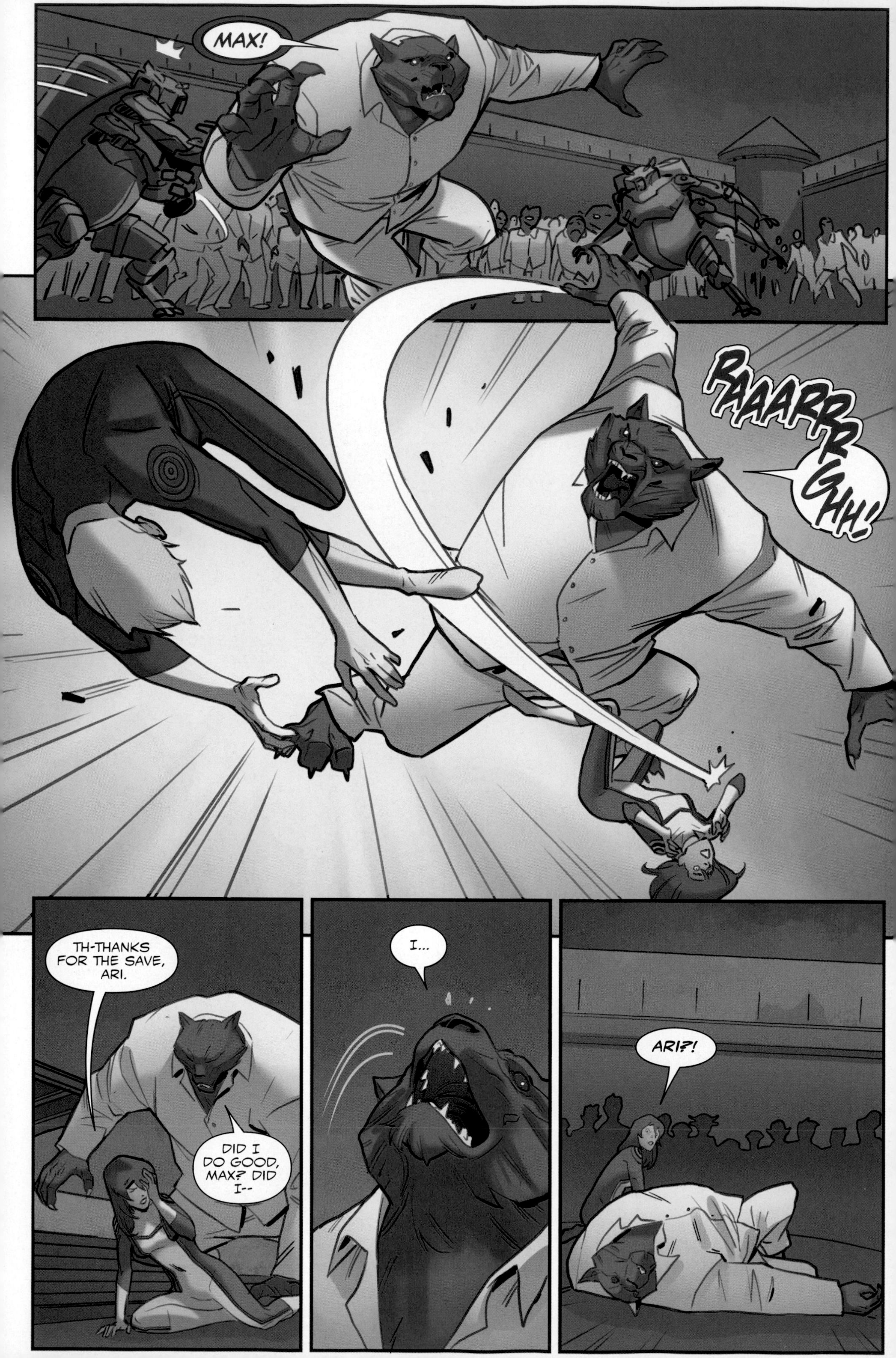
MAX!
RAAAARRRGHH!
TH-THANKS FOR THE SAVE, ARI.
DID I DO GOOD, MAX? DID I--
I...
ARI?!

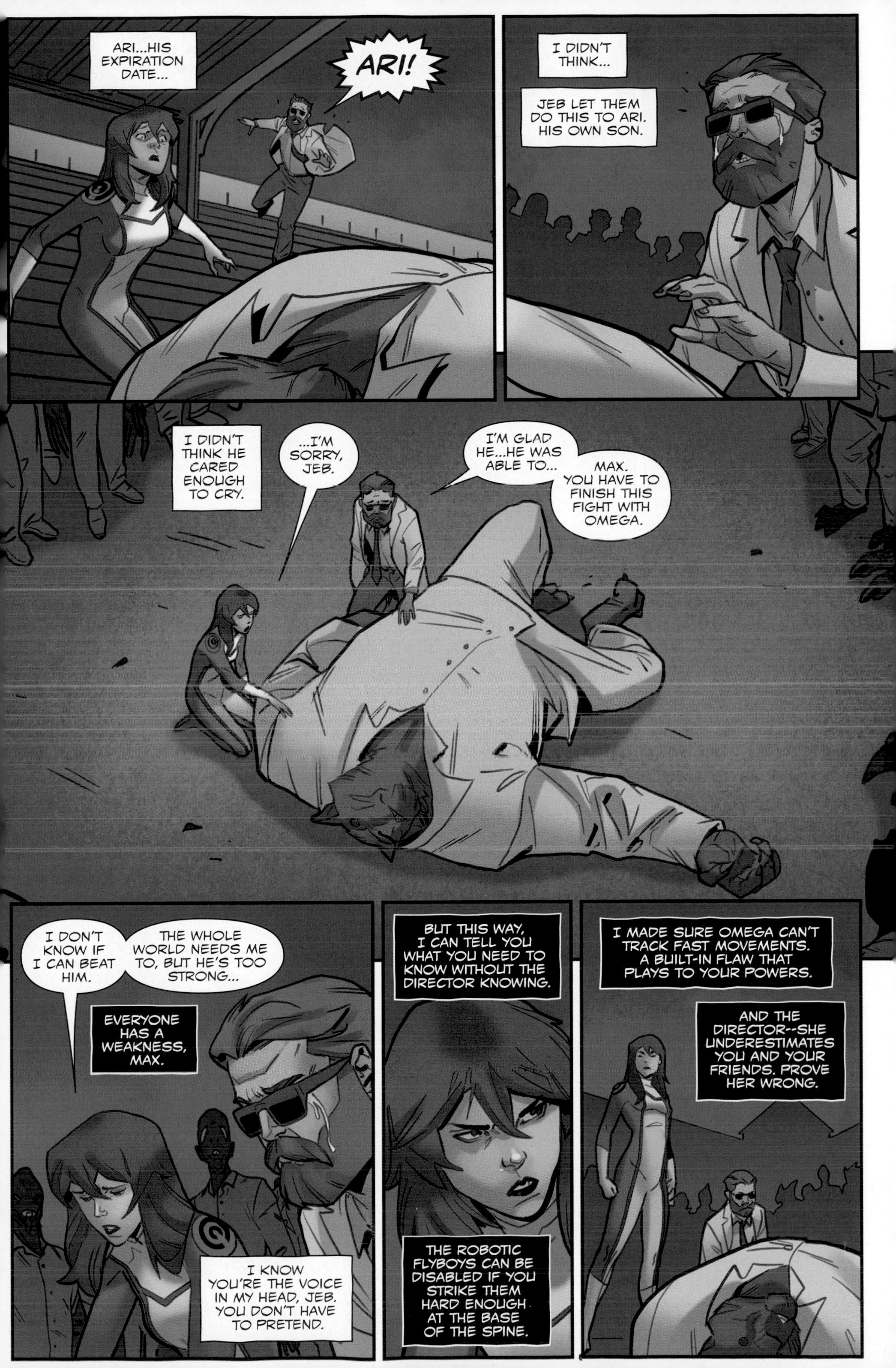

ARI...HIS EXPIRATION DATE...
ARI!
I DIDN'T THINK...
JEB LET THEM DO THIS TO ARI. HIS OWN SON.
I DIDN'T THINK HE CARED ENOUGH TO CRY.
...I'M SORRY, JEB.
I'M GLAD HE...HE WAS ABLE TO...
MAX. YOU HAVE TO FINISH THIS FIGHT WITH OMEGA.
I DON'T KNOW IF I CAN BEAT HIM.
THE WHOLE WORLD NEEDS ME TO, BUT HE'S TOO STRONG...
EVERYONE HAS A WEAKNESS, MAX.
I KNOW YOU'RE THE VOICE IN MY HEAD, JEB. YOU DON'T HAVE TO PRETEND.
BUT THIS WAY, I CAN TELL YOU WHAT YOU NEED TO KNOW WITHOUT THE DIRECTOR KNOWING.
THE ROBOTIC FLYBOYS CAN BE DISABLED IF YOU STRIKE THEM HARD ENOUGH AT THE BASE OF THE SPINE.
I MADE SURE OMEGA CAN'T TRACK FAST MOVEMENTS. A BUILT-IN FLAW THAT PLAYS TO YOUR POWERS.
AND THE DIRECTOR--SHE UNDERESTIMATES YOU AND YOUR FRIENDS. PROVE HER WRONG.

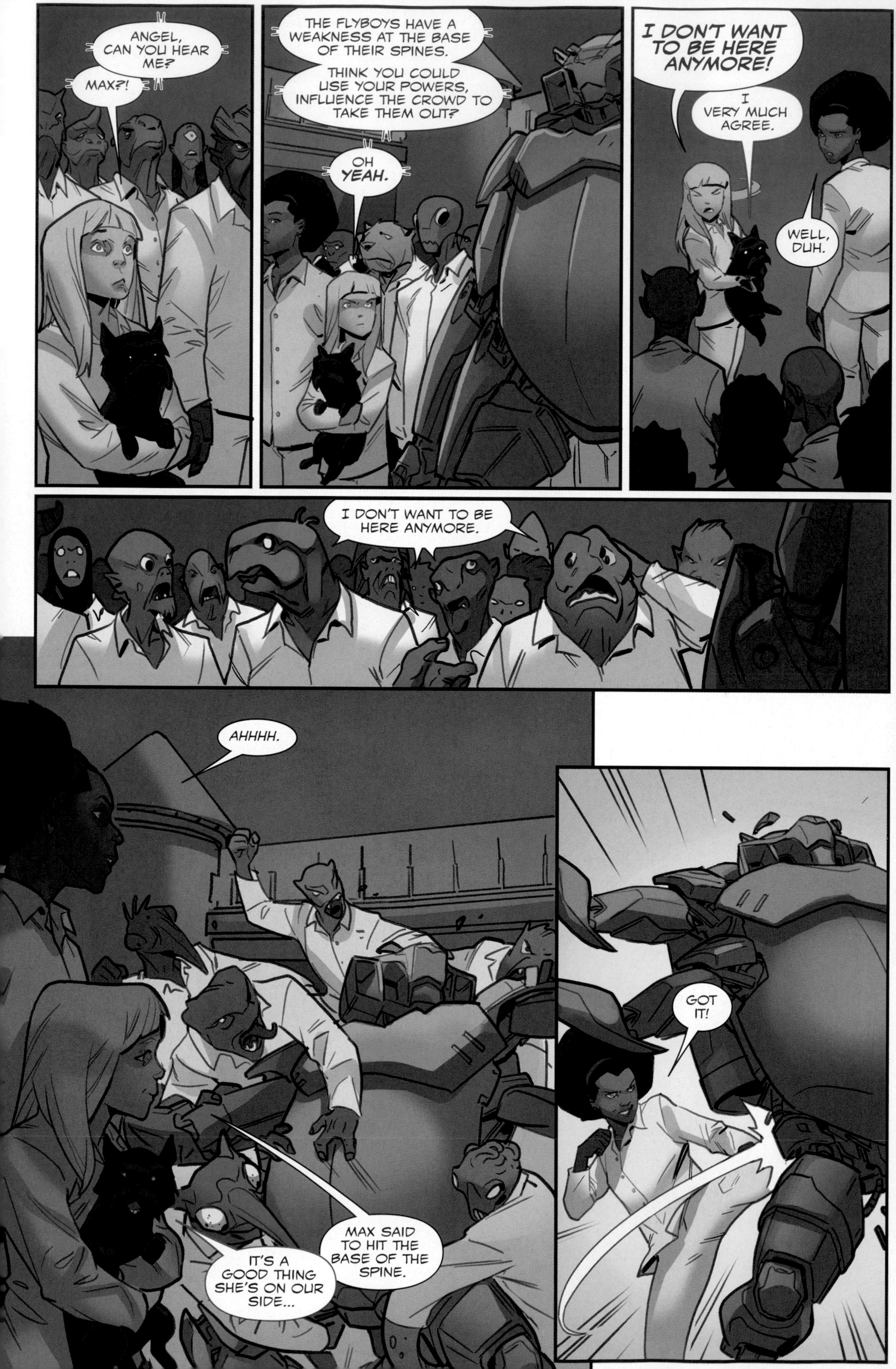
ANGEL, CAN YOU HEAR ME?
MAX?!
THE FLYBOYS HAVE A WEAKNESS AT THE BASE OF THEIR SPINES.
THINK YOU COULD USE YOUR POWERS, INFLUENCE THE CROWD TO TAKE THEM OUT?
OH YEAH.
I DON'T WANT TO BE HERE ANYMORE!
I VERY MUCH AGREE.
WELL, DUH.
I DON'T WANT TO BE HERE ANYMORE.
AHHHH.
IT'S A GOOD THING SHE'S ON OUR SIDE...
MAX SAID TO HIT THE BASE OF THE SPINE.
GOT IT!

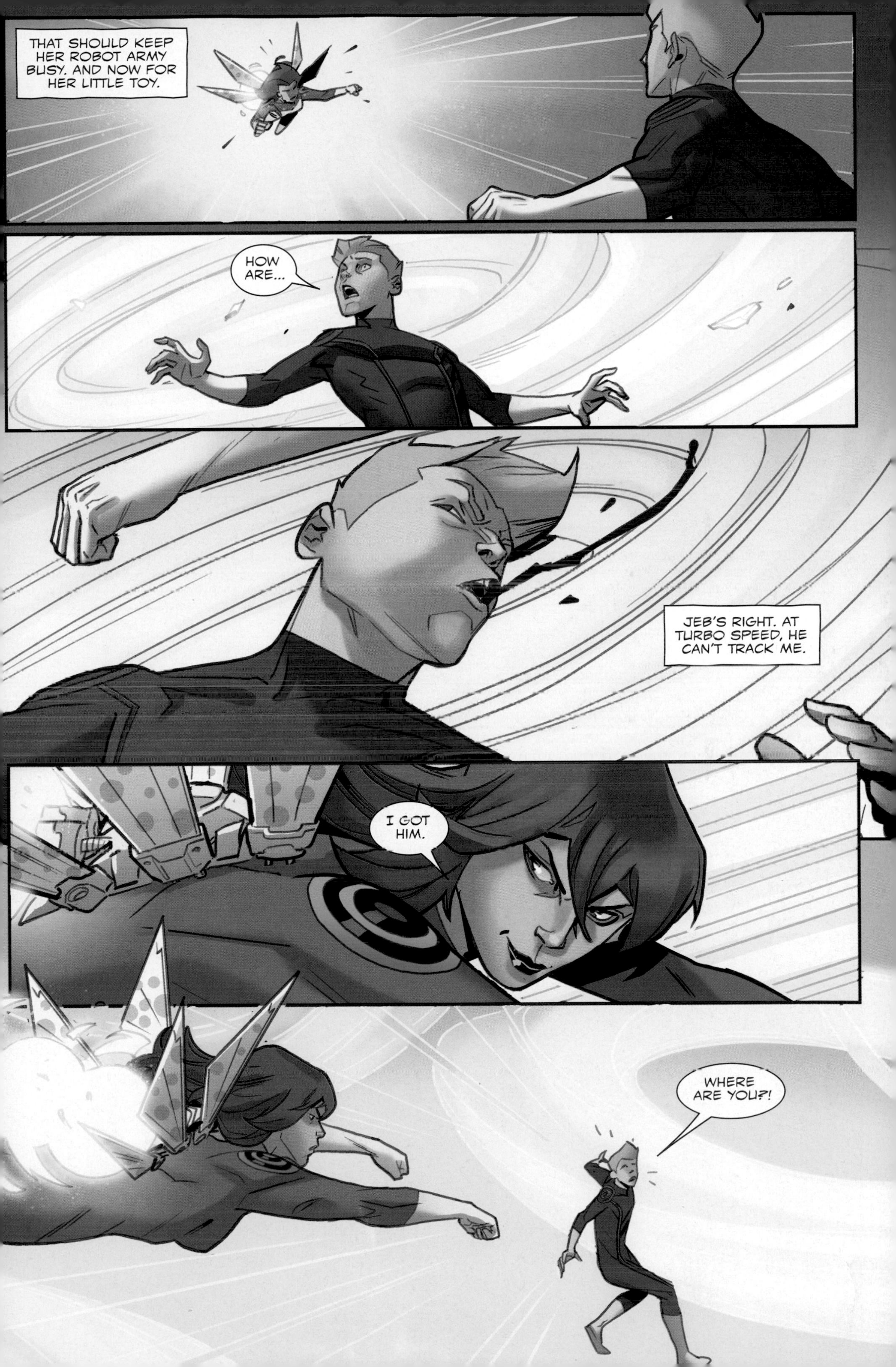
THAT SHOULD KEEP HER ROBOT ARMY BUSY. AND NOW FOR HER LITTLE TOY.
HOW ARE...
JEB'S RIGHT. AT TURBO SPEED, HE CAN'T TRACK ME.
I GOT HIM.
WHERE ARE YOU?!

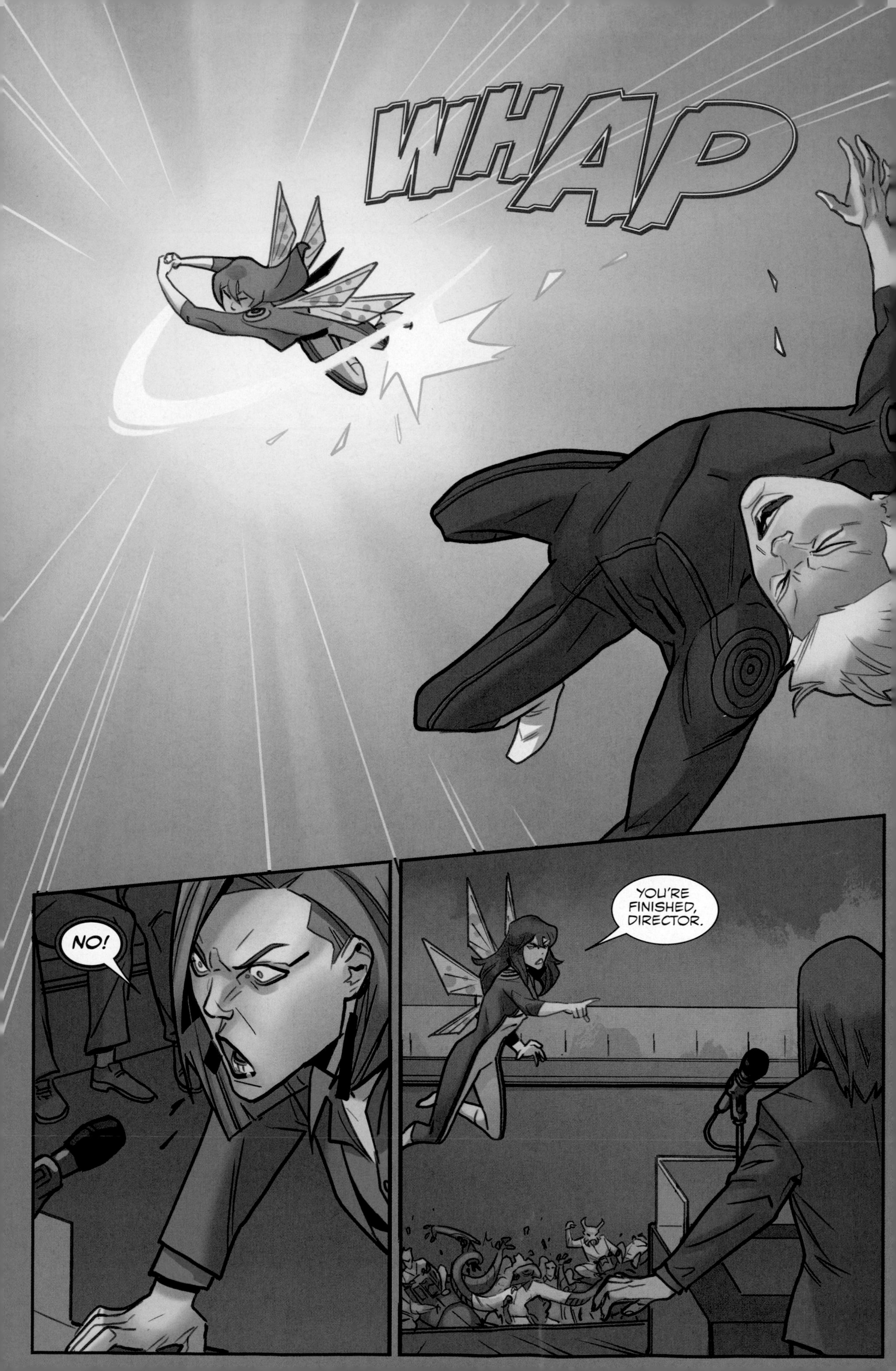
WHAP
NO!
YOU'RE FINISHED, DIRECTOR.

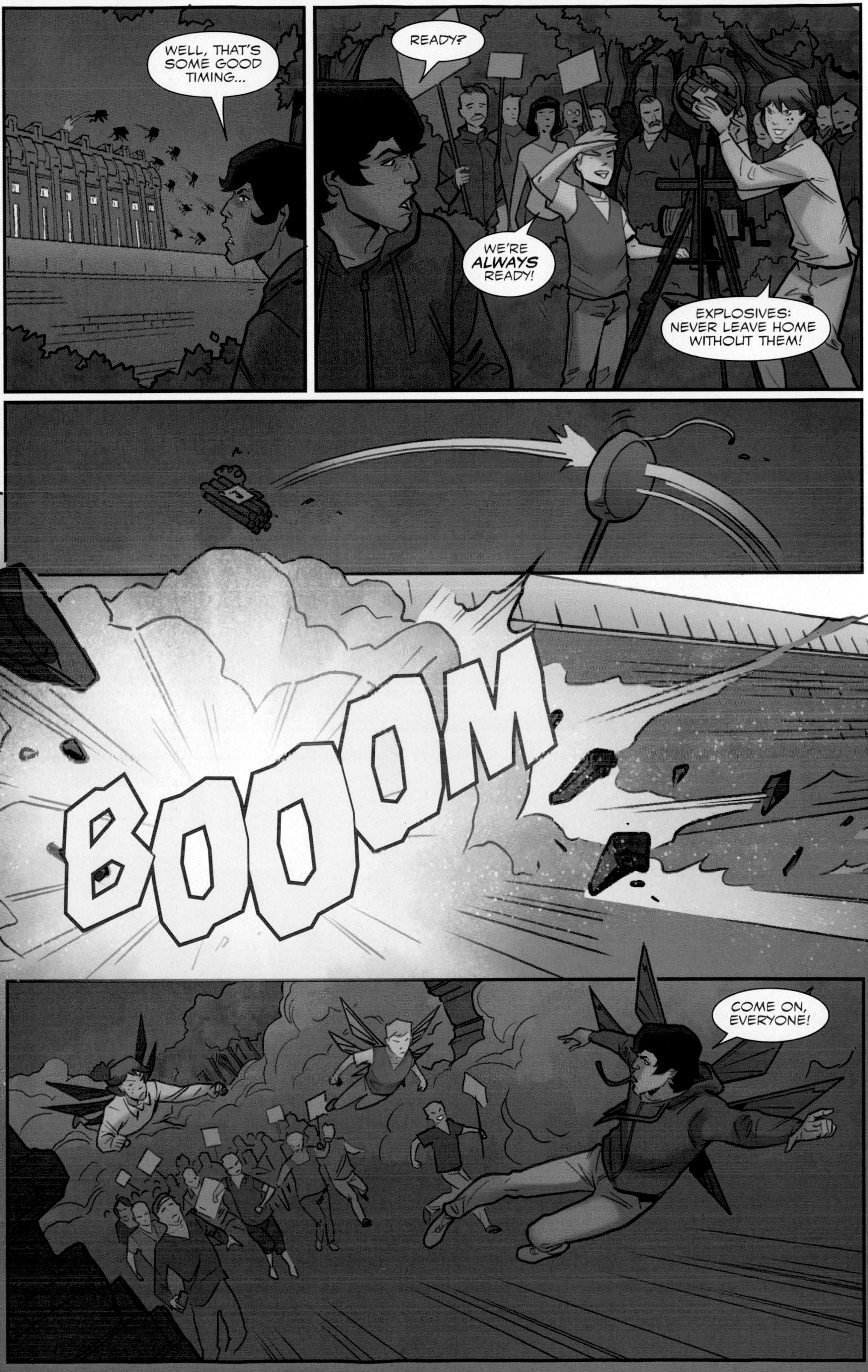
WELL, THAT'S SOME GOOD TIMING...
READY?
WE'RE ALWAYS READY!
EXPLOSIVES: NEVER LEAVE HOME WITHOUT THEM!
BOOOM
COME ON, EVERYONE!

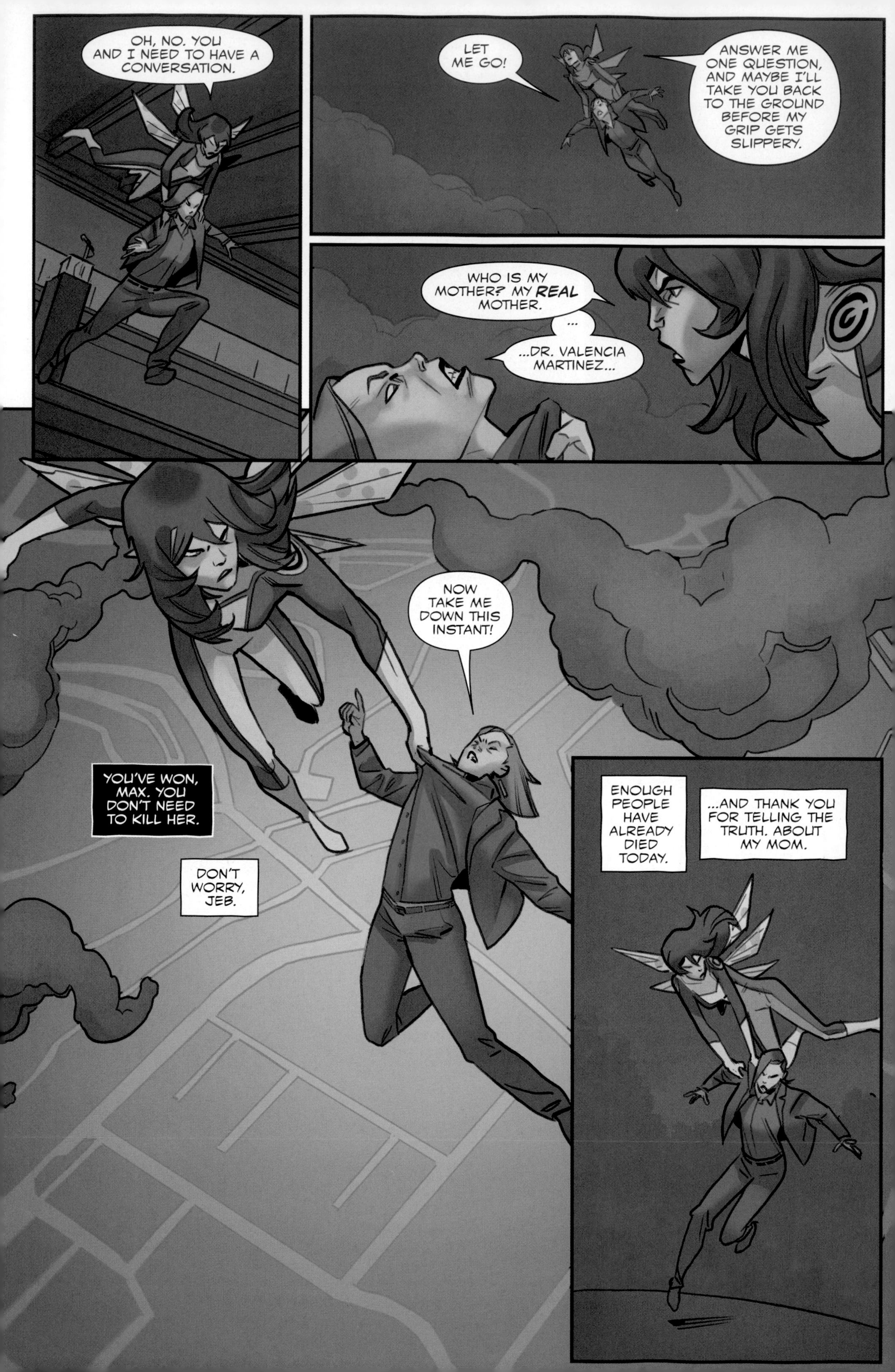
OH, NO. YOU AND I NEED TO HAVE A CONVERSATION.
LET ME GO!
ANSWER ME ONE QUESTION, AND MAYBE I'LL TAKE YOU BACK TO THE GROUND BEFORE MY GRIP GETS SLIPPERY.
WHO IS MY MOTHER? MY **REAL** MOTHER.
...
...DR. VALENCIA MARTINEZ...
NOW TAKE ME DOWN THIS INSTANT!
YOU'VE WON, MAX. YOU DON'T NEED TO KILL HER.
DON'T WORRY, JEB.
ENOUGH PEOPLE HAVE ALREADY DIED TODAY.
...AND THANK YOU FOR TELLING THE TRUTH. ABOUT MY MOM.

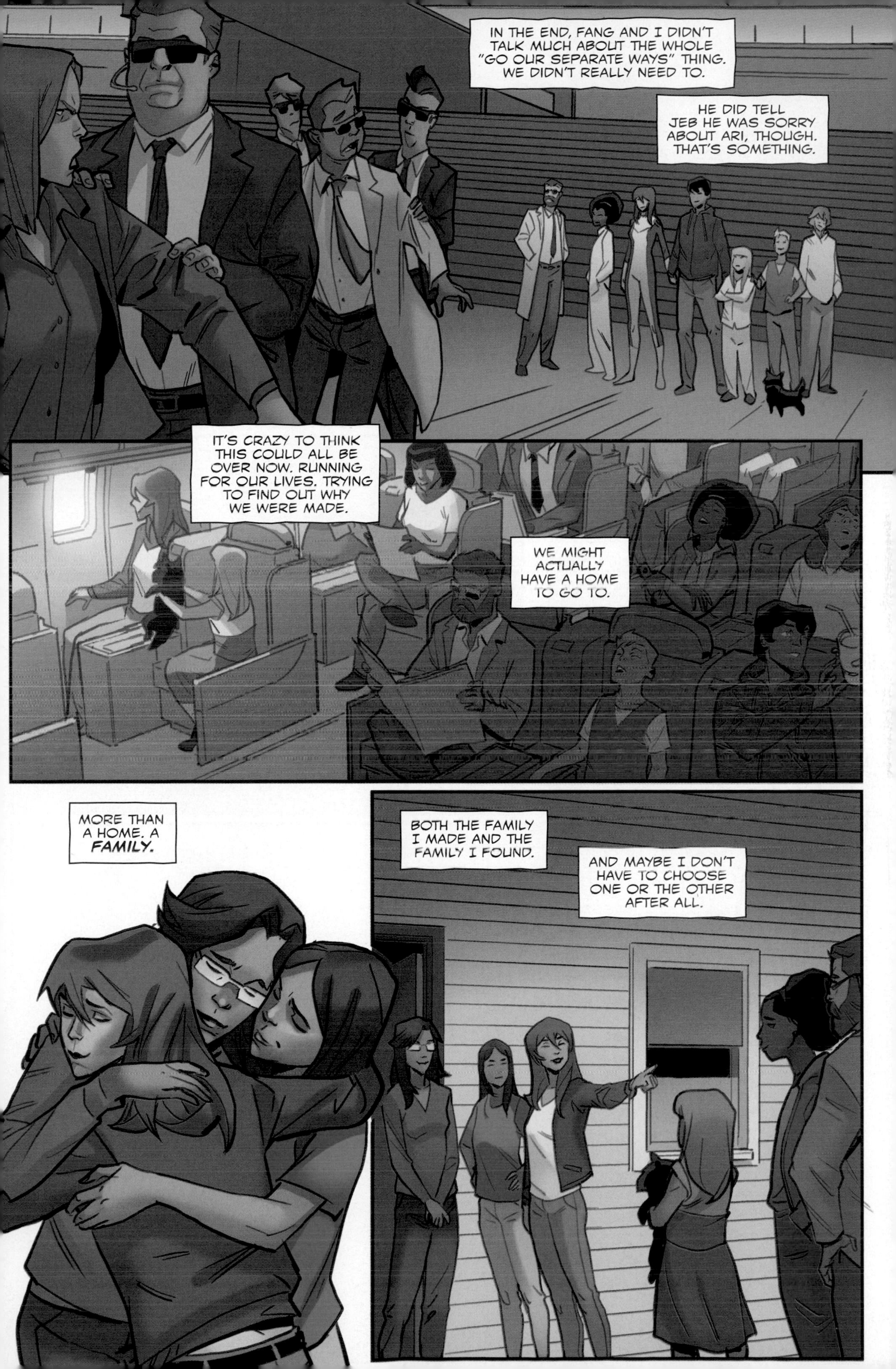
IN THE END, FANG AND I DIDN'T TALK MUCH ABOUT THE WHOLE "GO OUR SEPARATE WAYS" THING. WE DIDN'T REALLY NEED TO.
HE DID TELL JEB HE WAS SORRY ABOUT ARI, THOUGH. THAT'S SOMETHING.
IT'S CRAZY TO THINK THIS COULD ALL BE OVER NOW. RUNNING FOR OUR LIVES. TRYING TO FIND OUT WHY WE WERE MADE.
WE MIGHT ACTUALLY HAVE A HOME TO GO TO.
MORE THAN A HOME. A *FAMILY.*
BOTH THE FAMILY I MADE AND THE FAMILY I FOUND.
AND MAYBE I DON'T HAVE TO CHOOSE ONE OR THE OTHER AFTER ALL.

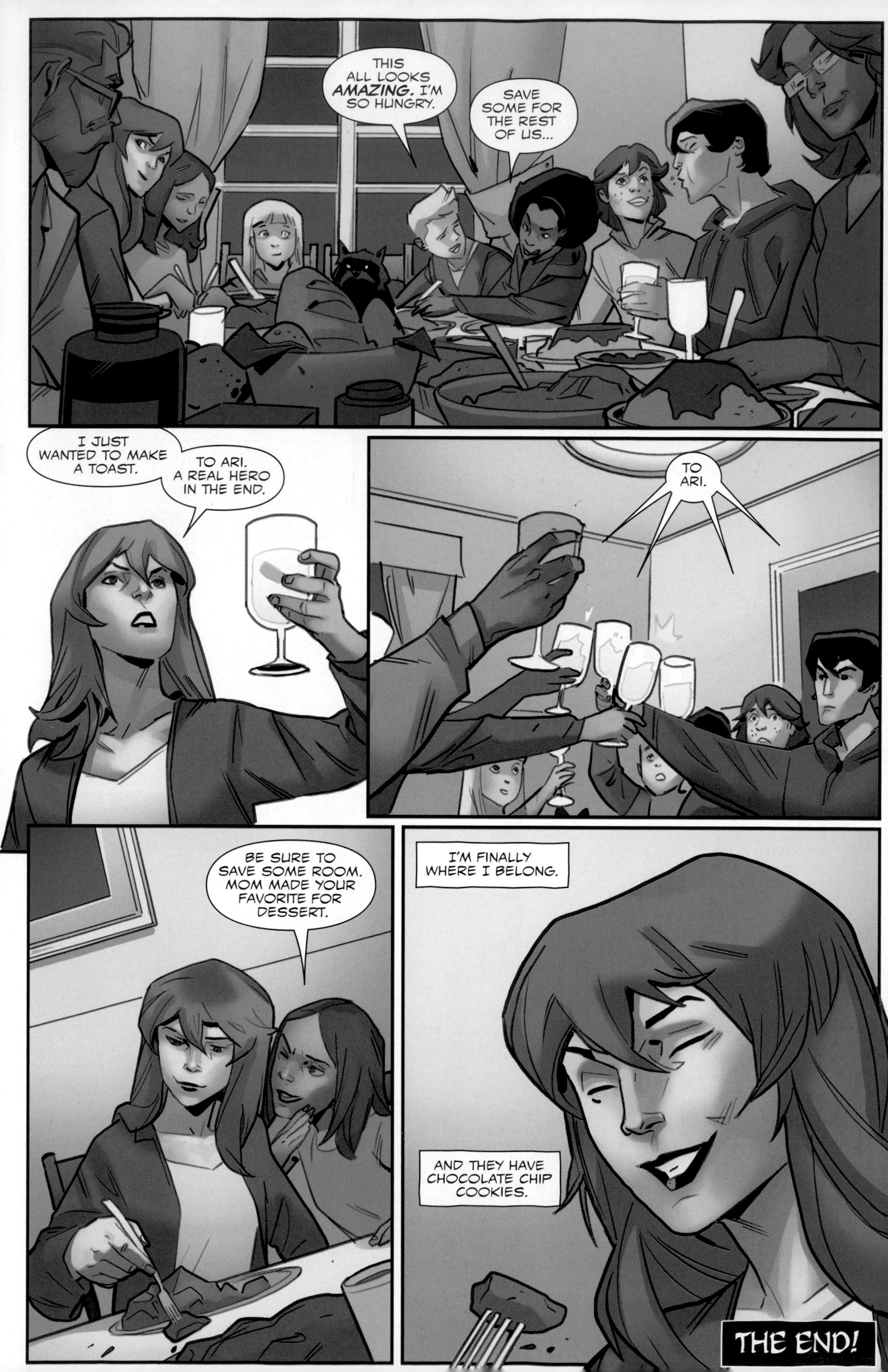

THIS ALL LOOKS AMAZING. I'M SO HUNGRY.
SAVE SOME FOR THE REST OF US...
I JUST WANTED TO MAKE A TOAST.
TO ARI. A REAL HERO IN THE END.
TO ARI.
BE SURE TO SAVE SOME ROOM. MOM MADE YOUR FAVORITE FOR DESSERT.
I'M FINALLY WHERE I BELONG.
AND THEY HAVE CHOCOLATE CHIP COOKIES.
THE END!

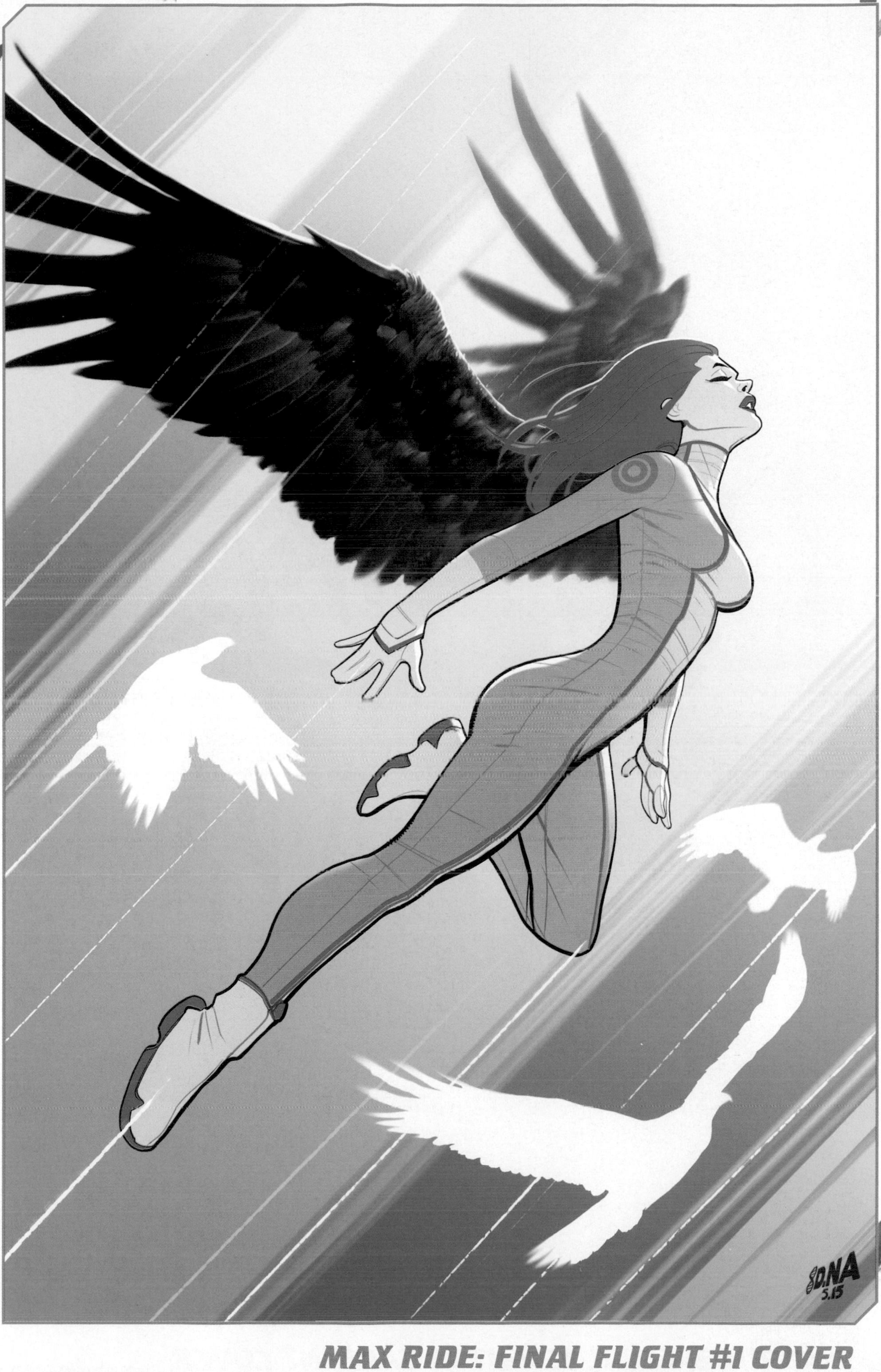
D.NA
5.15

MAX RIDE: FINAL FLIGHT #1 COVER

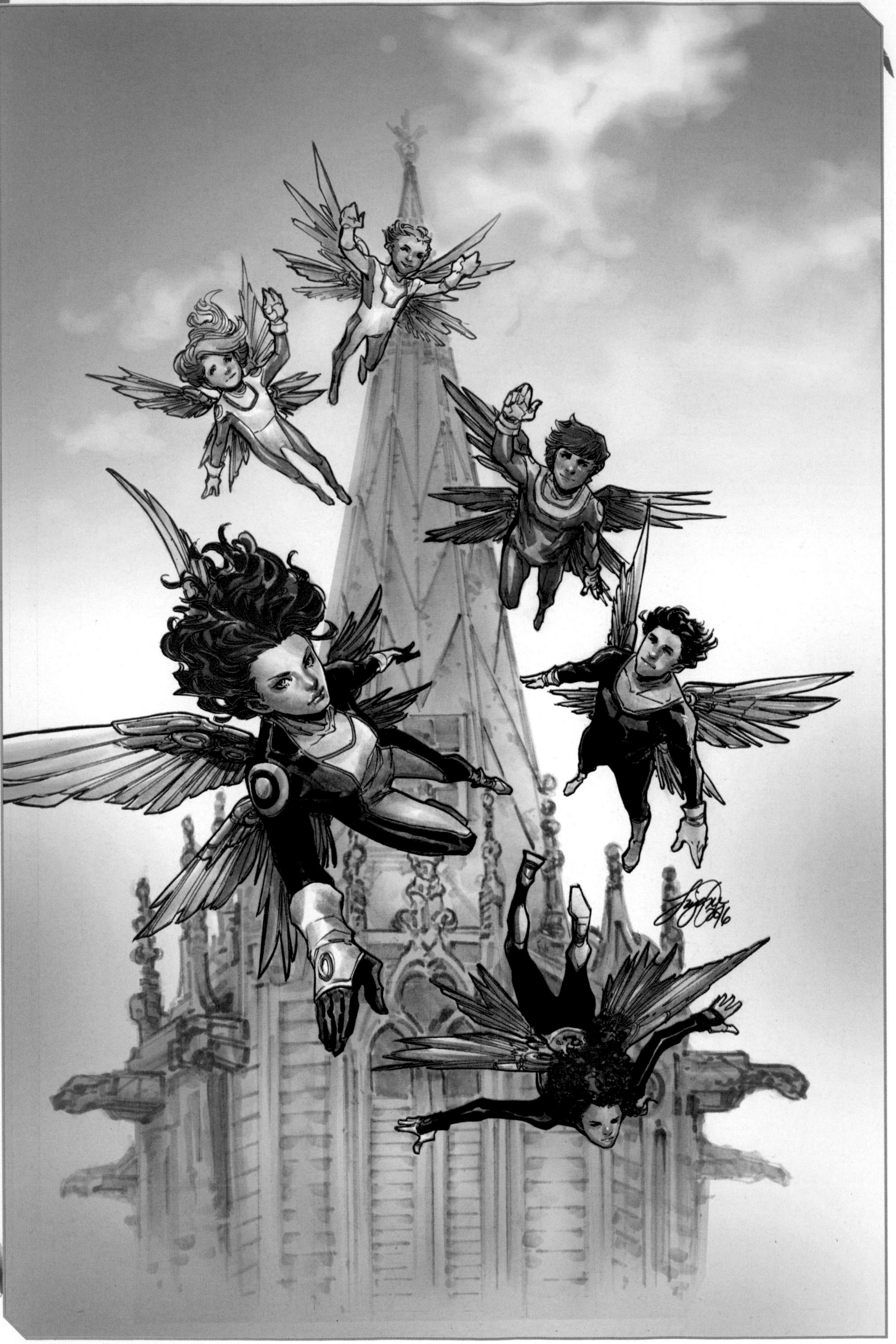

MAX RIDE: FINAL FLIGHT #1 VARIANT COVER
BY SIYA OUM

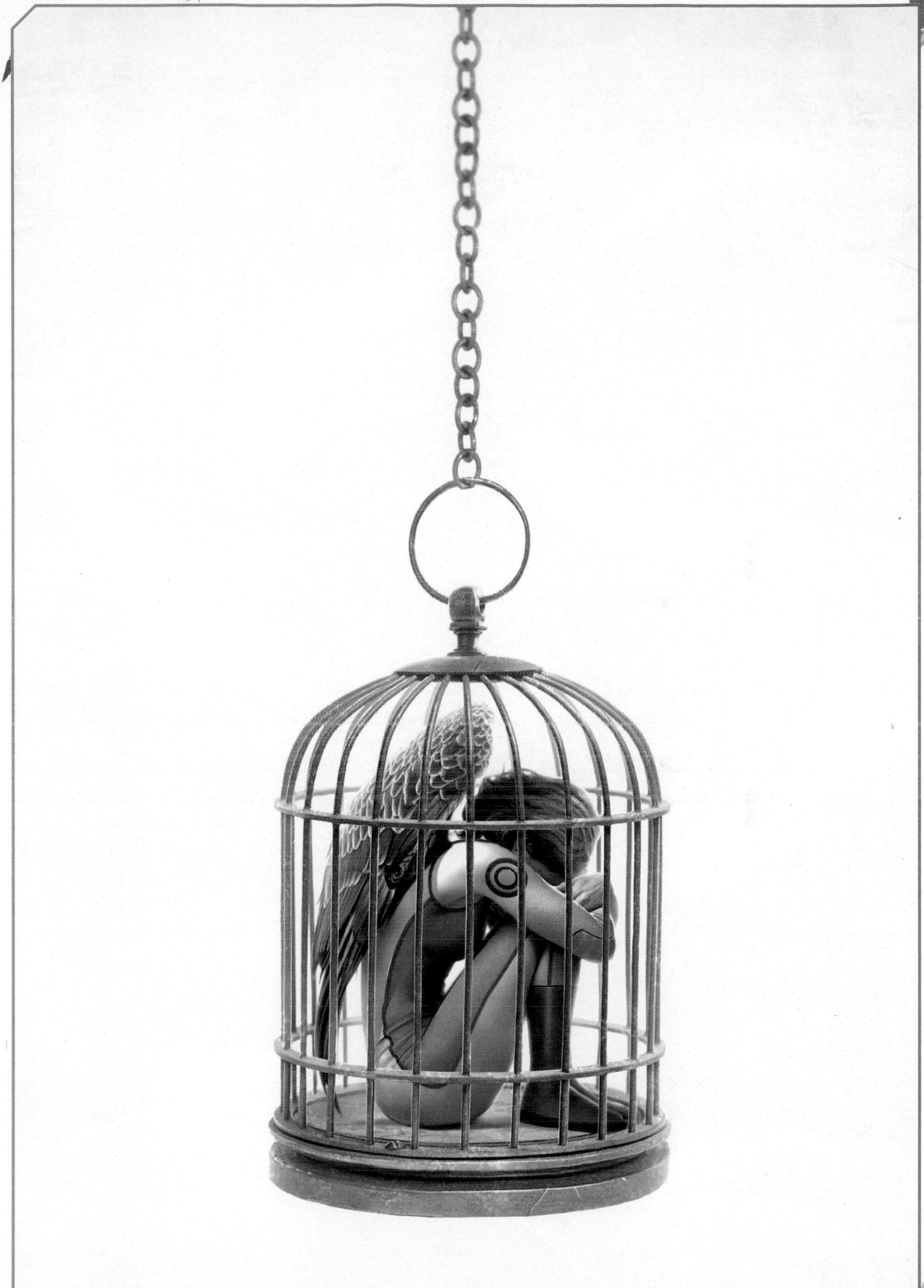
D.NA
6.15

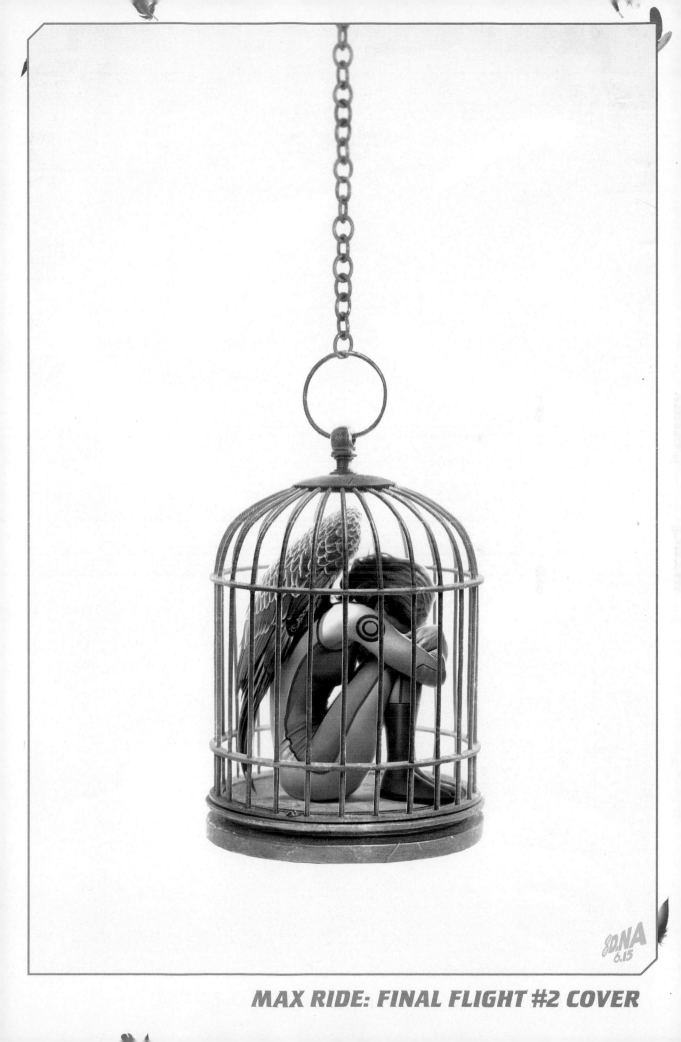

MAX RIDE: FINAL FLIGHT #2 COVER

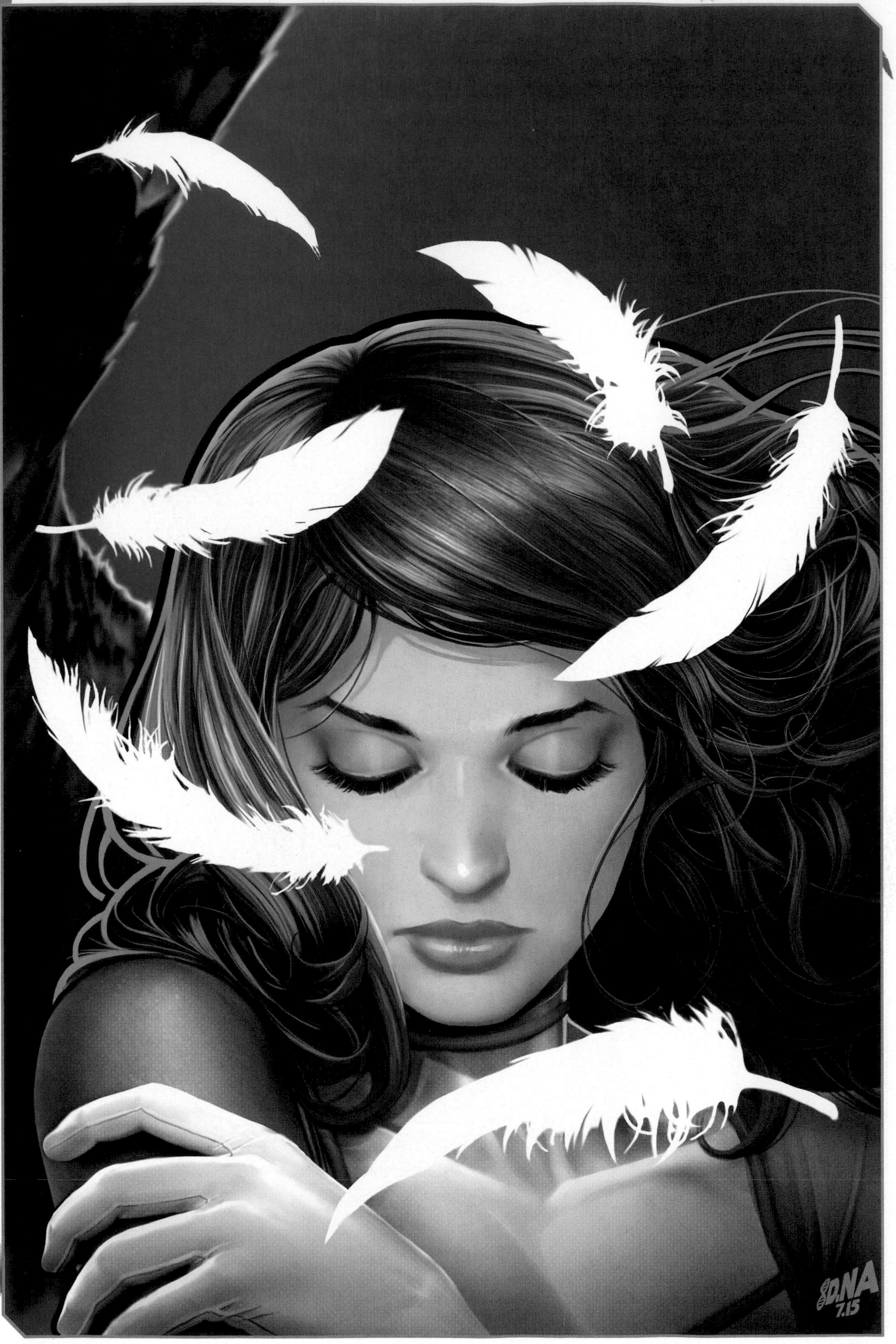
D.NA
7.15

MAX RIDE: FINAL FLIGHT #3 COVER

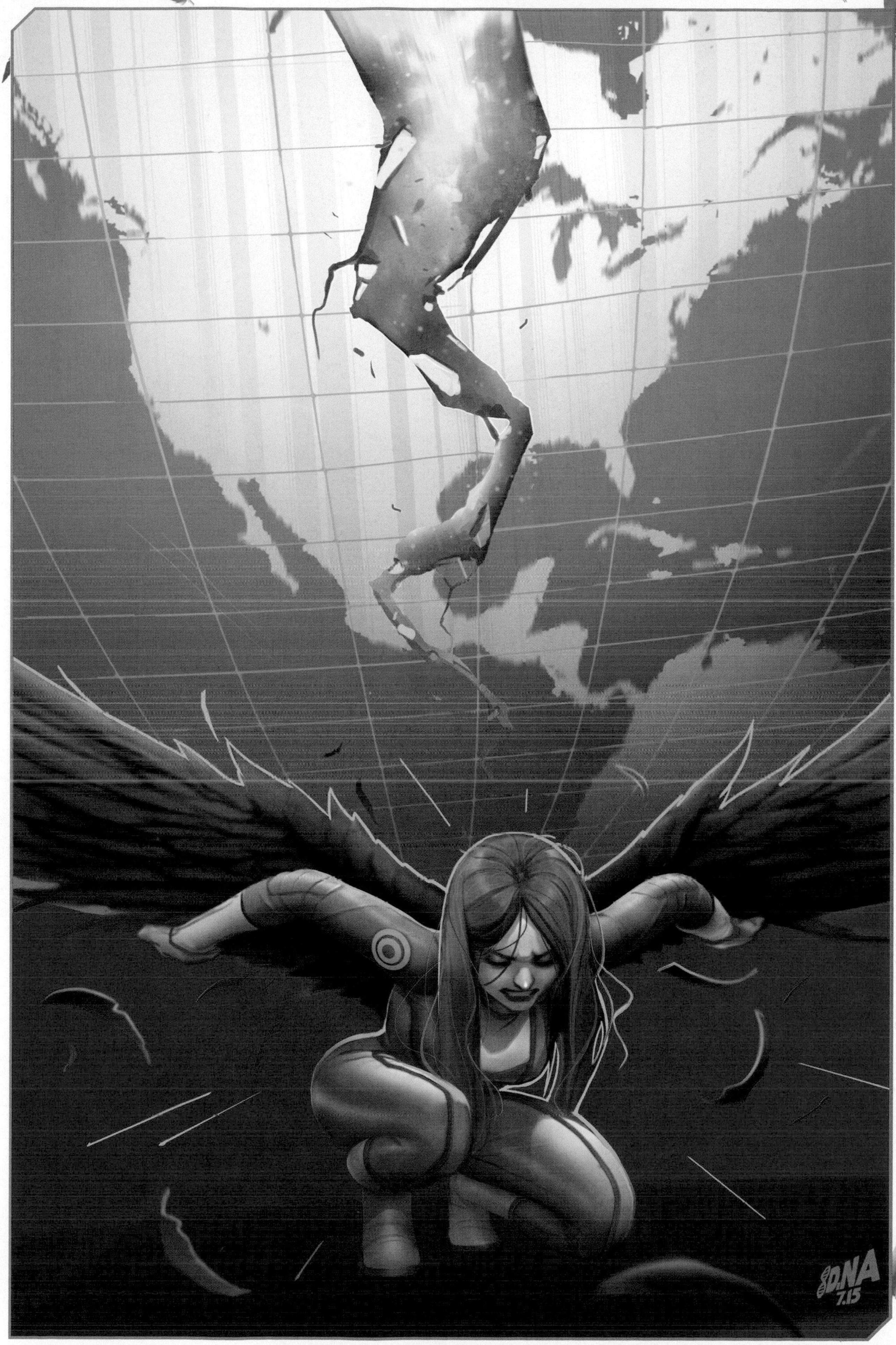
D.NA
7.15

MAX RIDE: FINAL FLIGHT #4 COVER

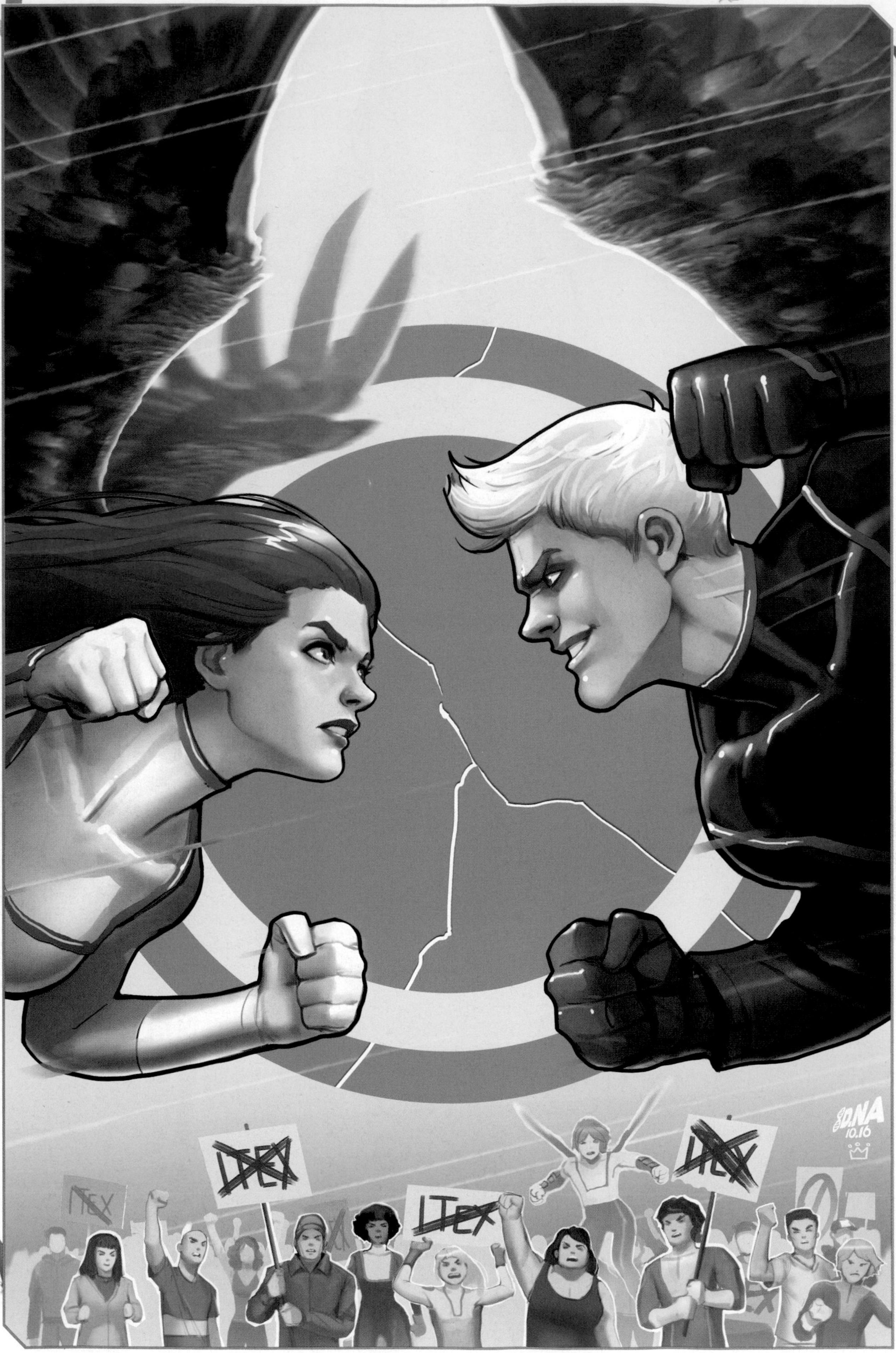

D.NA
10.16
ITEX
ITEX
ITEX

MAX RIDE: FINAL FLIGHT #5 COVER